A COMPREHENSIVE ASSESSMENT OF TAX CAPACITY IN SOUTHEAST ASIA

Aekapol Chongvilaivan and Annette Chooi

DECEMBER 2021

ADB

ASIAN DEVELOPMENT BANK

© 2021 Asian Development Bank
6 ADB Avenue, Mandaluyong City, 1550 Metro Manila, Philippines
Tel +63 2 8632 4444; Fax +63 2 8636 2444
www.adb.org

Some rights reserved. Published in 2021.

ISBN 978-92-9262-834-5 (print); 978-92-9262-835-2 (electronic); 978-92-9262-836-9 (ebook)
Publication Stock No. TCS210243
DOI: http://dx.doi.org/10.22617/TCS210243

The views expressed in this publication are those of the authors and do not necessarily reflect the views and policies of the Asian Development Bank (ADB) or its Board of Governors or the governments they represent.

ADB does not guarantee the accuracy of the data included in this publication and accepts no responsibility for any consequence of their use. The mention of specific companies or products of manufacturers does not imply that they are endorsed or recommended by ADB in preference to others of a similar nature that are not mentioned.

By making any designation of or reference to a particular territory or geographic area, or by using the term "country" in this document, ADB does not intend to make any judgments as to the legal or other status of any territory or area.

Please contact pubsmarketing@adb.org if you have questions or comments with respect to content, or if you wish to obtain copyright permission for your intended use that does not fall within these terms, or for permission to use the ADB logo.

Corrigenda to ADB publications may be found at http://www.adb.org/publications/corrigenda.

Note:
In this publication, "$" refers to United States dollars, unless otherwise indicated.

On the cover: Taxes are fundamental to the provision of services by governments. Many elements must come together to create an inclusive, broad-based tax system and it requires the contributions of individuals, communities, and sectors.

Cover design by Cleone Baradas.

Contents

List of Figures

Foreword

Prior to the coronavirus disease (COVID-19) pandemic, tax revenues in Southeast Asia were already insufficient to achieve the Sustainable Development Goals (SDGs). In 2018, the average tax-to-gross domestic product (GDP) ratio in the region stood at 14.8%, well below the average of 17.6% for developing Asia and 24.9% for members of the Organisation for Economic Co-operation and Development. Many economies in Southeast Asia are experiencing declining tax-to-GDP ratios and are failing to achieve a tax effort of 15% of GDP—the level considered to be the minimum for sustainable development.

High levels of public debt coupled with fiscal pressures induced by the pandemic mean many Southeast Asian countries are struggling to finance their COVID-19 response and recovery efforts in areas such as public health, education, and infrastructure. Domestic resource mobilization (DRM)—the ability of a government to mobilize its own resources and collect taxes—is suffering from a plunge in economic activities and trade as the pandemic continues to unfold. Various tax relief measures introduced to reduce the burden on taxpayers and to enhance cashflow for businesses are also contributing to lower tax revenue. Resource-dependent countries in the region face an additional challenge as non-tax revenues decline due to lower demand and prices for commodities. It is likely that low DRM will persist for some time in Southeast Asia as COVID-19 containment measures continue to suppress economic activity.

These developments offer a stark reminder of why it is essential to strengthen DRM and foster international tax cooperation in Southeast Asia. At the same time, the issue of tax revenue mobilization and administration, including institutional capacity, needs to be addressed from a longer-term perspective. Under its Strategy 2030, the Asian Development Bank (ADB) is committed to help its developing member countries build resilience and respond to economic shocks through support to strengthen governance and institutional capacity. Addressing emerging and evolving issues around DRM and international tax cooperation is crucial to foster a sustainable and inclusive economic recovery from the pandemic.

A Comprehensive Assessment of Tax Capacity in Southeast Asia examines technical, policy, and administrative tax capacity issues in ten countries and provides insights on potential capacity, institutional, policy, and legal reforms. The report underscores that there is no one-size-fits-all tax policy for Southeast Asia. Each country has a unique tax system with a distinct social and economic context and differing institutional and political settings. Therefore, customized and sequenced tax policy and administration reform options are required to strengthen tax capacities and address other emerging DRM and international tax cooperation challenges. These challenges include large informal sectors, high costs of tax compliance, overly complex tax systems, base erosion and profit shifting by multinational enterprises, and the digital transformation of tax authorities.

I believe this report will serve as a valuable reference for tax authorities, policymakers, researchers, and other stakeholders to better understand tax policy and administration issues and challenges in the region, as well as policy options to address them. Along with the recent establishment of the Asia Pacific Tax Hub, it will also guide ADB on how to boost assistance and operations to help its Southeast Asian member countries realize the potential of DRM and international tax cooperation.

Masatsugu Asakawa
President
Asian Development Bank

Acknowledgments

This report greatly benefited from views, insights, and suggestions of the experts and officials of the Southeast Asian tax authorities at the Webinar on Comprehensive Assessment of Tax Capacity in Southeast Asia on 27 November 2020. The authors thank the Domestic Resource Mobilization Trust Fund for funding support. Ramesh Subramaniam, Director General of the Southeast Asia Department; Bruno Carrasco, Director General and concurrently Chief Compliance Officer of the Sustainable Development and Climate Change Department; John Versantvoort, Head of the Office of Anti-Corruption and Integrity; and Jose Antonio R. Tan, Director of Public Management, Financial Sector, and Trade Division of the Southeast Asia Department, provided guidance and suggestions in preparation of this report. The authors would like to acknowledge coordination support by Daisuke Miura and Go Nagata, and the excellent research assistance by Gilliane A. De Gorostiza and administrative support by Jennalyn Delos Santos and Rodel S. Bautista.

About the Authors

Aekapol Chongvilaivan is an economist (Public Finance) at the Southeast Asia Department of the Asian Development Bank (ADB). Through ADB's lending and technical assistance, he supports governments in Southeast Asia for public finance management policy and reforms, including tax reforms, medium-term fiscal planning and budgeting, and public debt management. Prior to his current role, he was a country economist for the Philippines Country Office of ADB. He joined ADB in 2013 through the Young Professional Program and has worked with the Southeast Asia Department, Pacific Department, and Strategy and Policy Department. From 2008 to 2013, he was a fellow and coordinator of the Regional Economic Studies Programme at the Institute of Southeast Asian Studies in Singapore. He holds a doctor of philosophy degree in economics from the National University of Singapore. His economic research has been published extensively in international refereed journals.

Annette Chooi has over 30 years' experience in tax administration working for the Australian Taxation Office (ATO) and in the private sector, in a wide range of positions. In the ATO, she held senior roles in both the compliance and operations groups and led a number of major policy reforms, including a new tax system for small business, reforms to improve domestic tax policy and administration, and the implementation of tighter regulation for large businesses with international operations. She has held several senior appointments on the boards of both not-for-profit and unlisted companies, primarily in the financial services and social media sectors. Annette currently runs a consulting firm providing professional services in areas including business development for startups, corporate governance and risk management, and revenue administration. She has worked extensively across Asia and the Pacific as well as in Africa.

About This Report

This report examines technical, policy, and administrative tax capacity issues in 10 Southeast Asian countries with a focus on both national and international issues. In preparing this report, the authors referenced ADB in-house data, as well as a range of reports published by other agencies (such as the World Bank, the Organisation of Economic Co-operation and Development, and the International Monetary Fund). The report also draws on ADB's publication *A Comparative Analysis of Tax Administration in Asia and the Pacific: 2020 Edition* published in February 2020.

The objective of this report is to identify country-specific tax-related areas where ADB support may be beneficial in supporting resource mobilization. Support could include capacity building, and identification of institutional, policy, and legal reforms. The outcome is to shed light on domestic resource mobilization (DRM) measures that may be supported by existing programs and to identify areas where new investment may be needed to strengthen DRM in Southeast Asia.

The coronavirus disease (COVID-19) has impacted fiscal outlooks for every jurisdiction in the region and, indeed, across the world. The pandemic has required increased expenditure on health and stimulus packages, and reduced revenues due to economic shocks, making DRM challenges harder and more urgent. Nevertheless, the fundamental principles and the DRM opportunities and challenges outlined in this report continue to be highly pertinent, and all jurisdictions are encouraged to consider and, where relevant, implement the strategies identified as soon as practically possible. ADB stands ready to assist.

This report includes the following sections: I. Introduction; II. Tax Administration and Revenue Profile; III. Strengthening Revenue and Broadening the Tax Base; IV. Responsive Tax Administration; and V. Conclusion. It also includes an Appendix consisting of tax profiles for 10 Southeast Asian countries.

In considering the revenue data provided in this report, it is important to acknowledge that the tax ratios presented rely on both the denominator (gross domestic product [GDP]) and the numerator (net revenue collected), and that GDP is typically subject to periodic revision by the relevant statistical body to take into account updated data or new methodologies introduced to improve national accounts aggregates. As a result, variations in the tax ratios may occur as GDP data are revised.

It should be noted that, for some jurisdictions, including a number covered in this report, governments have access to significant non-tax revenues (e.g., sales of oil, minerals, and real property, and investment income) that lessen the need to rely on tax revenues to fund government programs and services. Economies in this category include Brunei Darussalam, the Lao People's Democratic Republic, Timor-Leste, and Singapore.

Abbreviations

ADB	Asian Development Bank
AML	anti-money laundering
BEPS	base erosion and profit shifting
CGT	capital gains tax
CIT	corporate income tax
DMC	developing member country
DRM	domestic resource mobilization
FDI	foreign direct investment
FY	fiscal year
GDP	gross domestic product
GNI	gross national income
GST	goods and services tax
HDI	Human Development Index
IMF	International Monetary Fund
IT	information technology
MNE	multinational enterprise
MOF	Ministry of Finance
MTRS	medium-term revenue strategy
OECD	Organisation for Economic Co-operation and Development
PIT	personal income tax
SSC	social security contributions
TADAT	Tax Administration Diagnostic Assessment Tool
VAT	value-added tax
WHT	withholding tax

Executive Summary

Economies across Southeast Asia are at various stages of development and growth. Demographic patterns and population movements observed in Southeast Asia resemble those seen in many regions across the world, with trends toward an aging population, increasing urbanization, improved internet access, and growing wealth and development. These shifts are likely to shape economic activities, giving rise to changing tax revenues and tax expenditures, including increasing demand for government services such as health care. With relatively low tax-to-gross domestic product (GDP) ratios across the region, resource mobilization is an imperative for most economies, with this pressure, heightened by the impacts of the global pandemic, likely to strengthen in coming years.

Tax policy and tax administration are important levers in meeting revenue challenges across the region. Considering the high levels of dependency on the tax administration for provision of government revenue across the region, strengthening the general capacity of revenue bodies, including fully utilizing digitization and improving staff processes and infrastructure, is likely to strengthen revenue results. Jurisdictions are at different stages, with diverse levels and types of economic development and revenue challenges, and solutions need to be tailored. Nevertheless, some common elements are apparent.

Increasing connectivity and access to technology will enable improvements in service and supervision. Increasing access to digital services and improving internal tax administration processes, as well as strengthening transparency of taxpayer dealings, are all likely to require digital transformation within revenue body operations and, in some cases, also across the community. Taking advantage of the opportunities presented by advancing technology and domestic networks may require further developments of business processes, infrastructure, and capability.

The shifts across the region toward increasingly open market economies may challenge corporate income tax revenue. As economies open up to foreign investment, weaknesses in the international taxation legal and administrative frameworks are likely to manifest, and the solutions will need to ensure that domestic revenue is protected. In addition, the appropriateness of tax incentives designed against a backdrop of low levels of development may need to be reconsidered.

Value-added taxes may be eroded by complexity in design, as well as difficulties in taxing cross-border sales of goods and services. Many jurisdictions have complex value-added tax (VAT) systems with multiple rates and exemptions, reflecting concerns to protect vulnerable citizens; however, these design features are also easily exploited. Increasing cross-border sales, which are difficult to tax, increases the pressure on VAT. Given the high reliance on indirect taxes, erosion of this revenue stream is highly problematic.

Increasing urbanization and the trend away from agriculture may highlight weaknesses in personal income tax design and administration. Many jurisdictions have numerous exemptions and low rates of taxes on salary and wages and personal business income. These design features may no longer be fitting in an environment of increasing wages and rising numbers of high-wealth individuals. Aging populations will increase pressure on social security systems, particularly where reserves are low. The design of these systems, and the role of the revenue body in administration, may need to be reconsidered.

The low revenue contribution of property taxes, and subnational taxes in general, presents an opportunity to broaden the tax base. Increasing wealth and investment in property also highlight an opportunity to increase equity by developing better approaches to more effectively tax immovable property. One important element of this is ensuring that land registries are well established, are digitized wherever possible, and that valuations are up to date.

Main Observations

This section summarizes several areas identified throughout this report that may support domestic resource mobilization (DRM) across the region, with particular focus on areas where ADB and other development partners may be valuable. Of course, not all jurisdictions will require support in each area and programs will need to be tailored according to need.

Corporate Income Tax

Tax Incentives

Countries in the region that are not already doing so may require assistance to evaluate tax incentives, in order to gauge the extent to which the desired benefits are being delivered; strengthen transparency, integrity and accountability; and, where necessary, redesign policies to better target incentives and improve benefits realization. In the short term, strengthening of governance within the existing frameworks may require support. Revenue bodies are often not directly involved in the administration of tax incentive regimes but may be best placed to perform this role.

International Taxation

The use of legal structures to hide assets highlights the role that ownership transparency plays in preventing and combating tax evasion, corruption, and other related financial crimes. Increased pressure on budgets and revenue outflows arising from the expenditures related to coronavirus disease (COVID-19), including stimulus packages, together with lower collections, makes the pursuit of greater tax transparency critical.

Assistance may be required in re-designing domestic legal frameworks and administration to support membership in international cooperative forums, as well as the formal steps required to become part of the global standard, including signing and ratifying the international instruments. Some jurisdictions may also need to build internal capacity to exploit the new opportunities that will arise from membership in these forums.

In addition, many jurisdictions may not be fully utilizing their existing legal provisions. Working within what is currently available by identifying revenue leakages and developing and implementing associated compliance improvement plans may also necessitate support for building capacity and confidence in managing the compliance of multinational enterprises (MNEs). The regional hub for domestic resource mobilization and international tax cooperation may be well placed to support these efforts.[1]

---

[1] The Asian Development Bank (ADB) on 17 September 2020 announced the establishment of a regional hub where developing members and development partners collaborate closely to promote domestic resource mobilization and international tax cooperation in the Asia and Pacific region. The regional hub will serve multiple functions, including a platform for (i) institutional and capacity development including exchange of information and ideas through a South–South dialogue; (ii) knowledge sharing across knowledge partners, international finance institutions, and other bilateral revenue organizations and Asia and Pacific developing countries; and (iii) collaboration and development coordination across development partners.

Changes in Production Structure

Economies in the region are at various stages in the evolution of production structures, from a high concentration in agriculture to higher levels of industry and ultimately to services. Both high growth and declining sectors have incentives for tax planning, and these activities may need to be more closely monitored in some jurisdictions. Revenue leakage may be better detected with sector-based monitoring. Assistance may support development of a better understanding of where production changes are occurring and revenue risks emerging, and in developing and implementing mitigation strategies.

Value-Added Tax

Multiple VAT rates and exemptions and, in some cases, relatively high registration thresholds, are common across the region. These VAT design features may contribute to higher administrative burdens and revenue shortfalls, due to both confusion about how the rules apply and deliberate manipulation. For those jurisdictions looking to redesign VAT laws, assistance may support creation of simpler and more robust regimes.

Paying legitimate VAT refunds, or offsetting the credits against other tax liabilities within a reasonable timeframe, is critical for business cash flow and viability. Many jurisdictions in the region are reported to have difficulty in processing refunds within acceptable periods. Support may be required in setting up processes that improve both the prompt payment of refunds and the prevention and detection of potentially fraudulent claims.

Personal Income Tax

Due to both policy and administration features, personal income tax (PIT) is underrepresented in tax revenues in many jurisdictions in the region. At a policy level, high thresholds, low rates, and multiple exemptions limit revenue, and may produce inequitable outcomes. As the earning power of individual workers increases, the emergence of more middle- and high-income earners follows. These individuals are often paying little or no taxes on relatively high earnings. Due to low current revenue, many jurisdictions may invest little or no resources in monitoring compliance with PIT. As earnings continue to rise, countries may seek assistance to redesign and strengthen the equity of law design and the administration of PIT.

Subnational Taxes

The strengthening of subnational administrations has the potential to improve revenue; this may be supported by targeted assistance. The relatively low percentage of revenue flowing from recurrent taxes on immovable property in Southeast Asian jurisdictions, compared with other parts of the world, suggests that there is considerable room for increasing revenue from this source.

Social Security Contributions

Aging populations across the region will put pressure on social security budgets. In many jurisdictions, the current systems are complex and multitiered and, despite the commonalities, are often administered separately from PIT. Often the same businesses are responsible for PIT withholding and for social security contributions (SSC), but may be required to administer different rules for each. There may be scope for greater cooperation between agencies to simplify policy and administration and to improve compliance.

Other Issues

Tax Havens

Tax haven usage is not confined to MNEs, and is also a popular vehicle for tax minimization by high-wealth individuals. Information on the use of tax havens in Southeast Asia is limited but, against a backdrop of growing wealth, this area is likely to require closer monitoring and improved supervision.

Shadow Economy

Many jurisdictions are concerned about the impact of the shadow economy and the costs of monitoring these hidden activities.[2] Emerging technologies will enable new techniques to better manage unreported transactions. Designing and implementing such systems may require international assistance.

Digital Economy

Effectively taxing the digital economy has proved to be problematic, with many international tax frameworks not adequately reflecting modern business practices. Traditional international tax rules are no longer appropriate to address new digitalized business models, such as where businesses are able to generate profits from participation in economic activity in a jurisdiction with or without a local physical presence. Several jurisdictions have introduced measures to address some issues and revenue losses, such as the introduction of digital services taxes, but more holistic redesign of the legal and administrative frameworks may be required.

Reducing Compliance Costs and Providing Certainty

Citizens are increasingly demanding higher levels of service, simpler rules, and more streamlined tax administration. Reducing and removing underlying complexity by, for example, reviewing the legal framework, reducing reporting requirements and simplifying processes may require support in legal and business process redesign, and will require strengthened infrastructure, including digital operations and improved information technology. Revenue bodies may require support to design and implement these changes. Assistance may also help to strengthen public and private rulings programs and work toward its delivery, and to build taxpayer trust in the fairness of the private rulings process and promote use.

---

[2] In this report, the term "shadow economy" is used to describe unreported activities that are legally required to be reported and are liable to taxation. This may include activities conducted by unregistered businesses and those conducted by registered businesses that are not returned.

I.   Introduction

Southeast Asia is one of the fastest-growing regions in the world. Prior to the coronavirus disease (COVID-19) pandemic, the region's gross domestic product (GDP) growth stood at 4.6% on average, outpacing the global average of 3.2%. Taken as a whole, the region has combined GDP amounting to approximately $2.5 trillion, which makes up 34% of the global total, and is set to become the world's fourth-largest economy by 2030. Notwithstanding the impressive economic performance, many countries in Southeast Asia have not fully translated economic growth into development outcomes. Countries such as Cambodia, Indonesia, the Lao People's Democratic Republic (Lao PDR), and the Philippines still have high poverty incidence and income inequality, especially in remote areas. To address these development issues, governments in the region have traditionally embarked on a fair and efficient tax system as an instrument for mobilizing domestic resources to spend them on priority sectors critical to ushering in economic and social development such as education, health care, and social protection. The need for domestic resource mobilization is ever-increasing amid COVID-19, as unprecedented fiscal resources become imperative to strengthen the health systems and shield the vulnerable groups and small businesses against the pandemic's ripple effects.

This chapter examines the regional trends that shape domestic resource mobilization in Southeast Asia. The assessment sheds light on the emerging tax policies and measures for improving effectiveness and fairness of tax administration in the region. The regional trends presented set the stage for the ensuing discussions on tax policy and administration issues in this report. These include (i) taxation in the aging society; (ii) strengthening revenue mobilization with rapid urbanization; (iii) emerging tax issues from sectoral shifts; (iv) tax policy for promoting competitiveness; and (v) digital transformation of revenue bodies.

A.   Taxation in the Aging Society

Population trends in Southeast Asia resemble those seen in many regions across the world, with a trend toward an aging population, increasing urbanization, and improving development. Figure 1 illustrates that Singapore and Thailand have the highest proportions of the population aged over 65 years and the fastest rate of aging in the region. Timor-Leste and the Lao PDR have the lowest proportion of the population aged over 65 and the slowest rates of aging in the region.

Aging populations have significant socioeconomic implications, including a decline in the size of labor forces, an increase in the age-dependency ratio, and a redistribution of income and wealth, which in turn present challenges for tax policy. Aging societies also mean greater fiscal strain on reserves held in social security funds, which are intended to provide for health care and income support for senior citizens. As Southeast Asia ages, redesigning the tax and social security systems is crucial to influence long-term saving behaviors and ensure effectiveness and fairness of the tax systems. In addition, the governments will also need to carefully take into consideration distributional impacts of tax policies.

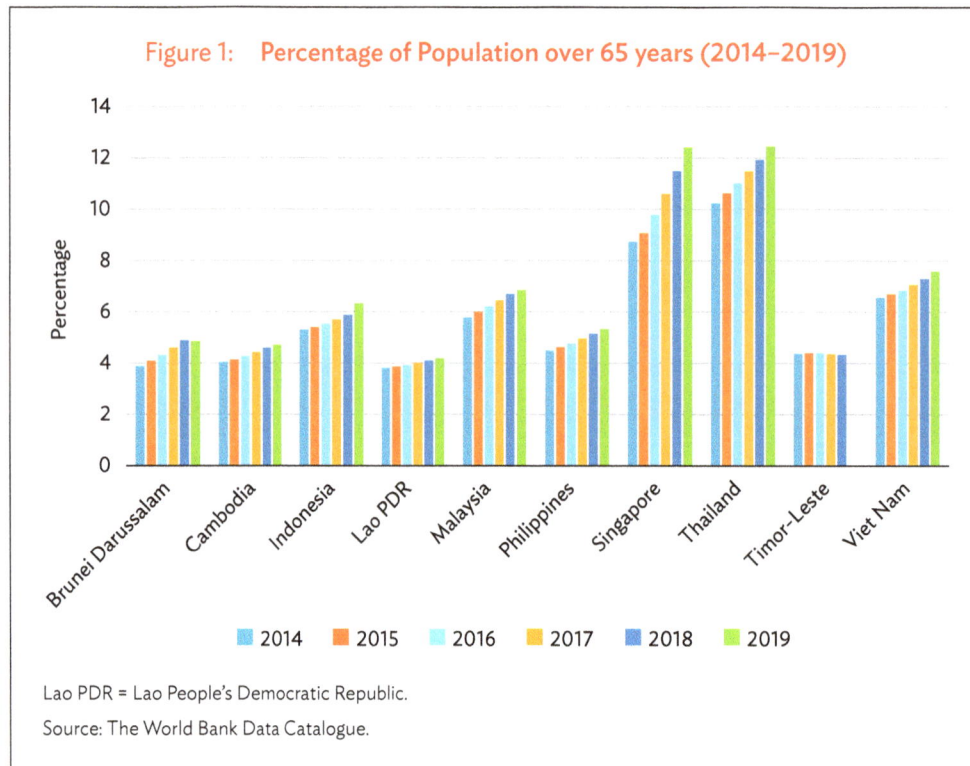

Figure 1:   Percentage of Population over 65 years (2014–2019)

Lao PDR = Lao People's Democratic Republic.
Source: The World Bank Data Catalogue.

B.   Strengthening Revenue Mobilization with Rapid Urbanization

Most countries in the region are relatively urbanized, with only Cambodia, the Lao PDR, and Timor-Leste having less than 40% of their population living in urban areas. The trend toward increased urbanization continues across the region, with most economies showing steady, but slight growth between 2014 and 2019, apart from the Lao PDR and Viet Nam, which both show slight declines. The human development indices have also increased consistently over the period, with all countries now reaching medium or higher development levels. Figure 2 shows the trends in urbanization and human development in Southeast Asia between 2014 and 2018–2019.

Although urbanization does not automatically lead to improvements in human development indicators, it has the potential to provide employment and enhance access to basic services. In Southeast Asia from 2014 to 2019, increasing levels of urbanization were generally associated with higher levels of human development. Exceptions to this trend are the Lao PDR and Viet Nam, both of which have active policies to promote and subsidize activities in rural communities to boost regional incomes. Cambodia has the lowest level of urbanization in the region and the lowest Human Development Index (HDI) rank, and Singapore has the highest level of urbanization and the highest HDI rank in the region.

Urbanization creates opportunities to expand the tax base. Increasing urbanization tends to be accompanied by a shift in employment patterns and may have ramifications for the personal income tax (PIT) system, at both policy and administration levels, especially where salary and wage earners are not required to file returns or may not be taxable at all. Employer withholding and social security contributions (SSC) will increase in importance too, and they may require greater attention. In addition, rapid urbanization has driven up residential property prices dramatically, thereby increasing the importance of effective property taxation. Property taxes, in nature, are wealth taxes and are the most dependable sources of domestic revenues for local governments. Hence, with urbanization

Figure 2:   Urbanization and Human Development in Southeast Asia (2014–2018)

Urbanization

Human Development Index

■ Urban Population (2014) ■ Urban Population (2019)

■ HDI (2014) ■ HDI (2018)

Lao PDR = Lao People's Democratic Republic.

Source: Key Indicators for Asia and the Pacific (ADB 2019).

Lao PDR = Lao People's Democratic Republic, HDI = Human Development Index.

Source: United Nations Development Program: Human Development Reports.

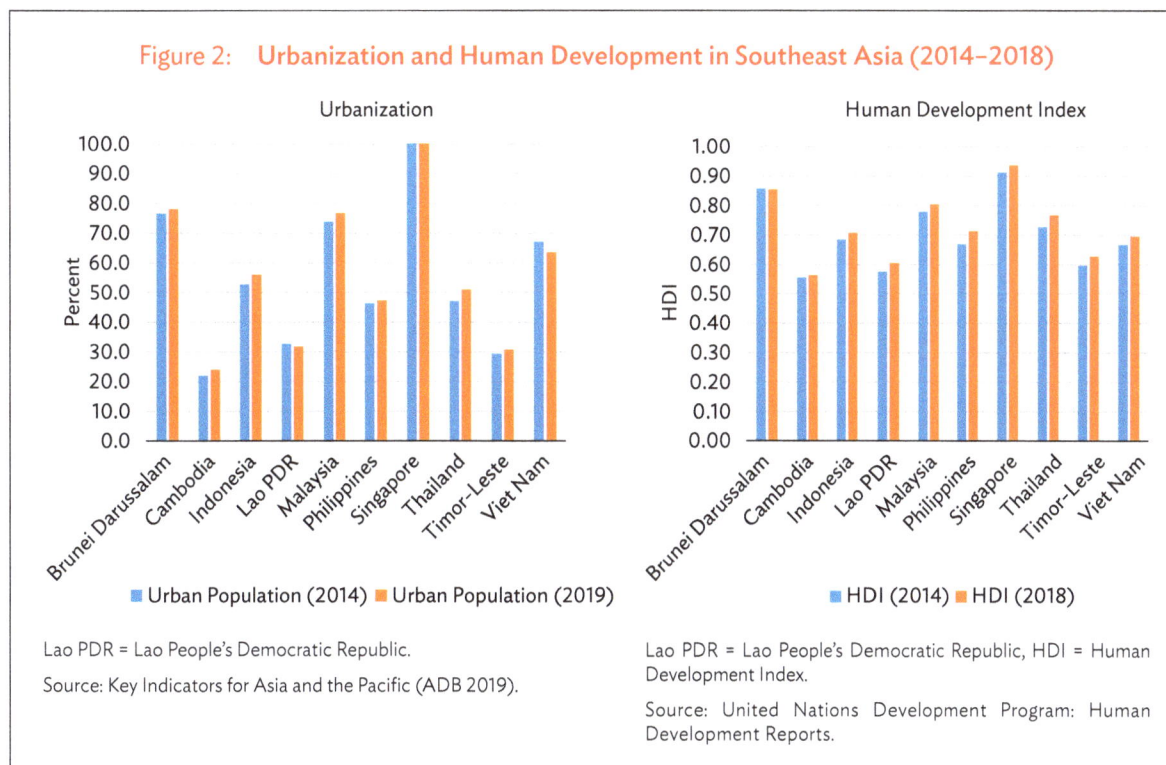

in the region, property taxes can be used as a policy instrument to usher in fairness of wealth distribution and enhance fiscal space of local governments for better service delivery.

C.   Emerging Tax Issues from Sectoral Shifts

Economic activity across the region has shown a sustained shift away from agriculture and into industry and services. Economies tend to follow similar patterns of sectoral changes as they develop. In the early phase of development, agriculture typically dominates; as development progresses, industry, particularly manufacturing, tends to expand. As industrialization proceeds, productivity in manufacturing improves, reducing the sector's intensity, while increasing the incomes of citizens and their demand for services. Service industries expand to meet this rising demand. Developing countries in Southeast Asia have broadly followed this pattern of structural change.

Figure 3 illustrates this shift in Southeast Asia, showing that, at a regional level, services are the dominant sector and growing. Industry is also growing against a lower base, and agriculture is declining. Economies across the region are at different stages of development, with Brunei Darussalam showing the most dramatic shifts out of the agriculture sector.

The structural shift toward industry and services poses new challenges to tax authorities in the region in various aspects. First, with the large informal sector, more and more firms are likely to grow but choose to stay outside the tax systems. The challenge for revenue bodies is how to incentivize these firms in the growing industry and service sectors to enter the tax systems, thereby expanding the tax base and domestic resource mobilization. Second, the revenue ramifications of these shifts include changes to tax compliance risks, including the likely emergence of

Figure 3:   Value Added by Sector (2014 and 2018)

ASEAN = Association of Southeast Asian Nations, GDP = gross domestic product, Lao PDR = Lao People's Democratic Republic.

Note: Singapore's agriculture sector has remained at 0% from 2014 to 2018.

Source: ASEAN Statistics and Data Portal: https://data.aseanstats.org/.

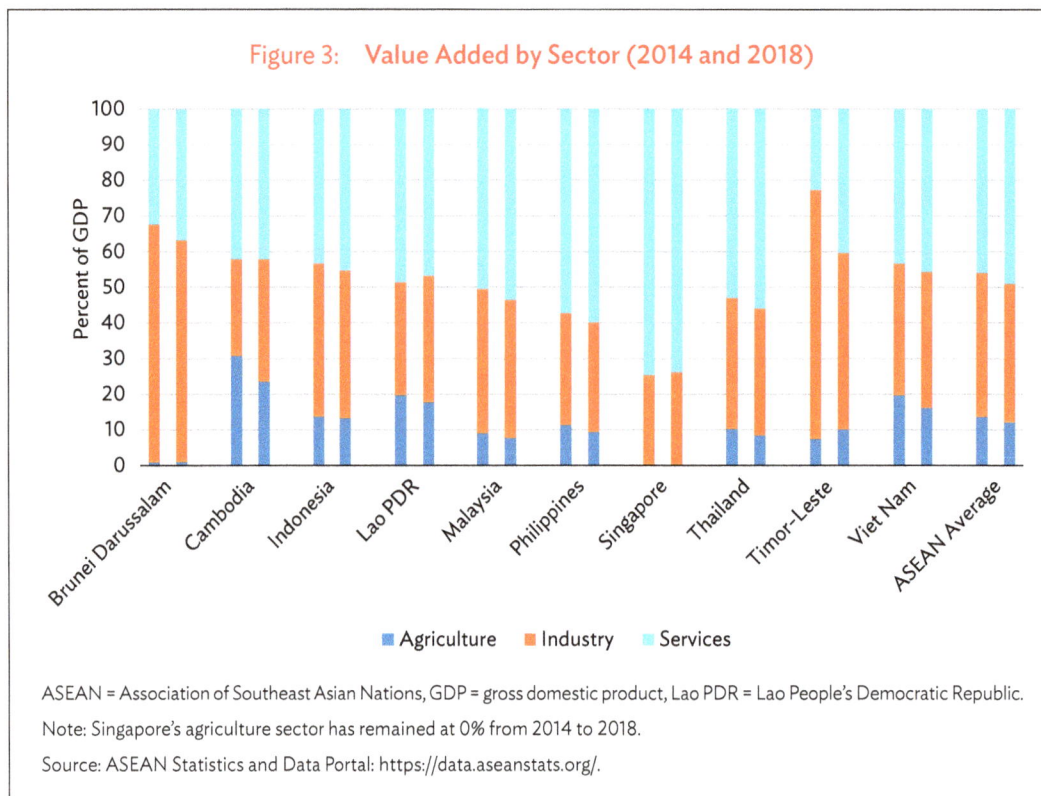

higher international taxation risks. Emerging and declining businesses tend to exhibit higher levels of taxation risks, which are likely to require attention. Last, tax policies for small and medium-sized enterprise (SME) development are likely to become increasingly important for policymakers. SMEs typically face higher compliance costs in comparison with large firms. Hence, simplification of tax compliance such as registration, filing, and payment of corporate income tax (CIT) and value-added tax (VAT) for SMEs tends to constitute the crux of tax policies and administration measures.

D.   Tax Policy for Promoting Competitiveness

Foreign direct investment (FDI) inflows into Southeast Asia are regarded as a catalyst of competitiveness and industrialization. FDI in the region grew by around 3% in 2018, to $149 billion. This is the third consecutive year in which FDI inflows into the region have increased. Singapore continued to attract the bulk of inbound FDI. Thailand recorded the largest increase in inbound FDI in 2018, growing by 62%. The main sources of investment were Japan and Hong Kong, China. Inbound FDI into Cambodia was up by 11% and Brunei Darussalam was up by 10% in 2018. Investment also recovered strongly in Timor-Leste, following a 10-year low in 2017. Intra-ASEAN investment played an important role in pushing up investment levels in the region. The Southeast Asian economies, particularly Indonesia, Malaysia, Thailand, and Viet Nam, have relatively low production costs and the ability to accommodate large-scale shifts of production. FDI is expected to strengthen as Southeast Asian countries continue to adopt measures aimed at attracting investment. Declines in inbound FDI were reported in the Lao PDR, Malaysia, and the Philippines. The Philippines saw the largest decline, with investment contracting by 26%.[1]

---

[1]   Based on the ASEAN Statistics and Data Portal. https://data.aseanstats.org/dashboards (accessed September 2020).

With increasing cross-border mobility of capital, policymakers in Southeast Asia are facing many challenges arising from globalization to stay competitive in the global markets. There has been rising tax competition in the region. The corporate income taxes have trended downward in Southeast Asia for the countries to remain competitive and attractive to FDI. At the same time, tax incentives for FDI, which are distortive and costly for tax compliance, have been widely utilized among Southeast Asian countries. More recently, the finance ministers of 20 of the world's largest economies (G20) agreed to set a minimum tax rate for corporate income of 15% and to shift where some taxes are collected to fit the modern digital economy and to address the base erosion and profit shifting. These trends will become emerging challenges for the Southeast Asian countries and will necessitate rethinking the existing tax incentives and redesigning tax policies for promoting competitiveness and the digital economy.

E.   Digital Transformation of Revenue Bodies

Access to internet services has been consistently improving in Southeast Asia (Figure 4). In all countries across the region, over 80% of the population are now within third generation or 3G (or higher) network coverage. However, when a broader range of key enablers of mobile internet adoption such as infrastructure, affordability, consumer readiness, and content and services are considered, material differences in mobile connectivity emerge.[2] Based on the mobile connectivity index, only Singapore ranks as a leader; Indonesia, Brunei Darussalam, Malaysia, Thailand, and Viet Nam are advanced; the Philippines is transitional; and Cambodia, the Lao PDR, and Timor-Leste are emerging. Driving higher levels of internet use and expanding the range of electronic services has the potential, especially in emerging and transitional countries, to ease meeting compliance obligations and to facilitate lower regulatory compliance costs across the system.

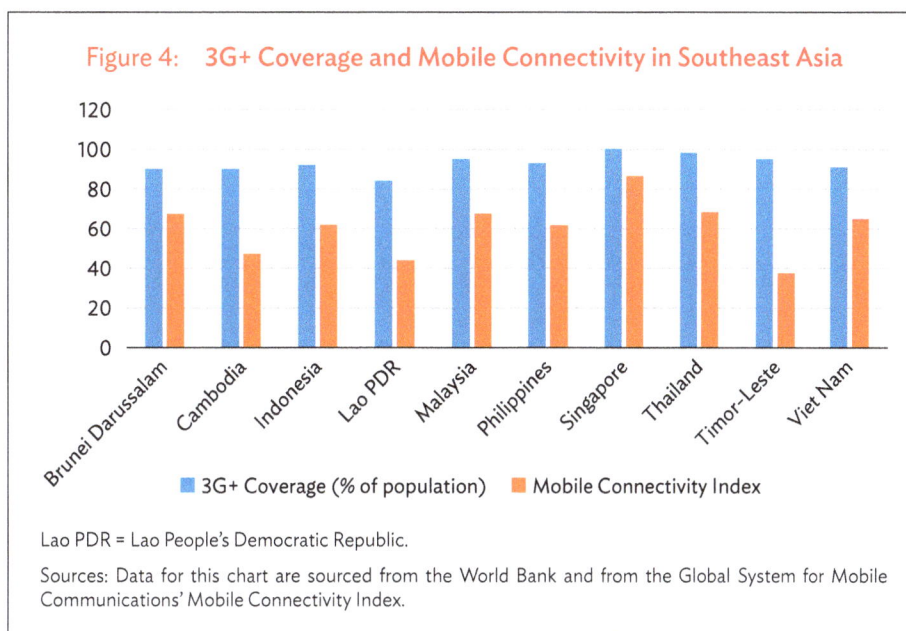

Figure 4:   3G+ Coverage and Mobile Connectivity in Southeast Asia

Lao PDR = Lao People's Democratic Republic.

Sources: Data for this chart are sourced from the World Bank and from the Global System for Mobile Communications' Mobile Connectivity Index.

---

[2]   Global System for Mobile Communications' Mobile Connectivity Index. https://www.gsma.com/mobilefordevelopment/resources/state-of-mobileinternet-connectivity-2018/ (accessed 14 July 2020).

Reflecting this strengthening infrastructure, e-service offerings from revenue bodies are increasing across the region, with most reporting at least some forms of electronic service delivery. Most jurisdictions offer, or have plans to introduce, electronic filing (or e-filing) and e-payment options. Fewer offer mobile apps to support taxpayer compliance or offer pre-filling services. All jurisdictions have plans to expand e-service offerings, promote (and in some cases compel) take-up, and most report plans to expand the use of technology in supporting better data management to assist in developing more effective approaches to compliance risk management.

The remaining chapters in this report identify avenues for tax policies and administration reforms in response to these emerging trends of domestic resource mobilization in Southeast Asia. Chapter 2 takes stock of tax administration of revenue profiles in Southeast Asia. It examines various country-specific aspects of revenue mobilization in each jurisdiction including the organizational and institutional setup, revenue mobilization performance, management of tax segments, and the states of the medium-term revenue strategies. Chapter 3 discusses the factors conducive to efficiencies of major tax types in Southeast Asia, especially PIT, CIT, and VAT. This chapter also touches upon cross-cutting tax issues including the use of tax havens, the shadow economy, and taxation in the digital economy. Chapter 4 examines policy options involving tax policies and administration reforms that would contribute to enhancing domestic revenue mobilization. This chapter underlines the pivotal roles of reducing compliance costs, establishing trust in and certainty of revenue bodies among taxpayers, and international tax cooperation. Chapter 5 concludes this report with short-, medium- and long-term policy recommendations and sheds light on the ways forward for ADB's engagement in domestic resource mobilization in Southeast Asia.

II. Tax Administration and Revenue Profile

A. Tax Administration Setup and Performance

The tax mix is relatively consistent across the region, with most revenue bodies collecting a typical range of domestic taxes (VAT, corporate income tax [CIT], and PIT) as well as various withholding taxes (WHTs), and some minor taxes such as on gambling and luxury goods. Five revenue bodies also collect excise, including environmental and so-called "sin" taxes. Brunei Darussalam has no VAT or PIT, Cambodia has no PIT, and Malaysia has recently abolished the VAT. As shown in Figure 5, the revenue collected by revenue bodies typically represents a relatively high proportion of total revenue collected, demonstrating a high level of dependency on the revenue body for government funds.

Tax administrations across the region are typically set up as a single organizational unit (e.g., department) within the Ministry of Finance (MOF).[3] Although there is no universally accepted best practice in establishing tax administration institutional arrangements, general advice from bodies such as the International Monetary Fund (IMF) and the European Commission suggest that some form of semiautonomous revenue agency is the preferred approach. In Southeast Asia, only two jurisdictions (Malaysia and Singapore) have semiautonomous

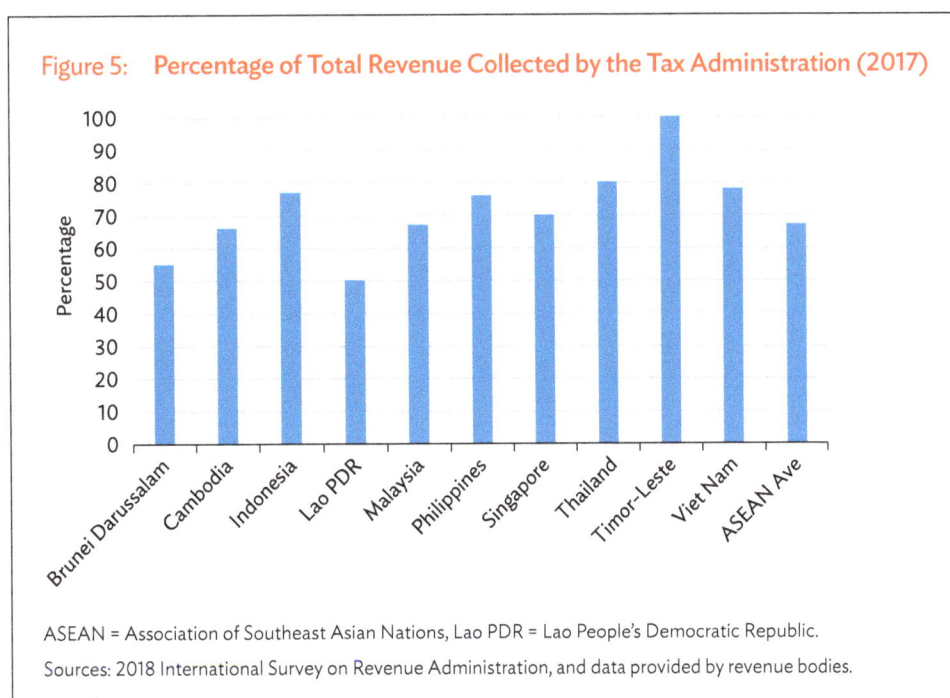

Figure 5: Percentage of Total Revenue Collected by the Tax Administration (2017)

ASEAN = Association of Southeast Asian Nations, Lao PDR = Lao People's Democratic Republic.
Sources: 2018 International Survey on Revenue Administration, and data provided by revenue bodies.

---

3   ADB. 2020. *A Comparative Analysis of Tax Administration in Asia and the Pacific*. Manila: ADB.

revenue bodies; in both cases, these bodies are overseen by an independent board, reporting to government. All other jurisdictions have tax administrations that are single organizations within the MOF. Only Timor-Leste has a revenue body responsible for overseeing both domestic taxes and customs.

As shown in Figure 6, revenue body staff coverage of citizens and workers varies considerably across the region, with Cambodia, and the Philippines having the highest numbers of labor force members per revenue body staff member, and Viet Nam, Malaysia, and the Lao PDR recording the lowest numbers. Malaysia reported the highest costs of collections and the Philippines the lowest. Cambodia, Indonesia, and Malaysia reported the highest levels of staff assigned to support functions, while Singapore and Thailand reported the lowest numbers.

Ideal revenue body staffing levels cannot be generalized as factors such as the design of the tax system and levels of automation play a major part in determining required staff levels. Nevertheless, some insights may be gleaned from considering factors such as the number of citizens and labor force members per revenue body staff member, the percentage of staff assigned to support functions, and the costs of collection. Each of these indicators tends to decline as institutions modernize, but extremely high and extremely low numbers should be cause for further investigation. High numbers may indicate inefficiencies, while very low numbers may suggest under-resourcing of the revenue body.

Across the region, there are relatively high levels of reliance on domestic revenue bodies for government revenue along with the demand for revenue mobilization, exacerbated by additional pressures arising from COVID-19-related spending. Governments must focus on sustaining and, where necessary, strengthening revenue body capacity and capability.

Figure 6:   Cost of Tax Collection for Labor Force Members and Full-Time Equivalent Staff

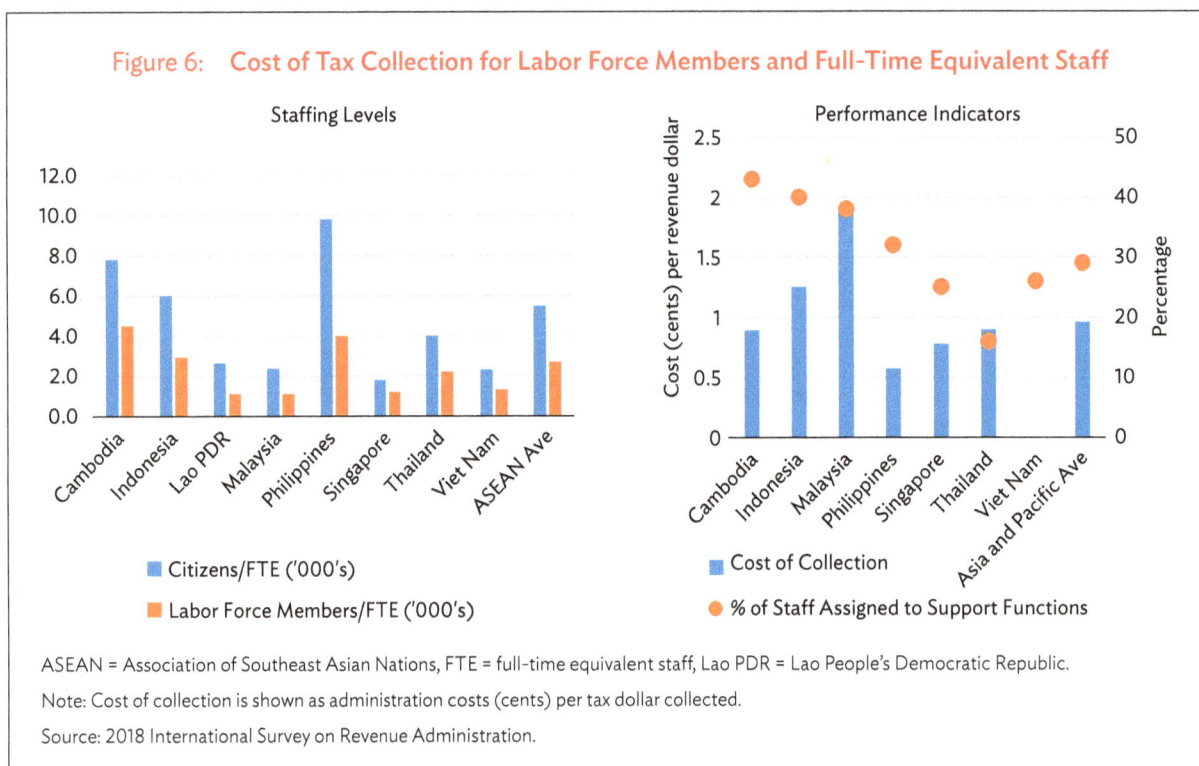

ASEAN = Association of Southeast Asian Nations, FTE = full-time equivalent staff, Lao PDR = Lao People's Democratic Republic.

Note: Cost of collection is shown as administration costs (cents) per tax dollar collected.

Source: 2018 International Survey on Revenue Administration.

B.   Revenue Profile

Regional Trends in Tax to GDP

Higher tax revenues mean a country is able to spend more to improve infrastructure, health, and education.[4] Figure 7 shows that, across the region, tax to GDP is typically slightly below the Asia and the Pacific average, and well below the averages for Organisation for Economic Co-operation and Development (OECD) member countries. Only three jurisdictions, Cambodia, Thailand, and Viet Nam, report tax to GDP as consistently exceeding 15%, that being the minimum level considered necessary to support sustainable economic growth and development.[5] However, it should be noted that Cambodia's GDP per capita is among the lowest in the region. No jurisdictions report tax to GDP consistently over 20%.

Trends across the region tend toward the downside and most economies have made slow progress in raising tax to GDP to the targeted levels. Tax to GDP has remained steady in Indonesia, Singapore, and Viet Nam, has improved in Cambodia and the Philippines (slightly), and has declined in the Lao PDR, Malaysia, and Thailand (slightly). Brunei Darussalam and Timor-Leste have more volatile tax-to-GDP patterns, largely due to the price volatility of oil and gas and the heavy reliance of these economies on oil and gas reserves.

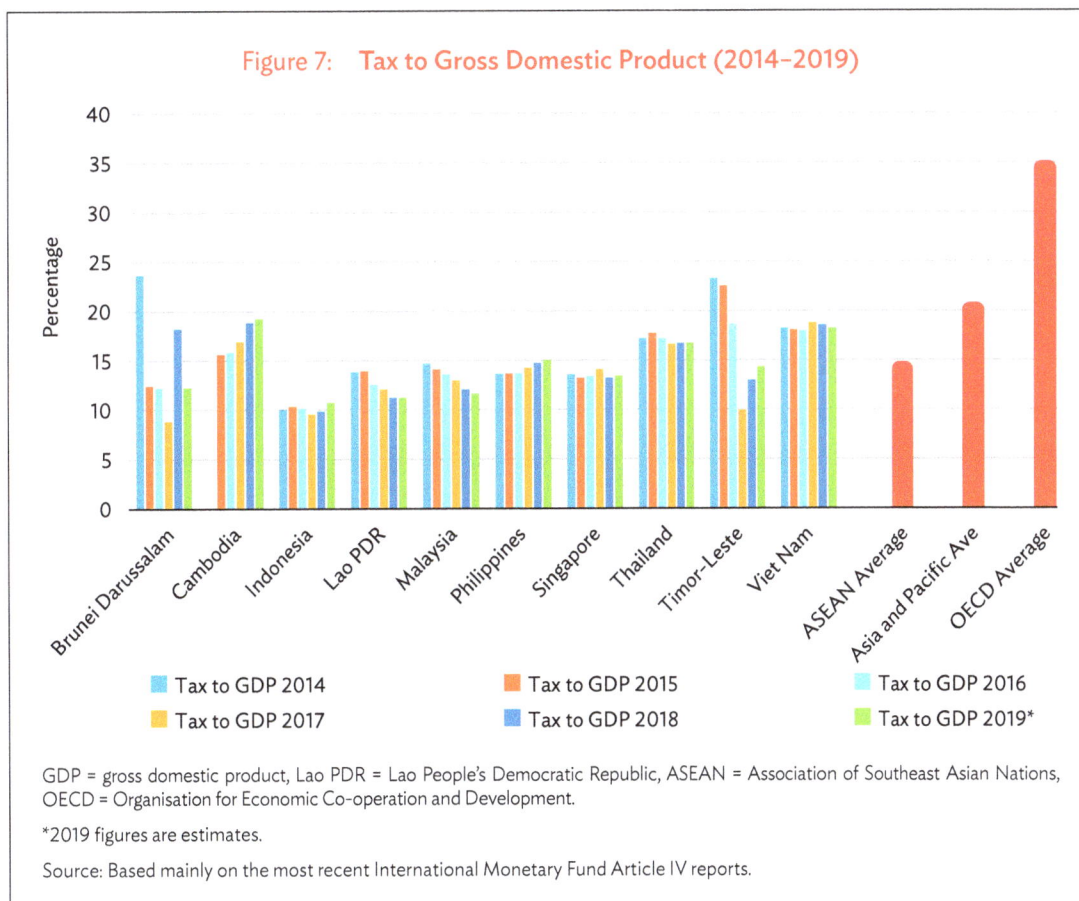

Figure 7:   Tax to Gross Domestic Product (2014–2019)

GDP = gross domestic product, Lao PDR = Lao People's Democratic Republic, ASEAN = Association of Southeast Asian Nations, OECD = Organisation for Economic Co-operation and Development.

*2019 figures are estimates.

Source: Based mainly on the most recent International Monetary Fund Article IV reports.

<hr>

[4]   For some jurisdictions, governments have access to significant nontax revenues (e.g., sales of oil, minerals, and real property, and investment income) that lessen the need to rely on tax revenues to fund government programs and services. Economies in this category include Brunei Darussalam, the Lao PDR, Timor-Leste, and Singapore.

[5]   IMF. 2016. Working Paper: *Tax Capacity and Growth: Is there a Tipping Point?* Vitor Gaspar, Laura Jaramillo, and Philippe Wingender. Washington, DC: IMF. https://www.imf.org/external/pubs/ft/wp/2016/wp16234.pdf.

Productivity of Taxes

The productivity or efficiency of the major taxes (such as CIT and VAT) may provide some guidance on areas where an increase in compliance focus or policy redesign, or both, may strengthen DRM and improve overall tax to GDP. Productivity is the amount of revenue produced per percentage point of the tax rate and is calculated as the ratio between the particular tax collection as share of GDP and the standard statutory rate for that tax.[6] Lower CIT or VAT productivity is to be expected in jurisdictions with low rates, and the converse is also true: where the rate is high, productivity is likely to be higher. Tax productivity that is out of alignment with the rate may point to erosion of the base. This may arise from weaknesses in design—such as high registration thresholds, multiple rates, high levels of exemptions or significant incentives—and weaknesses in tax administration—such as complex compliance requirements, poor risk management, and ineffective service and enforcement—leading to revenue leakage and higher tax gaps.

CIT productivity is illustrated in Figure 8. The statutory CIT rate is relatively high in Indonesia, Malaysia, and the Philippines, and relatively low in Brunei Darussalam, Singapore, and Timor-Leste. The increasing CIT productivity in Cambodia has been partly attributed to improved tax administration driven by the implementation of a revenue mobilization strategy in 2014.

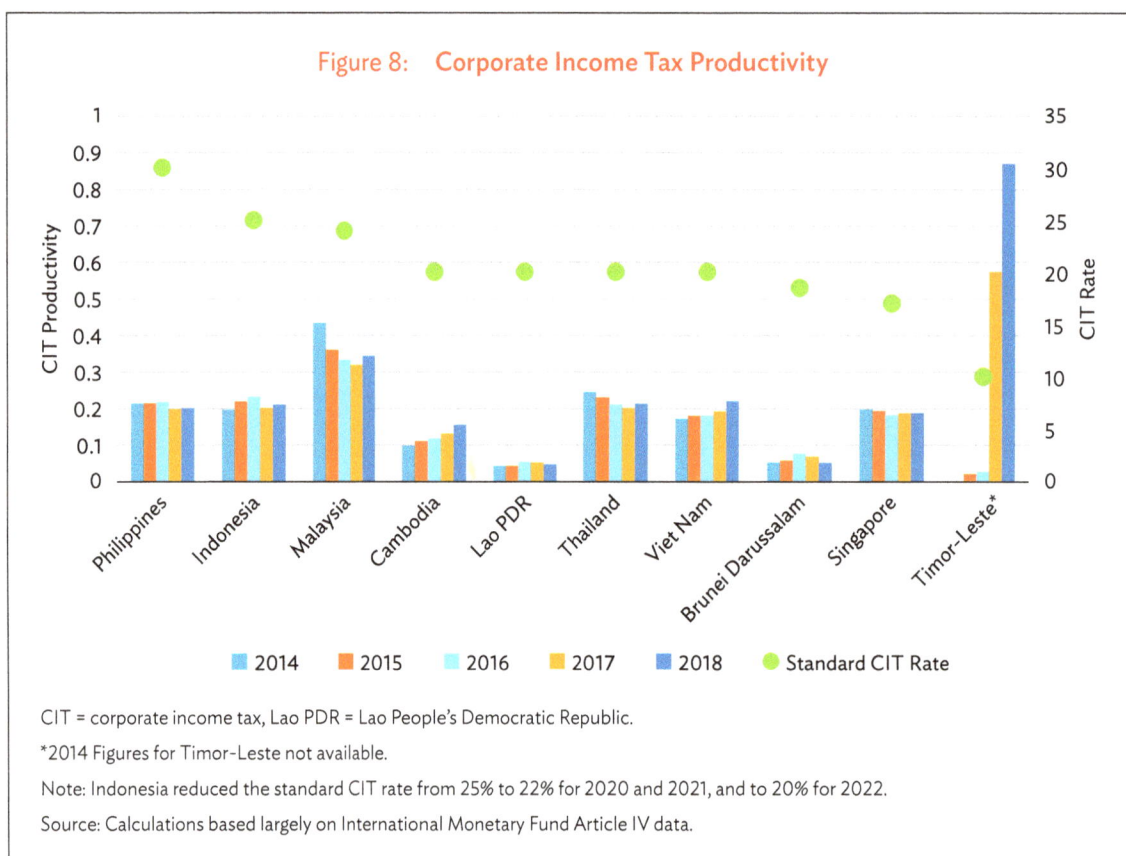

Figure 8:   Corporate Income Tax Productivity

CIT = corporate income tax, Lao PDR = Lao People's Democratic Republic.

*2014 Figures for Timor-Leste not available.

Note: Indonesia reduced the standard CIT rate from 25% to 22% for 2020 and 2021, and to 20% for 2022.

Source: Calculations based largely on International Monetary Fund Article IV data.

---

[6]   Productivity is measured as the ratio of revenue to the product of GDP and the standard rate. For example, VAT productivity is calculated as follows: VAT revenue ÷ (GDP × standard VAT rate). Productivity measures how much each percentage point of the standard tax rate collects in terms of GDP. Comparing this ratio over time or between countries can gauge relative revenue performance of the particular tax. A low ratio is typically taken as evidence of weak design (exemption and/or reduced rates) and/or weak enforcement. Source: IMF Tax Policy Assessment Framework (TPAF); https://www.imf.org/en/Data/TPAF. When making comparisons between countries, it is important to recognize that issues such as differences in the composition of GDP and the respective tax frameworks will impact this ratio. Other measures of efficiency, such as the C-efficiency ratio for VAT, may also be useful.

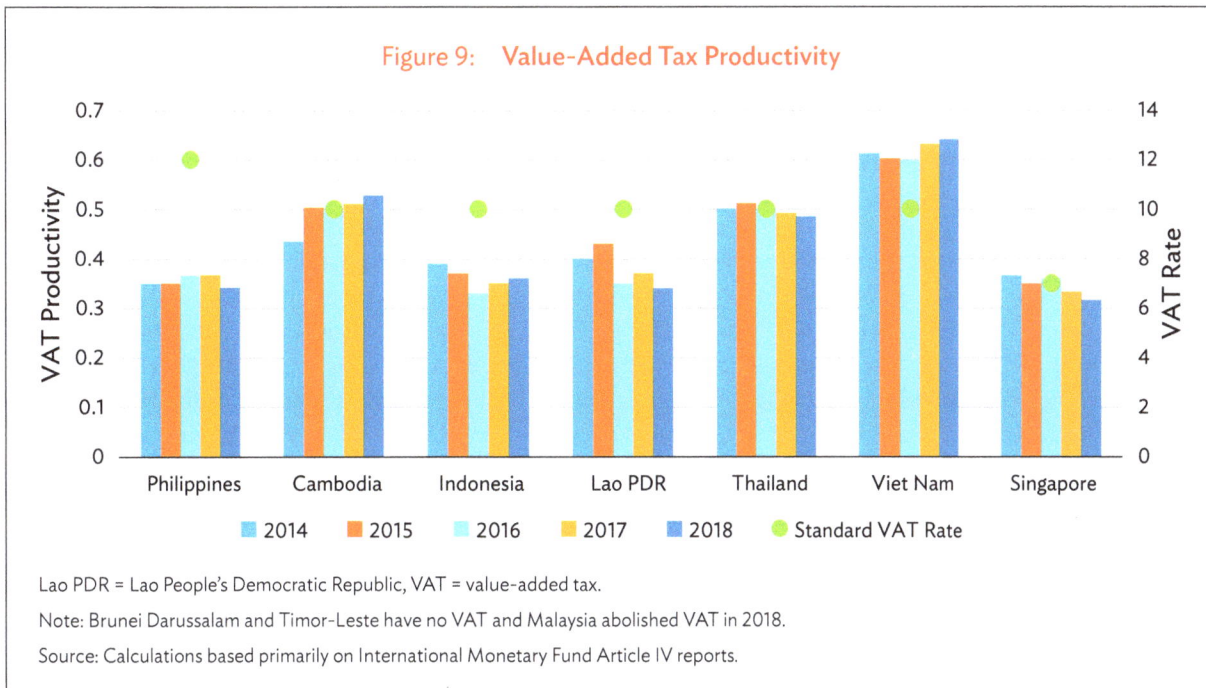

Figure 9:   Value-Added Tax Productivity

Lao PDR = Lao People's Democratic Republic, VAT = value-added tax.

Note: Brunei Darussalam and Timor-Leste have no VAT and Malaysia abolished VAT in 2018.

Source: Calculations based primarily on International Monetary Fund Article IV reports.

With respect to the relative CIT standard rates in Lao PDR, which is in the midrange, the CIT productivity is surprisingly low. This is likely to be partly impacted by the fact that around 80% of the corporate tax base is estimated to be exempt. The Philippines has a relatively high CIT rate, but CIT productivity is in the mid to low range. The pattern of CIT productivity in Malaysia more than likely reflects the introduction of a VAT in 2015, and its subsequent abolition in 2018. CIT productivity that is out of alignment with CIT rates may point to potential erosion of the CIT base, either due to policy design or higher levels of noncompliance, or both. These discrepancies may warrant further study.

VAT productivity is illustrated in Figure 9. At the lower end are the Philippines, Singapore, Indonesia, and the Lao PDR. VAT productivity in the Philippines is surprisingly low considering that the Philippines has the highest VAT rate and a registration threshold in the lower range for the region. Singapore has a relatively low VAT standard rate, and the low VAT productivity may in part reflect that, as well as the high registration threshold and the high level of exports (not subject to VAT). Indonesia and the Lao PDR both have midrange VAT rates, and both have registration thresholds that are slightly higher when compared to local incomes. It should be noted that ratios reflect both differences between VATs in terms of design and administration, as well as between the share of final consumption in GDP as this is the base upon which the VAT is levied. Differences between countries should be interpreted with caution.

The patterns in CIT and VAT productivity, particularly in the Philippines, Indonesia, and the Lao PDR suggest potential erosion of the base, which may be attributable at least in part to compliance issues, and extensive exemptions. Other factors, such as increasing hard-to-tax transactions including digital sales, may also contribute. These patterns may warrant further study.

C.   Management of Important Taxpayer Segments

The taxpayer segmentation is used to varying degrees by many revenue bodies across the world. Sometimes the revenue body is organized principally around segments of taxpayers (e.g., large businesses, small and medium-sized businesses, wage earners, etc.). In other cases, the focus is not structural but is reflected in the ways in which products, services, and verification activities are developed and delivered. The rationale for focusing on taxpayer segments is that each group has different characteristics, information needs, and compliance behaviors, and, as a result, presents different service needs and risks to revenue. Regardless of structural considerations, in order to manage these different segments effectively, the revenue body needs to develop and implement strategies (e.g., public rulings, taxpayer education and services, more targeted audits) that reflect the characteristics and compliance issues presented by each group.

In Southeast Asia, the most encountered segment focus is on large business taxpayers. The rationale is to provide greater attention to those taxpayers responsible for the largest proportion of revenue. Typically, the large business segment is defined in such a way as to encompass 50%–80% of revenue and often also includes major sectors, such as banking and finance, mining, and telecommunications. In Southeast Asia, as part of the 2018 International Survey of Tax Administrations, all jurisdictions surveyed reported having a large business unit, with most managing only corporate taxpayers.[7] Only Indonesia and Malaysia reported having a focus on individuals with high net worth.

D.   Tax Revenue Mobilization Plans

Stagnant or declining tax to GDP has prompted most countries in the region to develop, and in some cases implement, medium-term revenue strategies (MTRS). Some strategies are broadly based, while others are more targeted and aimed at specific areas where weaknesses have been identified. Most strategies include both policy and administrative focus areas. The following discussion provides a summary of each jurisdiction's planned approaches.

Brunei Darussalam has recently developed a medium-term fiscal plan, as part of the National Development Plan, to drive diversification and growth and reduce dependence on oil and gas revenues. The initiatives include privatization of state-owned assets, promoting public–private partnership, assessment of subsidies against objectives, fiscal management improvement, revenue diversification, and amalgamation of the government's asset management system. The plan focuses on five priority business clusters: downstream oil and gas, food, tourism, services, and information and communication technology. The government strategy encompasses corporatization, public–private partnership, and privatization, all of which may have taxation ramifications. Authorities are currently reviewing the tax policy and structure, and the feasibility to further broaden the current tax base. All these policy measures are likely to place additional demands on the tax administration requiring it to be proactive in planning and providing guidance and supervision to these emerging sectors and operations.

In Cambodia, the authorities have implemented the Revenue Mobilization Strategy 2014–2018 with significant revenue gains mostly through improved tax administration (additional 3% of GDP in 3 years). The Revenue Mobilization Strategy 2019–2023 was launched in 2019 to continue modernization and automation efforts, review tax incentives, and establish key performance indicators. Targets are for a further 0.3% of GDP through improved service quality and revenue body productivity. Property taxes is an area identified by the IMF, which recommended continuing efforts in using updated real estate valuations. Automation levels are relatively low and provide an opportunity to re-engineer business processes and strengthen institutional structures. Integrated IT systems and tax databases would improve efficiency, supported by risk-based audits, simplified regulatory procedures, and staff training.

The Directorate General of Taxes in Indonesia recently completed a reform plan including the implementation of administrative reforms designed to strengthen revenue collections. Steps have been taken to improve tax administration—such as risk-based audits, lifting bank secrecy, and ongoing development of IT system and data

---

[7]   Brunei Darussalam and Timor-Leste were not surveyed.

matching, all of which supported the positive revenue performance in 2018. These reforms are planned to continue under the directorate's MTRS, focusing on the design and launch of compliance improvement plans (CIPs) in key areas and backed by implementation of supporting initiatives and institutional reforms. The Directorate of General Taxes has announced focus areas for compliance improvement plans, including VAT, WHT (employer obligations), and wealthy Indonesians. Following up on tax audit reports and adopting risk-based auditing will also help focus scarce resources on the riskiest taxpayers. Further reforms are planned as part of the MOF's strategic program known as *Tax Reform Chapter III*, which focuses on five pillars: organization, human resources, information technology (IT) and databases, business processes, and regulation. In November 2020, the omnibus tax law was enacted to improve tax laws and make Indonesia more attractive to foreign investors.

The Lao PDR has developed, with the help of the IMF, an MTRS. Measures to improve revenue administration in 2019 included: an ongoing rollout of the electronic tax payment systems for VAT, income, road, and land taxes; strengthening taxpayer registration and risk-based administration systems; and refining organizational structural arrangements at provincial and national levels. The authorities have agreed to fiscal consolidation mainly through expenditure controls. Additional revenues may become available through increased automation and the planned review of tax laws, and this could further support fiscal consolidation. Strengthening the international taxation framework is considered by the IMF to be relatively urgent. Additional priorities in 2019 include implementation of three tax reform laws approved by the National Assembly in 2019 further revisions were made in August 2021: (i) income tax law, (ii) excise tax law, and (iii) tax administration laws.

Malaysia has a low tax revenue ratio, highlighting the need for revenue mobilization to support medium-term consolidation, and to help finance needed expenditure to achieve priorities identified under the Mid-Term Review of the Eleventh Malaysia Plan. Declining revenues in Malaysia have driven recent plans to develop an MTRS. The authorities will receive technical assistance from the IMF to support their efforts in formulating and implementing this MTRS to (i) reverse declining revenue trends and (ii) deliver sustainable higher revenue to finance priority expenditure. These efforts will build on the work of the Tax Reform Committee, which in August 2019 submitted for the government's consideration suggestions to improve tax administration, reduce tax leakages, and identify new sources of revenue. A Tax Reform Committee has been formed to oversee a wide-ranging review of Malaysia's tax system, including examining incentives, and considering new sources of sustainable revenue. The main task of the committee is to narrow the tax gap, improve efficiency, and to increase buoyancy.

In 2016, the Philippines commenced a program of reform with the passage of Package 1 of the Tax Reform for Acceleration and Inclusion (TRAIN) in 2017. Further measures involving excise tax increases for selected products and broadening the VAT base were implemented in 2018. A second package of the TRAIN initiative, known as the Corporate Recovery and Tax Incentives for Enterprises Act, was recently signed into law in March 2021 to lower corporate income taxes and rationalize tax incentives. A set of reforms known as Package 2+, focusing on so-called sin taxes, was approved in late 2019 and has been implemented. This package amended the laws to introduce phased increases in excise rates on tobacco and alcohol products from 2020. Package 3, dealing with property tax reform, has been approved in the House of Representatives and, as of June 2020, is currently the subject of review by a House and Ways Committee. Continued efforts to improve tax administration and revenue collection, together with further increases in excise taxes on e-cigarette and alcohol products, are the remaining revenue-raising priorities. The pending bill to rationalize and improve governance and design of the tax incentive regime, currently being discussed in Congress, would support higher levels of accountability and better targeted incentives to encourage business investment, job creation, and economic development. Development of legislation for TRAIN Package 4 on passive income tax reform is ongoing.

Singapore has built up its reserves over the years and the government can only spend up to 50% of the long-term expected real returns from Singapore's reserves under the Net Investment Returns framework. The remaining

50% continues to be invested for future returns. This ensures that investment returns are available for spending in a sustainable way. Apart from relying on returns from government assets, Singapore continues to review its tax structure to ensure its resilience and sustainability. For example, to support recurrent needs such as health care, security, and other social spending, the government has announced plans to raise the goods and services tax (GST) from 7% to 9%.

The Thailand Revenue Department is addressing revenue leakages arising from specific policy gaps, including in taxation of the digital economy. The recently introduced digital services tax is designed to partially address this gap. Authorities intend to strengthen revenue mobilization over the medium to long run, as part of a broader strategy to support government development programs and long-run social protection needs, including to prepare for aging-related expenditure pressures. According to the IMF, to do so, the revenue-to-GDP ratio needs to increase by about 3% of GDP on a permanent basis. The Thailand Revenue Department received IMF technical assistance in 2018 in the development of an MTRS and in 2019 to improve compliance in the hotel industry and e-commerce. Continued implementation of the medium-term revenue strategy, and a focus on revenue administration reforms are recommended. Other administration reforms to increase revenue include enforcement of the new Land and Property Tax Law and taxation of investment income from bonds through mutual funds. The new e-payment law, effective from the beginning of 2020, will help prevent local online vendors from avoiding income tax.

In Timor-Leste, authorities have acknowledged the need to increase domestic non-oil revenue mobilization. The Fiscal Reform Commission, which is a technical body, was established by the Government of Timor-Leste, and charged with evaluating all current and potential forms of revenue and enabling reforms. The commission will work with the new Tax Authority to reform tax administration, one of its three priorities. Over the coming 3 years, the plan is to completely reform tax administration. New laws and procedures for taxation set the legal basis for the reforms. New IT systems are planned to make the process of collecting and paying taxes easier and relevant officials will be fully trained in the use of new systems. The recruitment of additional staff will provide the Tax Authority with the required qualified human resources to properly implement the planned reforms. Current tax officials will undergo training over the next 2 years on new processes and laws, skills in auditing, taxpayer services, risk management, and return processing.

In Viet Nam, the authorities are confident that they will be able to broaden revenue bases based on administrative reforms, including the use of IT and digitalization. The General Department of Taxation (GDT) is researching options for improving property taxation and land registries. Administrative measures to improve revenue include (i) strengthening cooperation across government agencies such as the GDT, Customs Office, Ministry of Security, and other institutions to enhance coordination, strengthen supervision, and reduce tax arrears; (ii) adopting electronic tax transactions; (iii) adopting risk management in tax administration; (iv) requiring enterprises to use electronic invoices in transaction of sales of goods and service; and (v) strengthening measures to combat tax base erosion, tax evasion, and profit shifting.

III. Strengthening Revenue and Broadening the Tax Base

This section discusses factors that, at a broad level, may impact the CIT, VAT, and PIT revenue streams in Southeast Asian economies. It also discusses some specific compliance risks that may be relevant across a number of revenue streams, such as those relating to taxing the digital economy, managing the international taxation regime, and the potential of subnational taxes to further support revenue outcomes. Additional factors may include tax evasion, and tax planning and avoidance, which are likely to be present, albeit in different forms, across most segments of the business community.[8]

A. Corporate Income Tax and Value-Added Tax

Apart from resource-rich countries, CIT productivity across the region has remained relatively steady. Consistent improvements in Cambodia are noted. VAT productivity, which is typically higher than CIT productivity in the region, has also been stable over the last 5 years. Based on these steady productivity levels for both CIT and VAT, it is unlikely that any recent economic or business shifts have contributed to the observed soft tax-to-GDP ratios across most of the region. It is more likely that there are longstanding and systemic issues that are relevant in explaining the problematic nature of revenue performances. For example, international tax avoidance, weak tax administration, and the prevalence of extensive tax incentives, offered by every country in the region to attract foreign investment, undoubtedly erode the CIT tax base, and potentially the VAT base.

Tax Incentives

Tax incentives are widely used across Southeast Asia both to attract investment and the economic activity it generates, and to direct it into higher priority areas in order to selectively stimulate and strengthen certain areas of the economy. Although tax incentives have the potential to benefit the economy and support sustained growth, where governments do not estimate, report, and evaluate the fiscal cost of these tax expenditures, it is not possible to evaluate the success, or otherwise, of such measures in achieving goals.

Based on worldwide experience, tax incentives and other similar investment inducements offered by countries in Southeast Asia are likely to be costly and result in significant reductions of revenues, so it is important to know if they are delivering the outcomes sought. Where evaluations do occur, tax incentives are often found not only to be costly, but also to be relatively ineffective in generating future revenues and in stimulating sustainable economic activity. Further, revenue bodies also often express concerns that tax incentives are vulnerable to abuse and manipulation, and compliance with rules is often not effectively monitored. Often there is no clear responsibility for compliance monitoring.

---

[8] It should be noted that this review is based on available public information. Observations are prima facie only. Any conclusions drawn should be considered in more detail by the relevant authorities.

Most jurisdictions have not published tax expenditure analysis, so it is not possible to confirm the extent to which tax incentives have reduced revenues across the region. However, some jurisdictions are now beginning to examine these policies more closely. Brunei Darussalam has recently indicated that studies on the impact of incentives are planned. Indonesia has conducted and published extensive tax expenditure analysis since 2017, and recently announced an intended review.[9] Malaysia has announced a greater focus on public sector transparency, which may include publishing tax expenditures. The Philippines has published high-level tax expenditure details and recently announced an intention to rationalize tax incentives. The Lao PDR reported difficulties in finding records of tax incentives granted, resulting in difficulty in monitoring these expenditures.

Often, investment incentives are not designed holistically, but rather tend to evolve to address specific issues or needs. The result may be a somewhat haphazard system involving varied design features, different objectives, and frequently involving multiple government ministries. Although there may be good policy reasons to involve multiple ministries in the process of developing, promulgating, and approving various incentives, administering and estimating the costs of tax incentives in these circumstances is undoubtedly problematic. In many developing countries, central government agencies have experienced challenges in reviewing tax expenditures relating to investment incentives, at least in part due to incomplete or limited availability of data on tax and other incentives that may have been granted over the years. Against this backdrop, it is good practice to centralize some functions such as record keeping, monitoring and compliance review, and quality assurance, to facilitate both evaluation of various incentive programs and the monitoring of compliance with incentive conditions.

International agencies, such as ADB, the IMF, and World Bank, strongly encourage governments to pay closer attention to this area, both at a policy design and administration level, due at least in part to the considerable investment of tax revenue. Although understanding these tax expenditures at a whole-of-system level is important, of most concern is the identification of tax expenditures invested in legitimate incentives that may not be effective, and revenues lost due to incidents of abuse and manipulation of some schemes.

Countries in the region that are not already doing so may wish to evaluate current tax incentives with the view to better understanding the level of tax expenditures, improving effectiveness in delivery of desired benefits, and strengthening integrity and accountability. Such studies help to better design and target incentives, facilitate cost–benefit analysis, and identify areas where redesign may be required in order to improve effectiveness of incentives in generating long-term economic development. Studies also help pinpoint incentives that are not delivering desired outcomes and require modification or even abolition. Moving further in this direction would contribute to better outcomes and to easing governments' budget constraints, which is important for domestic revenue mobilization in developing countries.

Such reviews and policy changes are likely to take some time to deliver results; in the meantime, strengthening of current governance may be possible within the existing frameworks. Governments may or may not be satisfied with the incentive framework on offer, but even where the policy is considered to be sound, it is good practice to protect the system from potential abuses through governance and compliance monitoring. Where there is a lack of oversight, noncompliance with the conditions of incentives, and potential manipulations, such as to extend eligibility, may go unnoticed and unchecked.

In some jurisdictions, the revenue body has a role to play in monitoring compliance, but this is not always the case. Revenue bodies are often well placed to perform a monitoring role due to their access to relevant company

---

[9]   The report can be accessed at https://fiskal.kemenkeu.go.id/publikasi/tax-expenditure-report (in Bahasa Indonesian) and is also reported in the World Bank's 2020 publication: Indonesia Public Expenditure Review: Spending for Better Results at https://www.worldbank.org/en/country/indonesia/publication/indonesia-public-expenditure-review (accessed 1 September 2020).

records and accounts, as well as due to their expertise in verification and audit. Prompt implementation of a system of centralized reporting and record-keeping arrangements may be possible without material policy changes. Increasing the role of revenue bodies in compliance monitoring will help to detect revenue losses through abuse and improve the perceived effectiveness of compliance oversight, which is likely to increase voluntary compliance.

International Tax Issues

Multinational Enterprises and International Taxation

The approach and level of maturity of systems for managing international taxation risks associated with multinational enterprises (MNEs) varies significantly across the region. Figure 10 provides a snapshot of some pertinent features of the defensive and anti-avoidance measures in place across the region.

Six countries in the region have joined the OECD/G20 Inclusive Framework on base erosion and profit shifting (BEPS), and three have signed the Multilateral Convention to Implement Tax Treaty Related Measures to Prevent BEPS.[10] Only three jurisdictions have limited or no protective measures in place to defend against erosion of the domestic tax base. Some countries, including Thailand and Viet Nam, are still in the process of implementing the minimum standards required under the inclusive framework. Four countries (Indonesia, Malaysia, Singapore, and Viet Nam) have confirmed that domestic legislation is in place.

Tax Transparency

Eight of the 11 countries in the region are members of the Global Forum on Transparency and Exchange of Information for Tax Purposes (Global Forum), and 6 have signed the Multilateral Convention on Mutual Assistance in Tax Matters.[11] Singapore has been assessed to be fully compliant with the exchange of information requirements of the global forum, while Brunei Darussalam, Indonesia, Malaysia, and the Philippines have been assessed as largely compliant. Cambodia, Thailand, and Viet Nam are yet to be reviewed. For some jurisdictions, such as the Philippines, where proposed laws to reduce bank secrecy have not been accepted by Parliament (at the time of writing), attempts to introduce reforms to enable meeting of the exchange of information provisions of global forum membership have not yet been successful. There is an immediate need to consider measures to support revenue recovery following the pandemic and strengthening international taxation compliance is an obvious priority area for consideration.

The collection of beneficial ownership information supports tax transparency, and this remains a challenge for the region. ADB recently piloted a joint tax integrity and anti-money laundering (AML) initiative in the Philippines, Thailand, and Viet Nam. Resources from two technical assistance teams were used to strengthen national beneficial ownership transparency frameworks with a focus on plugging gaps in both AML and tax standards. The assistance on AML aims at supporting governments in strengthening their systems and financial institutions in fighting money laundering-related aspects of the shadow economy. The assistance in relation to tax aims to build the capacity of governments to work together toward enhancing regional tax transparency and fighting emerging BEPS-related issues caused by the increased digitalization of the economy. This blended approach demonstrates the benefits of a whole-of-government approach to streamline compliance and maximize the

---

[10]   OECD/G20 Inclusive Framework members are Brunei Darussalam, Indonesia, Malaysia, Singapore, *Thailand*, and Viet Nam. Signatories to the Multilateral Convention to Implement Tax Treaty Related Measures to Prevent BEPS are underlined and a jurisdiction that expressed an intent to sign the convention is shown in italics.

[11]   Global Forum members are Brunei Darussalam, Cambodia, Indonesia, Malaysia, the Philippines, Singapore, Thailand, and *Viet Nam*. Signatories to the Multilateral Convention on Mutual Assistance in Tax Matters are underlined and a jurisdiction that expressed an intent to sign the Convention is shown in italics.

effect of legal reforms that cut across both AML and tax integrity, thereby achieving greater impact in the fight against illicit financial flows.

Jurisdictions should, to the extent possible, participate in ongoing discussions at the OECD Inclusive Framework on BEPS. Enacting a sound domestic legal framework and participating in international forums to enhance consistency, cooperation, and information exchange, are important in supporting jurisdictions in their efforts to protect the domestic tax base from erosion, but they do not in themselves deliver this outcome. Many jurisdictions are currently preoccupied with participating in the expanding opportunities for international cooperation, but they should not overlook the need to also look inward and build their own internal capacity.

If revenue bodies are to be well placed to take advantage of new opportunities, which will arise from participation on international cooperative efforts, many other enablers are likely to be required. Strengthened staff capabilities in administering and enforcing international tax laws and access to modern technology to both support information exchange and fully capitalize on the data received from other jurisdictions, are just a couple of examples. Perhaps one of the best ways to identify gaps and to build capacity is to begin to work within the constraints of what is currently available by identifying areas of current revenue leakage, and to commence to develop and implement compliance improvement plans to address high priority risks. For example, most jurisdictions have some profit-shifting rules to control base erosion. Depending upon the rules in place currently, it may be possible to run pilots to select areas for compliance improvement pilots.

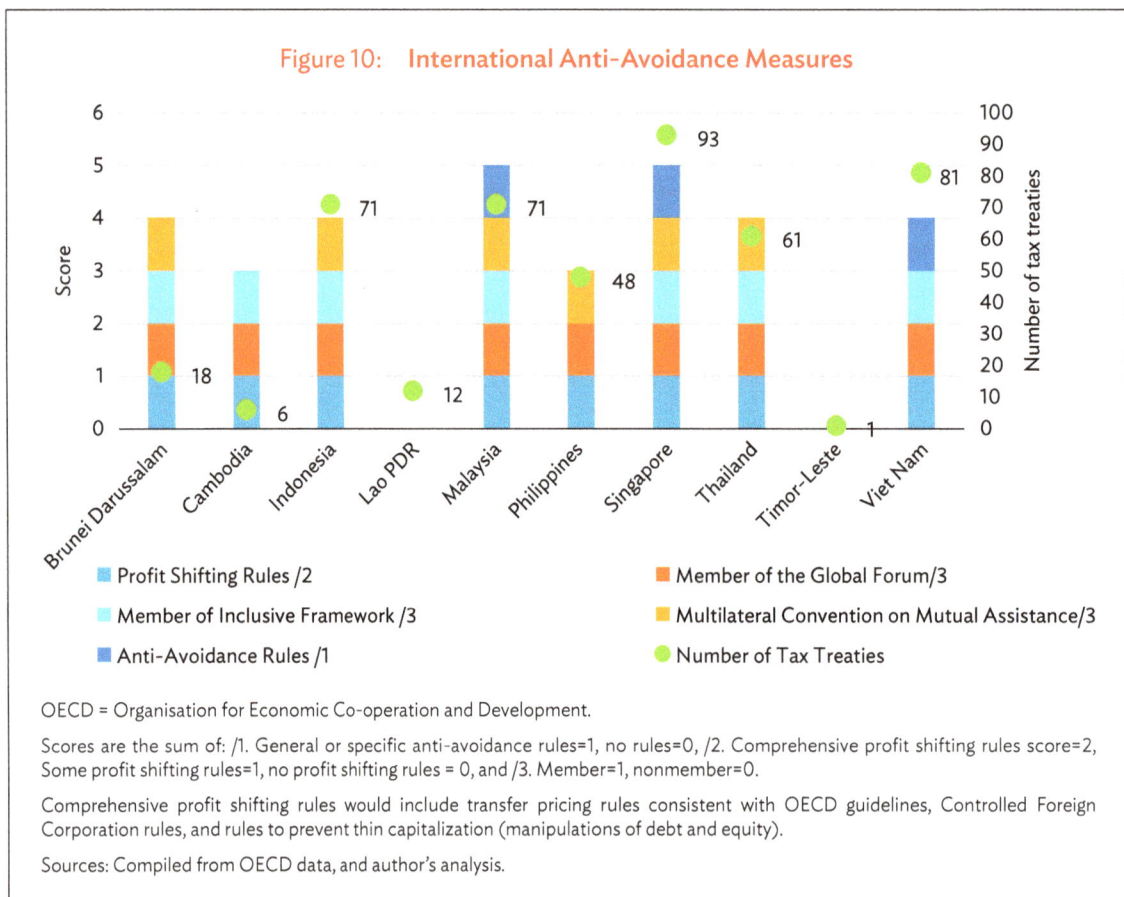

Figure 10:   International Anti-Avoidance Measures

OECD = Organisation for Economic Co-operation and Development.

Scores are the sum of: /1. General or specific anti-avoidance rules=1, no rules=0, /2. Comprehensive profit shifting rules score=2, Some profit shifting rules=1, no profit shifting rules = 0, and /3. Member=1, nonmember=0.

Comprehensive profit shifting rules would include transfer pricing rules consistent with OECD guidelines, Controlled Foreign Corporation rules, and rules to prevent thin capitalization (manipulations of debt and equity).

Sources: Compiled from OECD data, and author's analysis.

Waiting until all the enablers are fully developed before starting to work on international tax risks in earnest may be a lost opportunity to start building capacity, while *at the same time* building better enabling frameworks.

Production Structure Changes

In monitoring large business operations, including MNEs, changing production structures may guide revenue bodies toward areas of higher domestic and international tax risks. Monitoring shifts in production, both emerging and declining sectors, may help to narrow down areas where tax performance is out of step with levels of economic activity. Both high growth and declining sectors have incentives for both international and domestic tax planning and these activities may be more readily detected with sectoral-based monitoring. It is important to note though that analysis needs to be conducted at a relatively fine level, such as the subsector, industry, and sub-industry levels, in order to pinpoint particular compliance risks and identify risky taxpayers.

In Southeast Asia, emerging sub-industries include electronics; information and communication technology; textiles and apparel; and health care, biomedical sciences, and pharmaceuticals. FDI increases in emerging sectors may create opportunities for cross-border tax planning. Each revenue body would be well advised to conduct research on production structure shifts to better understand where changes are occurring and the risks that may emerge from those shifts. Analytics capabilities may need to be strengthened to support this assessment.

Value-Added Tax Systems

There is generally a relatively a high reliance on VAT revenue in the region, so there is vulnerability should this revenue stream be compromised. Design features such as high registration thresholds and widespread exemptions create vulnerability to revenue losses in some jurisdictions. Revenue leakage is also likely to be occurring from unreported sales associated with shadow economy activities, and emerging new business models, such as those involving cross-border internet sales of goods and services, which are difficult to detect and manage.

Value-Added Tax Design

VAT registration thresholds are generally set so as to strike a balance between costs of compliance and revenue. Setting the threshold too low risks imposing an administrative burden on very small enterprises where the revenue to be gained is relatively minor and compliance costs may have the counterproductive effect of driving some businesses into the shadow economy. Setting the threshold too high may incentivize manipulative practices (such as splitting businesses) to stay under the threshold, particularly if there is a lack of effective anti-avoidance rules and enforcement, which has the potential to disadvantage the few larger businesses that are required to register. Different models and design features have been adopted within Southeast Asian economies, as illustrated by the variation in registration requirements. The highest registration threshold in Singapore is set at over $700,000, while the lowest, in Viet Nam, is zero. Although other design features of the VAT regimes clearly impact decisions about the registration threshold, relative to the income levels many thresholds are quite high.

Multiple rates and exemptions are common across the region and these design features may contribute to further revenue shortfall and increased administrative burdens. Such features complicate the system requiring taxpayers to spend time ensuring that they properly classify goods in order to calculate the correct VAT rate, or to determine exempt status. These more complex designs are likely to generate higher error rates and may also facilitate manipulation. In addition, in such systems' revenue bodies must invest more resources in providing guidance and in conducting verification activities to detect errors and abuses.

Value-Added Tax Refunds

The inability of many revenue bodies to make timely refunds of excess VAT payments has been highlighted in research done by other bodies (e.g., large tax accounting professionals and the World Bank's Doing Business series). In Southeast Asia, four jurisdictions do not have a VAT system, and several others limit VAT refunds to international traders only. For these revenue bodies, the World Bank Doing Business series does not include a VAT refund case study. For the four revenue bodies reviewed as part of the World Bank series (Cambodia, Indonesia, Singapore, and Thailand), only Singapore issued VAT refunds in a shorter period (33 weeks) than the Asia and Pacific average of 41.5 weeks. No doubt these slow processing times are partly due to concerns about fraud.

Managing VAT refunds is challenging for most jurisdictions. Striking a balance between issuing refunds promptly, so as to minimize the impact on the cash flow of businesses, and protecting the revenue from refund fraud is challenging. Based on responses to the 2018 International Survey of Tax Administrations, VAT refund fraud is rated as a high risk by all jurisdictions with a VAT system.

Preventing VAT refund fraud starts at registration and ensuring that VAT registration applications require proof of identity checks to prevent fictitious traders from entering the VAT system. In processing refunds, it is usually recommended that a risk-based approach is used, rather than subjecting every refund request to a full audit. This approach is best supported by purpose-built automated risk assessment processes that are integrated with the compliance risk management system. All VAT refunds are automatically assessed against risk criteria to distinguish refund claimants with lower risk characteristics (such as a good compliance history) from those with higher risk characteristics (such as with poor or unknown compliance histories). High-risk refund claims are reviewed using pre-refund audits or other verification, while lower-risk refund cases may be reviewed post-refund verification or not reviewed at all.[12]

Paying legitimate VAT refunds, or offsetting the credits against other tax liabilities, within a reasonable timeframe (e.g., 30 calendar days from the date on which a refund claim is made) is important to support businesses and to improve the revenue body's credibility. As discussed above, it is possible to set up processes that support both the prompt payment of refunds and the detection of potentially fraudulent claims. In many cases, such processes are both more effective at reducing frauds and less costly to administer.

B.   Personal Income Tax Systems

Across the region, per capita incomes have risen, although inequality in income distribution is increasing in some countries. Human development indexes are improving and poverty levels are falling. There is a clear emergence of a middle class across the region. These trends toward increasing personal income and higher levels of development and consumption foreshadow the increasing importance of personal income taxes (PITs), particularly on salary and wages and professional income, and on capital gains. PIT is underrepresented in the tax mix in Southeast Asian economies. PITs account for less than 2% of GDP in all Southeast Asian countries (2016) compared to 8% of GDP in developed countries.[13] PIT rates have generally declined and deductions and exemptions have increased, to the point where some jurisdictions' PIT regimes collect few or no taxes from this source. The IMF noted that regimes in Southeast Asian countries are not comprehensive and have a narrow base.

This underrepresentation of PIT in tax revenues arises from both design and administration features. At a policy level, low rates and exemptions limit the revenue. At an administrative level, limited targeted supervision of high-wealth and high-income individuals, as well as smaller employers, is likely to result in material gaps in this revenue stream. It is important to ensure that the future policy design and administration of PIT and capital gains taxes (CGT) are appropriate for the changing conditions and reflect the increasing levels of earning power and wealth of individuals.

[12]   IMF. 2019. *Tax Administration Diagnostic Assessment Tool (TADAT) Field Guide*. Washington, DC: IMF. Prepared by the TADAT Secretariat.
[13]   Based on IMF Global Financial Statistics and World Development Indicators. Also reported in United Nations Economic and Social Commission for Asia and the Pacific. 2017. *Taxing for Shared Prosperity*. Policy Brief No. 46. UNESCAP.

C.   Subnational Taxation

Subnational governments in the region play an important role in delivering services to citizens and in raising revenues to support such services. Figure 11 illustrates the often-significant revenue raised at a subnational level in some economies in Southeast Asia where figures are available. It can be seen that, with the exception of Indonesia and Viet Nam, economies in the region raise considerably less revenue from this source than the Asia and Pacific average of around 8% of GDP.[14]

Some economies in the region have extremely complex networks of subnational organizations. For example, Indonesia has almost 84,000 subnational organizations across three levels of government, and Viet Nam has almost 12,000 subnational organizations, also across three levels of government. In contrast, Brunei Darussalam has no subnational governments, and although the Lao PDR has four levels of government, there are only 18 subnational government agencies. There is considerable variability in the levels of autonomy in determining the types of taxes and rates to be applied by sub-national organizations between jurisdictions.

The resources available at a subnational level are likely to be highly variable, especially in those countries with extensive subnational government networks, and this will inevitably impact the quality of revenue administration. Weak administration and lack of access to resources and technology impact subnational revenue across the board. There may be significant revenue potential from higher levels of support for subnational governments.

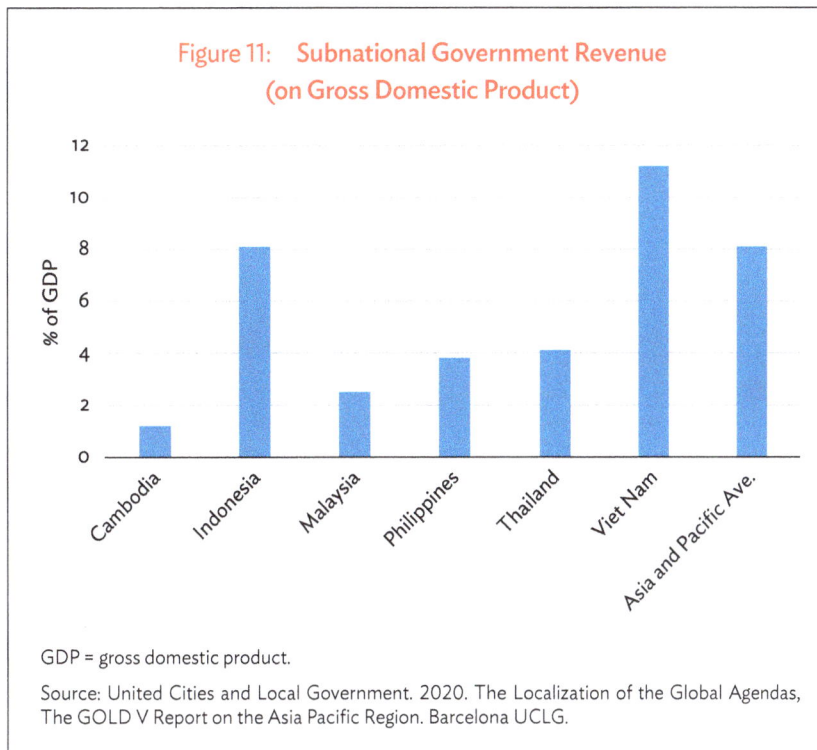

Figure 11:   **Subnational Government Revenue (on Gross Domestic Product)**

GDP = gross domestic product.

Source: United Cities and Local Government. 2020. The Localization of the Global Agendas, The GOLD V Report on the Asia Pacific Region. Barcelona UCLG.

---

[14]   The categorization of revenue as national and subnational is determined by each jurisdiction, so caution should be used in drawing comparisons between countries without closer examination of the make-up of the figures.

Figure 12:   Recurrent Property Tax Revenue (% of Gross Domestic Product)

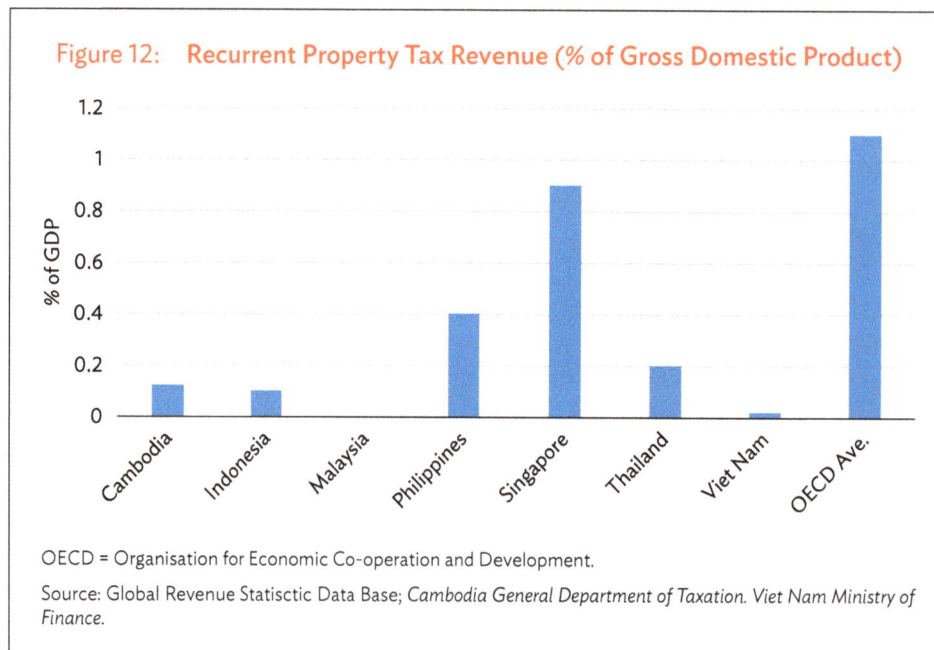

OECD = Organisation for Economic Co-operation and Development.

Source: Global Revenue Statisctic Data Base; *Cambodia General Department of Taxation. Viet Nam Ministry of Finance.*

Property Taxes

Taxes on immovable property often make up a significant proportion of subnational taxes and they are widely regarded as an efficient and equitable means of raising revenue. However, this revenue potential is largely untapped in many countries, due both to policy and administration issues.[15] As a matter of fact, in economies covered by OECD, the ratio of the revenue from recurrent taxes on immovable property to GDP in 2018 reached up to 1.1%, while in Southeast Asian jurisdictions such as Cambodia, Indonesia, Malaysia, the Philippines, Singapore, Thailand, and Viet Nam, the revenue from recurrent taxes on immovable property yields only less than 0.1%–0.9% of GDP (Figure 12).[16]

D.   Social Security Contributions

Considering the aging populations across the region, it may be expected that pressure on social security funds will increase over coming years. All countries in Southeast Asia have some form of social security contributions (SSCs) required to be made by employers and employees, and the employer contribution rates range from 3% to over 20%. Only the Timor-Leste revenue body has full responsibility for SSCs, but Indonesia has announced plans to integrate SSCs into the revenue body's role. Four other revenue bodies play support roles in the administration of SSCs ranging from information sharing in the Philippines and Viet Nam, to collection and verification in the Lao PDR.

In light of the increasing importance of these funds, there may be scope for greater levels of cooperation between the relevant agencies in administering the SSC system. According to the IMF's Tax Administration Diagnostic Assessment Tool (TADAT) Field guide, SSCs are increasingly collected by tax administrations.[17] This trend has been driven by the opportunity to streamline reporting and payment processes and to thereby reduce taxpayer

---

[15]   IMF. 2015. *Inequality and Fiscal Policy (Chapter 11, Taxing Immovable Property).* Washington, DC: IMF. https://www.elibrary.imf.org/view/IMF071/22448-9781513567754/22448-9781513567754/ch11.xml?language=en accessed on 27 July 2020.

[16]   2017 data are used for Cambodia and Viet Nam, as 2018 data are not available.

[17]   IMF. 2019. *Tax Administration Diagnostic Assessment Tool (TADAT) Field Guide.* Washington, DC: IMF. Prepared by the TADAT Secretariat.

compliance burden, as well as to strengthen the integrity of the SSC system through more effective compliance monitoring. Although this approach is not common in Southeast Asia, it is increasingly found in Central West Asia, Europe, and in sub-Saharan Africa.[18]

E.   Crosscutting Issues

The Use of Tax Havens

As the level of wealth in the region grows, high-wealth individuals and MNEs may seek to avoid PIT and CIT. The establishment of tax haven residency for individuals and MNEs, or the setting up of conduit entities and MNE subsidiaries, is a way to facilitate this process. The use of tax havens by individuals and entities to shift profits out of high tax jurisdictions and into low tax jurisdictions may involve a variety of profit-shifting techniques. All these techniques are designed to take advantage of mismatches between tax rates, and rules and regulations that exist (deliberately or otherwise) between countries.

The attraction of a tax haven is not only low tax rates or mismatches in the way that various transactions or structures are treated, but also higher levels of secrecy, which frustrate attempts to get behind the full transaction to understand its substance. This secrecy is often compounded by limited domestic mandatory financial transaction reporting to enable detection and trace the outflows of funds from the originating jurisdiction. Although some progress on international financial transparency has been made since the 2008 financial crisis, the use of tax havens still remains a popular tax minimization strategy, in part due to lack of financial reporting requirements and other regulations (such as sound domestic tax laws governing international transactions) in developing countries.

Recent estimates suggest that tax havens cost governments between $500 billion and $600 billion a year in lost corporate tax revenue. Low-income developing economies account for around $200 billion.[19] Tax haven usage is not confined to MNEs and is also a popular vehicle for tax minimization by high-wealth and high-income individuals and these figures do not include such revenue losses. Globally, it is estimated that individuals have around $8.7 trillion in tax havens.[20] Although there is limited information of the size of this problem in developing countries, and in particular information on the use of tax havens in Southeast Asia, it is likely to be an area requiring close monitoring and supervision. In developing strategies to manage and limit the abusive use of tax havens in Southeast Asia, further studies may be required at a country-by-country level.

The Shadow Economy

The shadow economy in most Southeast Asian countries is estimated to be over 20% of GDP, with only Singapore and Viet Nam having lower estimates (Figure 13). Although hidden activity impacts several revenue streams, VAT revenue is particularly vulnerable. As highlighted in Figure 9, VAT productivity in many jurisdictions is lower than would be expected, and this may in part flow from the design features discussed above, but is also likely to be linked to the relatively high shadow economy estimates, as detailed in Figure 13.

Most Southeast Asian revenue bodies reported in the 2018 International Survey of Revenue Administrations that the shadow economy is a concern and is rated among the higher compliance risks, with all but Viet Nam reporting a medium or higher risk rating. An examination of these ratings against the independent estimates of the size of the shadow economy would suggest that some revenue bodies may have underestimated the shadow economy risk. Although other jurisdictions may have strategies targeted at reducing the shadow economy, only Indonesia

---

[18]   2018 International Survey on Revenue Administration.
[19]   Crivelli, E., R. A. de Mooij, and M. Keen. 2015. Base Erosion, Profit Shifting and Developing Countries. *IMF Working Paper 15/118*. Washington, DC: IMF.
[20]   IMF, Finance and Development. 2019. The True Cost of Tax Havens. Washington, DC: IMF.

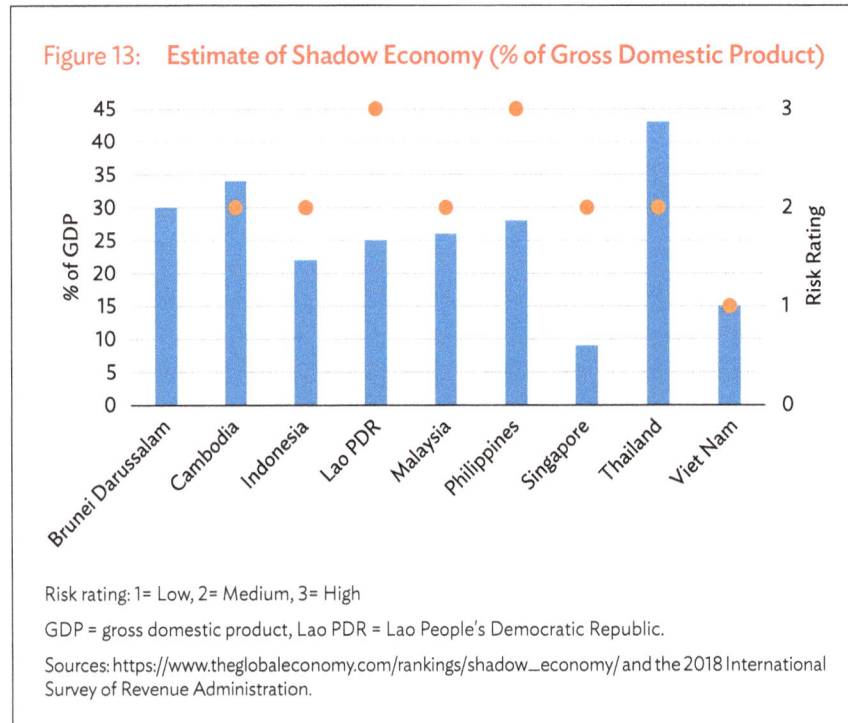

Figure 13:   Estimate of Shadow Economy (% of Gross Domestic Product)

Risk rating: 1= Low, 2= Medium, 3= High

GDP = gross domestic product, Lao PDR = Lao People's Democratic Republic.

Sources: https://www.theglobaleconomy.com/rankings/shadow_economy/ and the 2018 International Survey of Revenue Administration.

reported a focus on the shadow economy as part of their MTRS. Although dealing with the shadow economy has in the past been especially vexed, emerging technologies enable new approaches that may support better management of unreported transactions and identification of unregistered businesses. Maximizing the use of these new capabilities, together with steps to accelerate trends away from the use of cash, may be exploited to support more cost-effective monitoring and control over this risk. Strengthening system design features such as improving the revenue body's access to bulk data on financial and business transactions, increasing mandatory withholding and reporting, and enhancing data management capabilities, all have the potential to reduce opportunities to operate in the shadow economy.

Taxing the Digital Economy

Under current international tax rules and those prevalent in Southeast Asia, MNEs generally pay corporate income tax where production occurs, rather than where consumers or users are located. In a digital economy, businesses are able to derive income from users/consumers anywhere in the world, without a physical presence in the country concerned, and this has raised issues about a misalignment between value creation and payment of taxation. In response to these concerns, the OECD has for some years been hosting discussions that aim to adapt the international tax system to the changing business practices in a digitalized economy. The current OECD proposal, which is not yet finalized or agreed, would realign international taxing rights with (new) measures of value creation. This would allow the reallocation of income to the users'/consumers' jurisdictions, requiring multinational businesses to pay at least some CIT in the jurisdiction where those consumers or users are located.

In response to concerns about ongoing loss of revenue on cross-border sales and increased, at least in part, by the additional revenue demands associated with COVID-19-related expenditures, many countries are considering various tax policy responses, ahead of the OECD developments. Several countries in the region have decided to move ahead with a different form of digital taxation—namely, digital services taxes (DSTs)—partly as a proxy for corporate taxation, and to plug VAT gaps. These taxes are typically based on the revenues derived from certain

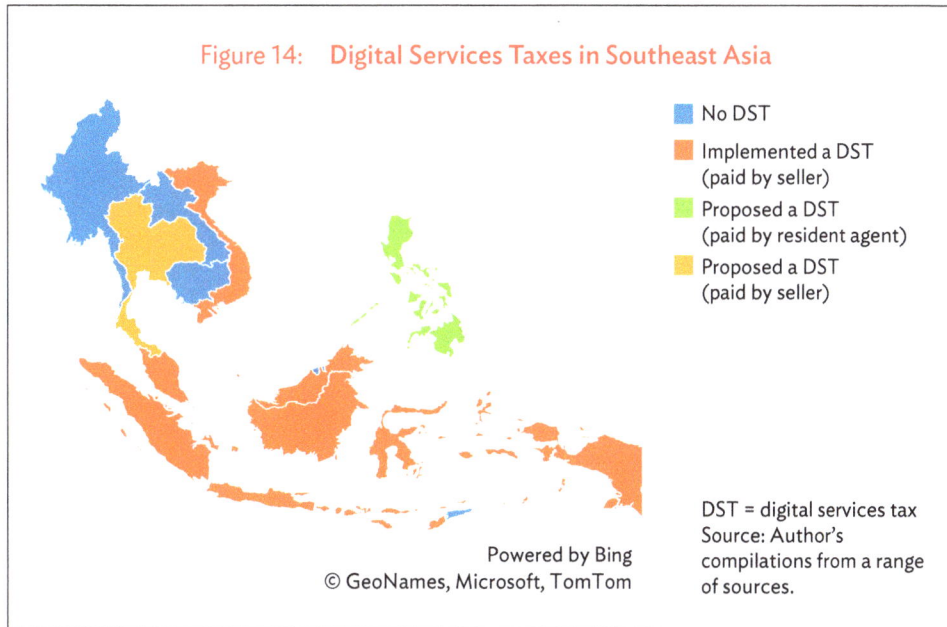

Figure 14:   Digital Services Taxes in Southeast Asia

No DST

Implemented a DST
(paid by seller)

Proposed a DST
(paid by resident agent)

Proposed a DST
(paid by seller)

DST = digital services tax
Source: Author's
compilations from a range
of sources.

Powered by Bing
© GeoNames, Microsoft, TomTom

digital services provided to domestic users or consumers. In the region, Indonesia, Malaysia, and Viet Nam have recently introduced various types of digital services taxes, while the Philippines and Thailand have announced their intention to do so (Figure 14). From 1 January 2020, Singapore has introduced a goods and services tax on imported services, as these services are for consumption in Singapore.

Most of the models adopted in the region involve setting a registration threshold above which the multinational is required to register and remit taxes on domestic sales. Viet Nam already has a withholding tax (WHT) system for foreign entities or individuals involved in business-to-business or B2B transactions. The new arrangements will extend to those performing e-commerce activities or doing business via digital platforms in the business-to-consumer or B2C market. These businesses must directly register to file tax in Viet Nam or authorize other parties to do so on their behalf. Those already included in the existing WHT arrangements may continue or migrate to the new system. If the supplier does not comply with the requirements to self-declare and pay taxes as specified, the General Department of Taxation (GDT) has the right to enforce tax collection via commercial banks. The new requirements were introduced because the current WHT does not capture cross-border B2C transactions.[21] The Philippines plans to adopt a model where the multinational must appoint a domestic representative or agent, and e-commerce platforms (including peer-to-peer) will be required to withhold. The DSTs are typically positioned as part of the VAT system. Rates range from 12% in the Philippines to 6% in Malaysia (administered by the Royal Malaysian Customs Department).

---

[21]   GDT has issued a draft circular, which is not yet finalized.

IV.   Responsive Tax Administration

Revenue bodies recognize that they cannot enforce their way to compliance. Not only is such an approach too costly, but the community is also unlikely to accept such high levels of intervention. Although supervision and monitoring are important to protect the integrity of the system, far higher levels of revenue are likely to be generated, often at lower cost, through activities designed to support and improve voluntary compliance. There is a significant body of research indicating that the way in which taxpayers are supported by the revenue body, how they perceive the service levels, and the professionalism of tax administration and the system as a whole, impact the levels of voluntary compliance. This section discusses some approaches adopted by revenue bodies in their attempts to strengthen voluntary compliance.

A.   Reducing Compliance Costs

Making it easy to comply through the provision of simple and streamlined compliance processes, including an extensive suite of electronic services, supports taxpayers to correctly meet their tax obligations and reduces the costs of compliance for both taxpayers and the revenue body.

Paying Taxes

A useful measure for assessing ease of compliance is the World Bank's Paying Taxes series. Figure 15 outlines two of the paying taxes indicators: the overall rank among the jurisdictions measured and the assessment of the total hours required for businesses to comply with tax obligations.

Six of the 11 countries in Southeast Asia rank in the bottom half of those assessed against the paying taxes measures. Only Singapore, which is among the world's best, ranks in the top third. Most countries in the region have seen little shift in rankings in 2020, with only Indonesia, the Philippines, and Viet Nam showing improvements.

Digital Transformation

Many jurisdictions see an upturn in the paying taxes rank in the year following the introduction or expansion of electronic services or e-services such as e-filing and e-payment. For example, Brunei Darussalam jumped 20 points in ranking after introducing the System for Tax Administration and Revenue Services or STARS e-Services system in 2017. In Indonesia, following the introduction of an e-filing and payment system in 2018, the ranking jumped over 30 places. The improvements seen in Viet Nam in 2020, although not related to e-services, have been attributed to improved compliance processes flowing from an upgrade of the internal processing systems within the revenue body.

Brunei Darussalam, Indonesia, Malaysia, Singapore, and Thailand all offer a wide range of electronic filing and payment options. Singapore also has an extensive prefilling system, where returns are prepopulated for taxpayers from information held by, or reported to, the revenue body. It may be no coincidence that these five jurisdictions also record the best ranking on the World Bank's Paying Taxes.

Figure 15:   World Bank Paying Taxes Series

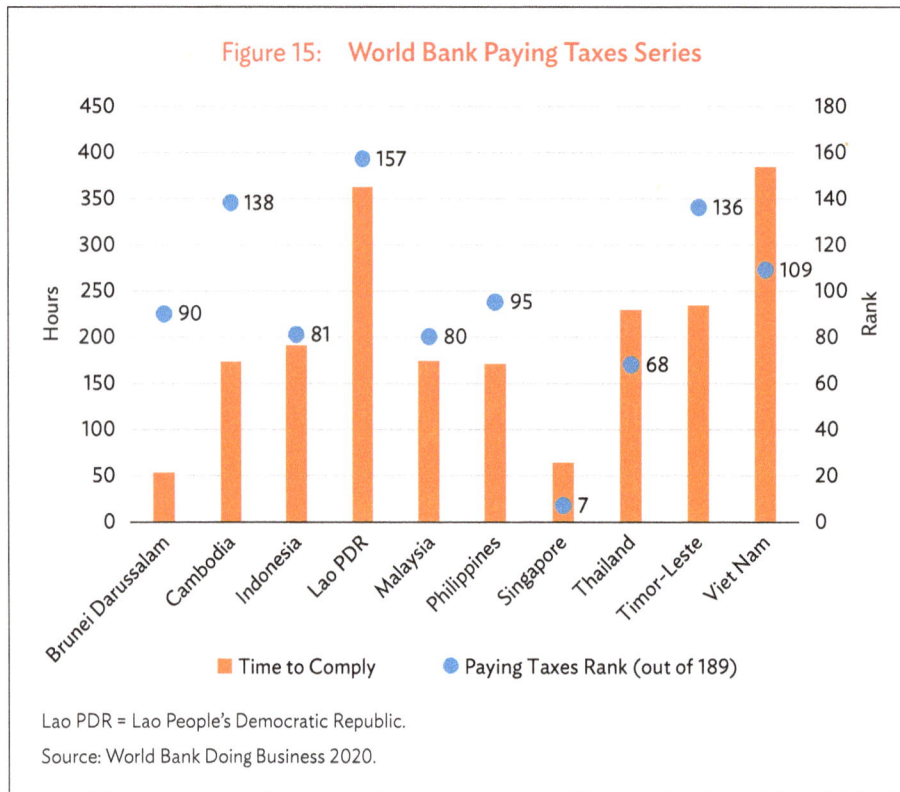

Lao PDR = Lao People's Democratic Republic.

Source: World Bank Doing Business 2020.

Viet Nam has announced plans to expand e-filing and e-payment. Other jurisdictions may also be considering upgrading e-services, and they may be well advised to do so based on the trends observed.

Strengthening and maintaining well-functioning e-service offerings appears to be a key to improving the ease of compliance, but such services may not have the desired effect if they are introduced against the backdrop of complex legal frameworks or if the systems do not operate smoothly and reliably. Attention must also be paid to continuous improvement of these offerings, as taxpayer expectations typically rise following the introduction of improvements. Useful additional services include access to consolidated accounts and using e-services to mask complexity through simple calculators and decision support tools.

Use of innovative technologies may reduce costs to the revenue body and improve security and reliability of taxpayer data. Figure 16 outlines a range of such approaches and new technologies either in use or contemplated in Southeast Asia.

According to the 2018 International Survey of Revenue Administration, most countries in Southeast Asia have in place a formal organizational unit to nurture innovative practices. The majority also routinely test new digital products with end users prior to release. A range of technologies are increasing in popularity across the region. For example, the use of blockchain technologies to secure and authenticate data is contemplated in many jurisdictions, as is the use of artificial intelligence to improve services and to enhance compliance management. Although many jurisdictions are making advances in this area, there is potential to both reduce costs and improve revenue through further exploitation of emerging opportunities.

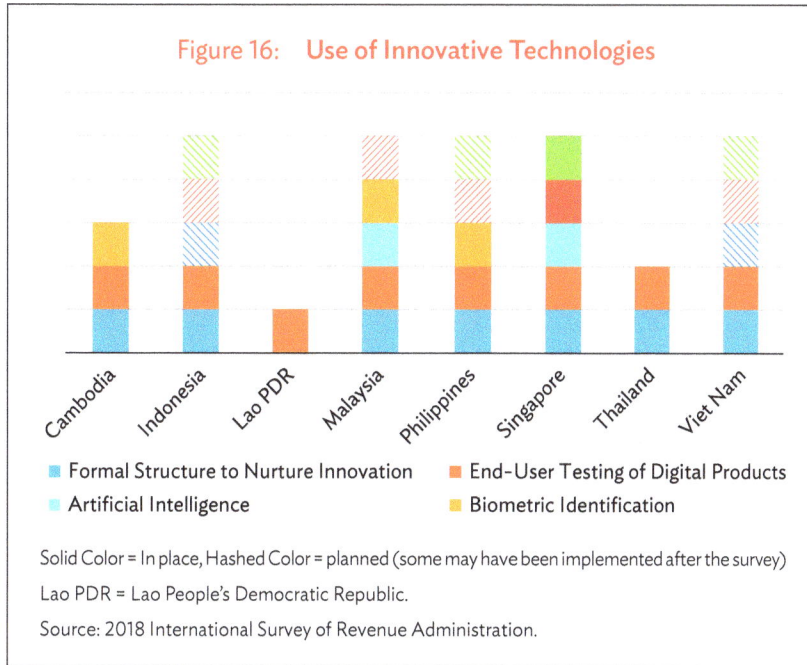

Figure 16:   Use of Innovative Technologies

■ Formal Structure to Nurture Innovation   ■ End-User Testing of Digital Products
■ Artificial Intelligence   ■ Biometric Identification

Solid Color = In place, Hashed Color = planned (some may have been implemented after the survey)

Lao PDR = Lao People's Democratic Republic.

Source: 2018 International Survey of Revenue Administration.

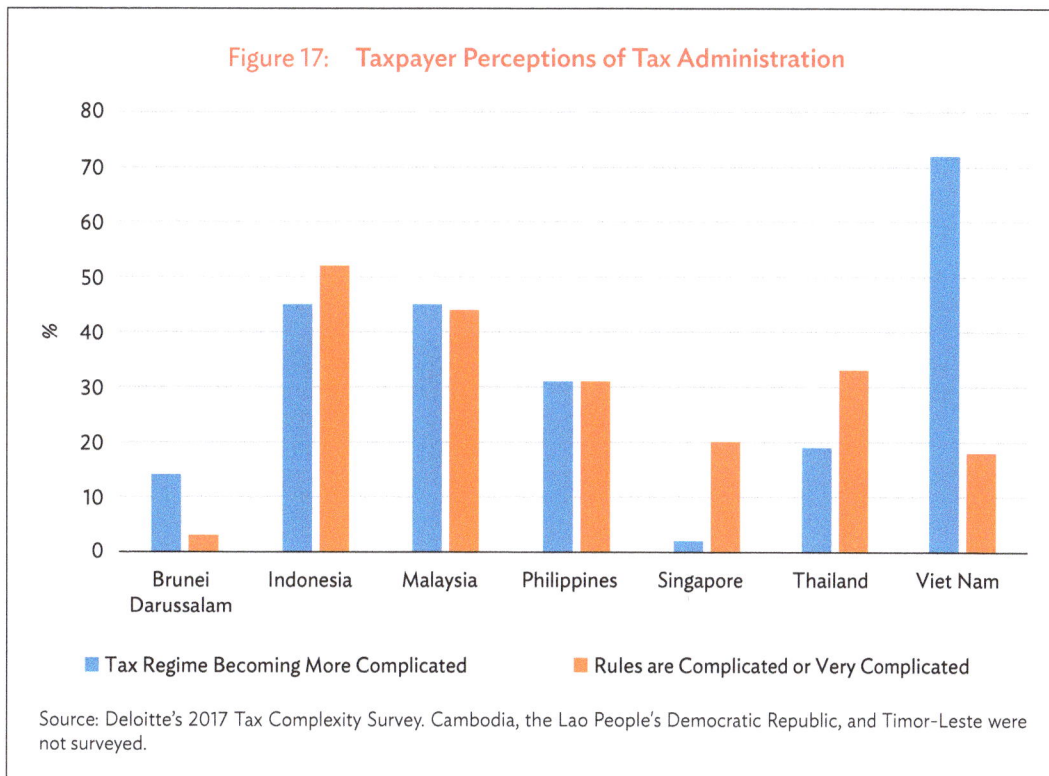

Figure 17:   Taxpayer Perceptions of Tax Administration

■ Tax Regime Becoming More Complicated   ■ Rules are Complicated or Very Complicated

Source: Deloitte's 2017 Tax Complexity Survey. Cambodia, the Lao People's Democratic Republic, and Timor-Leste were not surveyed.

Reducing Complexity

According to the most recent Deloitte survey on tax complexity, which measures perceived level of difficulty, as shown in Figure 17, the percentage of taxpayers in the jurisdictions surveyed who observed that tax rules are already complicated, and are becoming more so, is surprising. This is particularly notable in Viet Nam where over 70% of the survey respondents said the regime is becoming more complicated. In Indonesia, Malaysia, and the Philippines, the figure was over 30%, against a backdrop of a system already perceived as complex.

E-services make accessing information, filing returns, and making payments easier. But attention must also be paid to removing underlying complexity by, for example, reviewing the legal framework, streamlining reporting requirements, and simplifying processes, whether they are offered electronically or via other channels. In addition, broadening the suite of advice products, including binding rulings and reforms policies, to reduce complexity is advisable.

B.   Providing Certainty

Certainty is important to taxpayers, especially in a self-assessment system. Knowing the revenue body's position on how they will administer the law in various situations provides a higher level of confidence for taxpayers in managing their tax affairs, and allows them to make business decisions with more confidence. For those taxpayers wanting to adopt a conservation position, certainty is offered through well-functioning public and private binding ruling systems, and through the publication of taxpayer rights and obligations. As shown in Figure 18, 9 of the 10 jurisdictions in Southeast Asia offer public binding rulings, 7 have published statements of taxpayer rights, and 7 offer private binding rulings. Against this backdrop of apparent sound legal frameworks, it is somewhat surprising to see the results on measures such as the Deloitte survey and the Paying Taxes indicators. No doubt other factors are at play, which require further study.

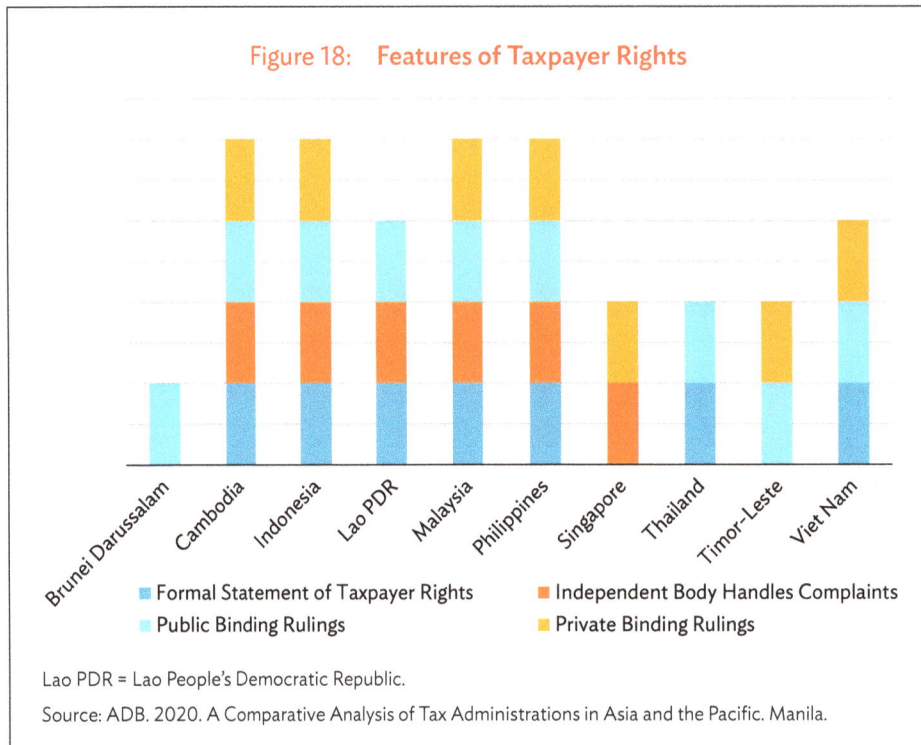

Figure 18:   **Features of Taxpayer Rights**

Lao PDR = Lao People's Democratic Republic.

Source: ADB. 2020. A Comparative Analysis of Tax Administrations in Asia and the Pacific. Manila.

The Deloitte tax complexity survey asked taxpayers to rate revenue bodies on the perceived fairness of audits and appeals, and the relationship with the revenue body. Only taxpayers in Singapore rated each of these parameters as good. All other revenue bodies were rated as neutral or low.

One of the best-performing revenue bodies in the region, and indeed the world, is the Inland Revenue Authority of Singapore (IRAS). Yet, Singapore has no formal statement of taxpayer rights, and no public rulings system. It seems that the limited suite of products to support certainty does not have a detrimental impact on taxpayer perceptions of the administration in Singapore, or the IRAS's performance in the World Bank Doing Business and paying taxes rankings. This may be partly due to the sound and widely promulgated advance ruling system (private binding rulings), and the provision of expansive advice (albeit nonbinding), as well as the reported good relationship with the revenue body, and perceptions about the fairness of its operations. IRAS also publishes a commitment to service, providing standards and publishing results against those standards, and a service quality policy.

Although many jurisdictions in the Asia and Pacific region have the legal provisions to allow for such rulings, issuing of public rulings are often infrequent and targeted at procedural matters, rather than legal ones. Take-up rates for private rulings, where reported, are often low. It is not enough to simply have the legal framework in place. Tax administrations need to actively develop a public rulings program and work toward its delivery, and to build taxpayer trust in the fairness of the private rulings process and promote use.

C.   Increasing Trust and Perceptions of Professionalism

The question of what induces better voluntary tax compliance appears simple enough. But the answer is likely to include a complex web of factors, which will most likely vary depending upon the situation and the cultural norms within the jurisdictions under consideration. A number of studies have identified factors that influence taxpayer compliance behavior in particular situations and jurisdictions, including opportunities to evade and perceptions of the likelihood of detection. There is a growing body of research indicating that perceptions of the fairness of the tax system and trust in regulators plays a significant part.

There are likely many factors influencing this perception, including observations of corruption in public administration, views about the way in which taxes are spent, and perceptions about whether others, such as large businesses, high-wealth and high-income individuals, and prominent citizens are thought to be compliant and effectively supervised by the revenue body. Figure 19 examines one of these factors: perception of corruption.

Perceptions of Corruption
The profile across Southeast Asia shows that the region has some of the best and worst performers on this measure. For those revenue bodies with high corruption perception, there may be considerable benefits in terms of improved community perception, and likely improved voluntary compliance, through investment in measures to strengthen integrity.

The Role of International Tax Cooperation
Perceptions about equity in the distribution of tax burdens are important in strengthening overall community confidence in the tax system. One way to bolster these perceptions is to demonstrate effective supervision over the wealthiest taxpayers in the community, particularly MNEs and high-wealth and high-income individuals, who are often perceived by the general community to engage in aggressive tax planning, including the use of international profit shifting, to minimize their taxation. Effective supervision of these taxpayers depends on several factors, including domestic legal frameworks, and the capacity of the revenue body.

Figure 19:   Corruption Perception Rank (Score Out of 180)

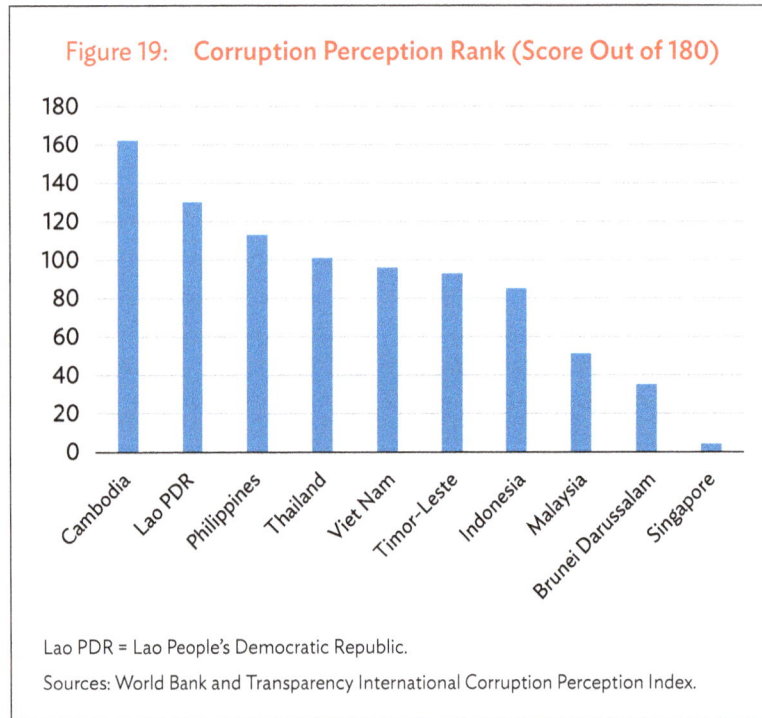

Lao PDR = Lao People's Democratic Republic.
Sources: World Bank and Transparency International Corruption Perception Index.

One critical factor in both encouraging voluntary compliance and strengthening supervision of MNEs and wealthy citizens is the level of transparency of their international dealings. Membership in international cooperative forums supports revenue bodies to gain access to important information, via exchange of information protocols, designed to improve transparency of international dealings and to establish beneficial ownership of legal entities holding assets offshore. Across the region, this is likely to require a higher level of participation in international initiatives such as the Inclusive Framework on BEPS and the Global Forum on Transparency and Exchange of Information for Tax Purposes. Many jurisdictions may not be currently fully utilizing these opportunities, at least in part due to lack of internal capacity.

The regional hub for domestic resource mobilization (DRM) and international tax cooperation (ITC), which was recently announced by ADB, may be well placed to support efforts in building capacity and community confidence in the revenue body's management and oversight of the compliance of MNEs and other taxpayers using international profit-shifting techniques. The regional hub will focus on promoting DRM and international tax cooperation through close collaboration among finance and tax authorities of developing economies; international organizations such as the IMF, the OECD, and World Bank; and regional tax associations. The regional hub will also seek to bring together practitioners from tax policy bodies and tax administration bodies to achieve meaningful progress in tax reform.

V. Conclusion

Like other parts of the world, Southeast Asia has been hard hit by the coronavirus disease (COVID-19) pandemic. Governments in the region have swiftly responded to the pandemic in various fronts with a wide array of coordinated health, social, and economic interventions. However, lockdowns, travel bans, community quarantines, and other restrictions imposed to contain the spread, coupled with subdued global demand, painted a bleak picture on the prospect of economic growth in the region. In 2020, the gross domestic product (GDP) of the Southeast Asian economy experienced a sharp contraction of 4.0%. Thanks to vaccine rollouts in the region and revival of tourism and international trade and investment underway, the *Asian Development Outlook 2021* projected that the region stands to rebound to 4.4% growth in 2021 and 5.1% in 2022—the growth levels witnessed in the pre-pandemic period.

All economies in Southeast Asia have appropriately pursued countercyclical fiscal policy, posting fiscal deficits of anywhere between 2% and 7% of GDP, depending on avenues through which to source deficit financing. The governments have geared fiscal spending toward scaling up public health systems to meet the immediate need of controlling and preventing the outbreak, including ensuring adequate supplies of medical equipment and vaccines. A series of social assistance programs have been implemented to safeguard the most vulnerable groups from falling back into poverty through interventions such as cash and in-kind transfers, reemployment programs, and enhanced social protection against COVID-19. Fiscal stimulus has also been provided to shield local businesses and workers against economic shocks through capital injections, loan restructuring, tax deferrals, deductions, and credits.

However, the biggest challenge for the governments is how to efficiently and adequately mobilize domestic resources to sustain the fiscal stimulus needed to restore buoyant growth trajectories. In the context of Southeast Asia, domestic resource mobilization has been part and parcel of fiscal challenges even before the pandemic struck. It is not uncommon for most Southeast Asian countries to consistently experience a declining trend of the tax-to-GDP ratio hovering below 15%—the minimum level of tax revenues widely considered to be imperative for increasing GDP per capita and achieving higher development levels and the Sustainable Development Goals (SDGs). The generally low tax-to-GDP ratio in Southeast Asia not only signifies the low capacity of tax authorities to raise tax revenues, but also translates to the inability of the government to provide sufficient public services. Given the magnitude of the pandemic-induced shocks, a further decline in tax revenues is most possibly substantial. In addition, the post-pandemic economic recovery is by and large uneven and uncertain due to mixed progress on vaccine rollouts and emergence of new COVID-19 variants.

Learning from the past crises, governments should not embark on fiscal consolidation too prematurely as there is still an utmost need to strike a fine balance between sustaining fiscal stimulus and mobilizing fiscal revenues for long-term development. These emerging challenges to fiscal policy reiterate ever-increasing importance of domestic resource mobilization in Southeast Asia. The post-pandemic era is an unprecedented time for the governments to rethink and refine their tax policy and administration measures to not only address short- to medium-term development challenges, but also to build back better and usher in inclusive and sustainable development.

A Comprehensive Assessment of Tax Capacity in Southeast Asia is among the pioneering attempts of the Asian Development Bank (ADB) to examine the different stages of tax policy and administration among countries in the region, based on the most recent publicly available data. The findings point to common issues and challenges surrounding domestic resource mobilization, while recognizing that tax policy options need to be customized to address different sets of issues and challenges and take into consideration the country-specific political, institutional, and socioeconomic landscape. The assessment reveals that there is a set of "low-hanging" tax policy and administration measures that can help the governments quickly boost tax revenues without compromising the momentum toward an economic recovery. At the same time, it is indispensable for the governments to realize that the COVID-19 pandemic is a structural shock to the global economy and will shape the new roles of tax and fiscal policy. Therefore, while the countries are struggling to restore strong growth trajectories, the governments should start contemplating structural tax reform strategies and road maps for addressing a country's long-term socioeconomic challenges such as aging population, climate change, and inequality.

A.   Short- and Medium-Term Policy Recommendations

This publication shows that one root cause of the generally narrow tax base in Southeast Asian countries is attributed to a relatively large informal sector (shadow economy). Economic activities that operate outside the tax system are as large as 43% of GDP in Thailand, 35% in Cambodia, 28% in the Philippines, 25% in the Lao People's Democratic Republic, and 23% in Indonesia.

There are various reasons for a large informal economy—such as weak tax enforcement, inefficiencies of tax administration, and tax avoidance behaviors among others. Yet, high costs of tax compliance, such as costly, time-consuming tax registration, tax filing, accounting, and tax payment, are together a key factor that discourages small taxpayers, especially micro, small, and medium-sized enterprises (MSMEs), to operate in the tax systems and comply with tax rules and regulations. Therefore, in the context of the Southeast Asian countries, there is a huge opportunity for tax authorities to leverage on tax administration measures that aim to reduce costs of compliance and promote voluntary compliance by simplifying tax registration, filing, and payment for individual taxpayers and MSMEs.

These tax administration measures can be applied readily within the existing legal frameworks for key tax types, especially personal income taxes (PIT), corporate income taxes (CIT), and value-added taxes (VAT). The Tax Administration Diagnostic Assessment Tool (TADAT) of the International Monetary Fund (IMF) would offer a diagnostic tool for the Southeast Asian tax authorities to assess tax administration performance and identify gaps. In addition, it is important for tax authorities to recognize that efforts to lower costs of compliance, such as simplified PIT and CIT rates, the use of cash-based accounting for CIT and VAT filing and reporting, and less frequent VAT reporting, may entail lower tax revenue flows from each taxpayer; however, improved tax compliance means an expanded tax base—more and more taxpaying individuals and firms entering a tax system—thereby enhancing total tax revenues.

Digital transformation of tax authorities is another area of tax administration that can help the government quickly boost revenues without amendments of the existing rules and regulations. This report underlines the opportunity for tax authorities in Southeast Asia to leverage on new information technology (IT) for tax administration, such as big data and blockchain technology, to improve taxpayers' services and gain more control and access to data for monitoring of noncompliance risks.

In addition, the use of digital technology will also reduce transaction costs and enhance transparency of tax authorities, resulting in more efficient revenue mobilization. Following the use and adoption of electronic services or e-services, such as e-filing and e-payment, many Southeast Asian countries see an increase in tax collection. Almost all Southeast Asian countries offer a wide range of electronic filing and payment options. Singapore also has an extensive pre-filing system, where returns are prepopulated from the records of the revenue body. Expectedly, these jurisdictions recorded the best ranking in the World Bank's Paying Taxes database.

Strengthening subnational taxation may offer the other tax administration lever for boosting domestic resource mobilization. Real property taxes are the main and stable source of local governments' tax revenues. However, real property tax revenue is low in Southeast Asia, less than 1% of GDP in Cambodia, Indonesia, the Philippines, and Thailand. The challenges of low real property tax revenues in the region rest with an inefficient and outdated property transaction database, which results in outdated market values of properties for real property tax assessment. In addition, the business processes for property valuation and real property tax payment are manual.

The lack of centralized monitoring and reporting systems imply that subnational governments administer real property valuation and real property tax collection independently; consequently, they are subject to local political pressure to keep property values lower than what they should be in the market. Given these issues and challenges, the Southeast Asian countries have potential to tap on digital technology platforms and IT tools to modernize business processes of real property taxation, ranging from a transaction database and valuation functions. These real property tax measures are progressive in nature as they generate tax revenues from wealthy property owners and are likely to yield significant gains in the short term.

B.   Long-Term Policy Recommendations

Tax reforms that have so far been implemented in Southeast Asia are complex and will take time to complete. Country contexts and challenges vary considerably, and national development priorities and SDGs are also country-driven. The governments will need to strengthen their policy and institutional frameworks to manage these challenges. Government authorities will have to work with key stakeholders including the private sector, civil society organizations, and the public to make these happen.

Southeast Asia's tax reform journey presented in this report underlines that meaningful and successful tax reforms necessitate the government's long-term perseverance and commitment to addressing overarching development challenges such as poverty, income inequality, environmental issues, and macroeconomic and fiscal sustainability. International organizations such as ADB, International Monetary Fund (IMF), and the Organisation for Economic Co-operation and Development (OECD) encourage tax bodies to develop and implement the medium-term revenue strategies (MTRSs) to address the unpredictable and inconsistent tax reform efforts that often fail to deliver any benefits. In the aftermath of the COVID-19 pandemic, rethinking tax reform priorities and refining the existing MTRSs to address emerging development challenges such as income inequality, climate change, and aging society will likely constitute an integral part of fiscal consolidation and domestic resource mobilization strategies for Southeast Asia.

With an exponential increase in digital service transactions amid the COVID-19 pandemic, the governments in Southeast Asia have moved toward unilaterally imposing digital service taxes on multinational digital companies. For example, Indonesia, Malaysia, the Philippines, and Thailand have imposed or are introducing new levies on digital service providers. These measures are part of the global attempt in bringing the borderless digital economy into domestic tax systems, in response to increasing scrutiny of whether these multinational digital service providers are fairly paying taxes on their earnings.

The OECD/G20 Inclusive Framework on Base Erosion and Profit Shifting (BEPS) offers an exceptional opportunity for the Southeast Asian countries to take part in the global efforts and address this issue collectively at the multilateral level. The governments should, to the extent possible, participate in ongoing discussions at the OECD Inclusive Framework on Base Erosion and Profit Shifting (BEPS) and the Global Forum on Transparency and Exchange of Information for Tax Purposes. Enacting a sound domestic legal framework and participating in international forums to enhance consistency, cooperation, and information exchange, are important in supporting jurisdictions in their efforts to protect the domestic tax base from erosion.

Carbon taxation is another emerging area for harnessing domestic revenue mobilization to address the increasingly severe impacts of climate change. In Southeast Asia, energy-related carbon emissions are expected to rise by as much as 61% between 2014 and 2025, and effective pricing of externalities presents an opportunity to facilitate energy transition and strengthen environmental tax regimes. Currently, excise taxes on fuel products (or phasing out of energy subsidies) are a common approach to pricing carbon in the region. However, excise taxes on fuel products typically incur high administration and compliance costs and are often subject to fuel smuggling, tax leakages, and distortive effects on fuel markets.

Southeast Asian countries have large potentials to develop the emission trading scheme (ETS), also known as the "cap-and-trade" system, first introduced in the European Union. Under the ETS, a cap is set by the government on the total amount of greenhouse gases to be emitted. Then, a market where emission allowances are traded is created. For each year, a business will have to surrender enough allowances to fully cover its emissions; otherwise, heavy fines are imposed. However, the progress has been slow and quite patchy in the region. Indonesia, the Philippines, and Thailand have started introducing the ETS. Private sector support is often limited, and the private sector participates in the ETS on a voluntary basis due to the absence of domestic legal framework, coupled with limited technical knowledge and infrastructure of the responsible government agencies.

C.   Ways Forward for ADB Engagement in Southeast Asia

Domestic resource mobilization is instrumental for Southeast Asia to usher in COVID-19 economic recovery and create sufficient fiscal space to finance public expenditures necessary for realizing the long-term national development plans and achieving the SDGs. Recognizing this, ADB stands firm to continue to be a long-term partner of its developing member countries to strengthen governance and institutional capacity for domestic revenue mobilization in line with ADB's Strategy 2030. ADB will continue to work with its Southeast Asian member countries to ramp up revenue performance and to tailor the various policy options to suit country-specific priorities and contexts.

The relevance of each approach will vary across jurisdictions, and more detailed country-by-country evaluation will be necessary to determine the extent to which each of the areas identified is relevant. ADB is well positioned to help assess resource needs, evaluate options, customize approaches, and provide support to develop capacity and progressively implement agreed strategies to strengthen domestic resource mobilization.

The establishment of the ADB Asia Pacific Tax Hub could help develop multilateral, consensus-based solutions to support domestic revenue mobilization and foster international tax cooperation. It will serve as an open and inclusive platform for (i) strategic policy dialogue, (ii) knowledge sharing, and (iii) development coordination among our members, development partners, and ADB. The regional tax hub can also help countries formulate consistent policies, thereby preventing unilateral tax measures, which could lead to double or triple taxation, threatening cross-border trade and investment.

The COVID-19 pandemic gave a glimpse of what the future of tax policy and reform could look like in Southeast Asia. To make up for lost ground and reinstate a strong growth trajectory, the governments have an exceptional opportunity to reshape their tax systems and find new ways of mobilizing domestic resources to create more equitable and environmentally sustainable societies. This is no easy task. The path toward a fair and efficient tax system conducive to inclusive and sustainable development necessitates the governments' long-term commitment to tax reforms and working with stakeholders and development partners including ADB.

Country Tax Profiles

Brunei Darussalam
Cambodia
Indonesia
Lao People's Democratic Republic
Malaysia
Philippines
Singapore
Thailand
Timor-Leste
Viet Nam

BRUNEI DARUSSALAM

AT A GLANCE

	Measure	2014	2015	2016	2017	2018	2019
Demographic Overview *(refer Note 1)*	Total Population	409,769	414,907	419,800	424,473	428,962	459,500
	Age profile (Years)						
	0–14	24.48	24.09	23.88	23.50	23.03	20.59
	15–64	71.65	71.84	71.82	71.94	72.10	74.58
	65+	3.88	4.07	4.30	4.57	4.87	4.83
	Literacy level (% of population)	...	...	...	...	97.21	...
	Urbanization (% of population)						
	Urban Population	76.33	76.66	76.99	77.31	77.63	77.90
	Rural Population	23.67	23.34	23.01	22.69	22.37	22.10
	Employment to population (%)	61.44	60.65	59.95	59.36	59.19	58.78
	Agriculture	0.55	0.75	1.01	1.36	1.37	1.36
	Industry	18.63	17.75	16.90	16.13	15.97	15.88
	Services	80.82	81.50	82.10	82.51	82.66	82.76

Industrialization Indices	2012	2013	2014	ASEAN Ave.	World Ave.
Industrialization Intensity Index	0.2	0.2	0.2	0.54	0.65
Share of Medium & High Tech	0.04	0.04	0.04	0.44	
Main Economic Sectors	Due to its extensive resources of oil and gas and its small population, Brunei Darussalam is among the world's richer countries. The oil and gas sector dominates, generating the bulk of export earnings and government revenues. The largest single employer is the public sector (financed by oil and gas revenues).				

	Measure	2014	2015	2016	2017	2018	2019	ASEAN Ave.
Trends in Income and Inequality *(refer Note 1)*	Income Index	1	1	1	1	1	...	0.734
	Inequality in Income (%)	...	...	...	...	...	...	20.35
	Gross National Income (GNI) per Capita	76,778	79,110	77,492	77,188	76,389	...	23,069
	Human Development Index Rank				43/189			

	Measure	Description
Take-up of Technology *(refer Note 2)*	E-commerce trends	76% of Bruneians are using e-commerce to shop, bank, and pay bills.
	Internet coverage: Southeast Asia (SEA) average = 66%	In 2020, around 95% were reported to have access to the internet and around the same percentage used social media. Mobile Connectivity Index = 67.3 (ranked 4th in SEA).
	Take-up of internet and mobile banking	Credit or debit cards were the preferred method of payment for 84% of e-commerce users; other methods include online bank transfers (36%), e-wallets (27%), and offline payment or cash on delivery (19%).[1]
	Take-up of e-filing	System for Tax Administration and Revenue Services (STARS) e-Services provides taxpayers with self-service capabilities such as e-filing, e-payment, viewing statement of account, and submission of requests for refunds; 64% of business tax returns are filed online.

---

[1]   Based on the results of a survey conducted by the Authority for Info-communications Technology Industry of Brunei Darussalam in February 2018.

BRUNEI DARUSSALAM: EMPLOYMENT BY SECTOR

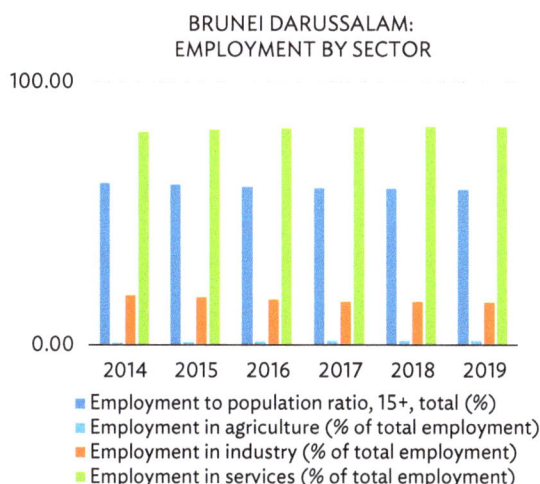

- Employment to population ratio, 15+, total (%)
- Employment in agriculture (% of total employment)
- Employment in industry (% of total employment)
- Employment in services (% of total employment)

BRUNEI DARUSSALAM: TAKE-UP OF TECHNOLOGY

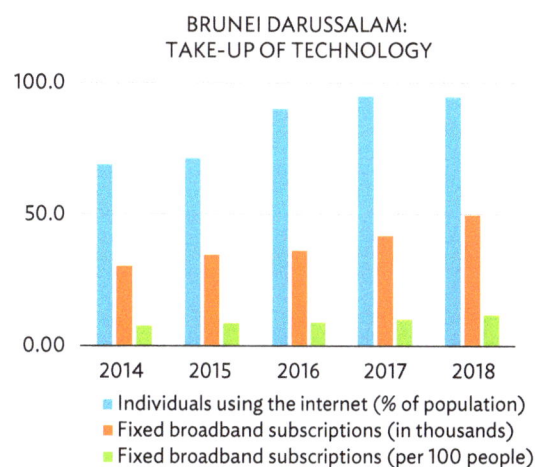

- Individuals using the internet (% of population)
- Fixed broadband subscriptions (in thousands)
- Fixed broadband subscriptions (per 100 people)

PRODUCTION STRUCTURE

		Exports ($ million)				
	Region	**2014**	**2015**	**2016**	**2017**	**2018**
Exports - Overall (refer Note 3)	Brunei Darussalam	12,311	11,750	6,751	5,652	6,012
	SEA	1,606,681	1,630,770	1,508,470	1,498,265	1,676,341
	US	2,273,428	2,371,704	2,266,800	2,220,609	2,356,726
Main sector 1 Fuels	Brunei Darussalam	11,049	9,725	5,907	4,284	4,989
	SEA	220,922	207,952	135,574	109,869	140,057
	US	148,866	156,185	104,639	93,753	139,261
Main sector 2 Chemicals	Brunei Darussalam	92	472	138	235	202
	SEA	106,838	110,838	96,840	95,613	104,422
	US	208,586	211,639	205,857	197,107	206,730
		Imports ($ million)				
	Region	**2014**	**2015**	**2016**	**2017**	**2018**
Imports - Overall (refer Note 3)	Brunei Darussalam	4,226	4,303	4,318	5,693	5,693
	SEA	1,506,926	1,372,220	1,354,024	1,525,565	1,701,449
	US	2,879,362	2,786,645	2,739,415	2,932,062	3,148,464
Main sector 1 Machinery and Transport Equipment	Brunei Darussalam	1,387	1,273	884	1,054	1,602
	SEA	462,822	456,028	462,749	520,106	576,718
	US	956,716	989,206	969,943	1,040,707	1,103,063
Main sector 2 Food	Brunei Darussalam	555	507	498	463	505
	SEA	83,402	80,109	85,591	92,665	98,492
	US	133,230	134,912	137,511	146,441	155,557
Observations	Exports grew by around 6% in 2018 compared with a regional average growth of 10.1%. Imports remained steady in 2018 compared with a regional average growth of 10.3%. Brunei Darussalam owns major stakes in foreign suppliers of essential services such as food (Australia) and cement (Indonesia). The top exports are oil and gas, and the top imports are aircraft and refined petroleum.					

	Sector	2014	2015	2016	2017	2018
Flows of Inward Foreign Direct Investment (FDI) to ASEAN Sourced from Brunei Darussalam, by Economic Sectors ($ million) (refer Note 4)	Agriculture, forestry, and fishing	0.23	0.92	0.66	0.14	0.03
	Mining and quarrying	0.58	0.33	(0.16)	0.68	1.09
	Manufacturing	29.80	54.92	112.05	23.67	3.55
	Electricity, gas, steam, and air conditioning supply	0.39	9.70	0.88	4.30	0.33
	Water supply; sewerage, waste management and remediation activities	0.11	0.06	3.25	0.29	0.05
	Construction	1.84	2.54	3.87	0.58	0.24
	Wholesale and retail trade; repair of motor vehicles and motorcycles	(1.14)	4.56	5.42	3.56	34.82
	Transportation and storage	0.30	0.50	5.88	0.20	0.07
	Accommodation and food service activities	(2.17)	(2.51)	(0.25)	(2.72)	(2.80)
	Information and communication	0.17	0.26	2.48	0.20	0.02
	Financial and insurance activities	(4.13)	(44.81)	11.39	(11.47)	(100.70)
	Real estate activities	15.30	17.33	20.47	5.91	3.49
	Professional, scientific, and technical activities	0.87	(0.46)	6.93	0.12	(2.86)
	Administrative and support service activities	0.01	0.18	1.07	0.06	0.04
	Education	0.13	0.10	0.40	0.06	0.02
	Human health and social work activities	0.70	0.05	0.35	0.20	0.03
	Arts, entertainment, and recreation	(0.14)	0.01	2.20	0.02	0.23
	Other services activities	0.01	0.13	37.35	8.83	0.43
	Unspecified activity	–	8.27	16.50	0.00	–
	TOTAL activities	593.14	52.48	231.65	38.54	(63.22)
IMF Article IV	Net FDI inflows (in percent of GDP)	3.3	1.3	(1.3)	3.9	3.8
	Net Direct Investment (FDI) – in $ million	575	171	(150)	468	512
General Observations on FDI	Brunei Darussalam allows 100% foreign ownership and offers a range of investment incentives. In 2015, the government introduced a package of measures designed to promote FDI, including offering an attractive tax regime, including some of the lowest corporate taxes in the region. After declining significantly, FDI showed signs of recovery in 2017 and 2018. The main drivers of the recovery were the wholesale and retail trade and manufacturing. However, according to UNCTAD's World Investment Report 2020, Brunei Darussalam's FDI inflow stands at $275 million in 2019, down from $382 million in 2018. The stock of FDI is rising, reaching $7.1 billion in 2019. The mining and quarrying sector receives the largest share of FDI. The largest foreign investment is a methanol distillery, partially financed by the Japanese Mitsubishi Gas Chemical Company. Brunei Darussalam has attracted sizable FDI in its five priority business clusters, mainly in the downstream oil and gas sector. A joint venture with investors from the People's Republic of China (PRC) to develop a petrochemical project on Pulau Muara Besar was one of the largest FDI-funded projects in 2017–2018. The project cost over $15 billion. Trade agreements, for example, the Comprehensive and Progressive Agreement for Trans-Pacific Partnership (CPTPP) may further enhance Brunei Darussalam's attractiveness for FDI. The International Monetary Fund (IMF) recommends more efforts to generate stronger positive spillovers from FDI to the domestic economy, including by integrating local micro, small, and medium-sized enterprises (MSMEs) into the supply chains. Brunei Darussalam would also benefit from further improving trade facilitation, such as advance rulings, information availability, and reducing formalities. The authorities report that they are making progress in advance rulings as part of the preparation to ratify the CPTPP.					

Component Sector	2014	2015	2016	2017	2018	ASEAN Ave.	US 2018
Gross domestic product (GDP)	100.0	100.0	100.0	100.0	100.0	100	100
Final consumption expenditure	36.9	44.8	47.4	47.0	43.7	68.04	87
Household consumption expenditure (including NPISH)	15.5	19.8	21.2	20.5	19.5	54	70
General government final consumption expenditure	21.4	25.1	26.2	26.5	24.1	14.51	17
Gross capital formation	**27.4**	**35.2**	**34.6**	**34.8**	**41.1**	**28.58**	**18**
Gross fixed capital formation	27.3	35.0	34.4	34.6	40.9	27.74	17
Changes in inventories	0.2	0.2	0.3	0.2	0.2	1.04	1
Exports of goods and services	68.2	52.2	49.6	49.6	51.9	63.65	13
Imports of goods and services	(34.2)	(37.7)	(37.7)	(35.6)	(42.0)	(61.1)	18
Total value added	**100.0**	**100.0**	**100.0**	**100.0**	**100.0**	**100**	**100**

Industry Structure: GDP by type of expenditure (refer Note 5)

Observations: Capital formation is a lead indicator of economic performance and compares favorably with both the ASEAN average and US figures. Tax outcomes flowing from investment may be significantly impacted by tax incentives.

NPISH = nonprofit institutions serving households.

Component Sector	2014	2015	2016	2017	2018	ASEAN Ave.	US 2018
Agriculture, hunting, forestry, and fishing	0.8	1.1	1.2	1.1	1.0	12.11	167
Industry	66.8	60.2	56.5	58.7	62.2	38.84	1,512
Mining, manufacturing, and utilities	64.9	57.8	54.0	56.3	59.8	32	673
Manufacturing	15.9	14.3	11.3	12.5	13.8	17.29	2,321
Construction	1.9	2.4	2.5	2.5	2.5	6.99	839
Services	32.3	38.7	42.4	40.2	36.7	49.05	2,579
Wholesale, retail trade, restaurants, and hotels	5.0	6.0	6.5	6.2	5.8	16.75	2,338
Transport, storage, and communications	3.4	3.8	4.0	3.9	3.5	7.02	658
Other activities	23.9	28.9	31.9	30.1	27.5	25.28	437

Industry Structure: Value Add by kind of economic activity ($ million) (refer Note 5)

Observations: There is a heavy, although declining, reliance on mining due to the export of crude oil. The government recognizes that the reliance on crude oil revenue to supplement taxation needs to be reduced. Government revenue has been badly hit by falling world oil prices over recent years. GDP growth declined at an average annualized rate of 1.3% between 2012 and 2016, making Brunei Darussalam the only Southeast Asian country to record 4 straight years of economic recession.

TAX SYSTEM AND TAX ADMINISTRATION DESIGN FEATURES

Tax Rates, Thresholds, and Overall Revenue Contribution (see Note 6)

Taxes	Rates of Tax (%) /1		Threshold		Share of All Tax Revenue (latest year) /2
	Basic/Standard	Other	Local Currency	$	
Corporate income tax (CIT)/3	18.5%		B$100,000 = 18.5% of B$25,000 plus B$100,000 – B$250,000 – 18.5% of B$75,000 plus B$ > 250,000 = 18.5% of amount over B$250,000	$71,500 $71,500– $180,000	10.4% (2019) (includes WHT and Excise)
Oil and Gas	55.0%				89.6% (2019)
Export Tax /4	1.0%		No threshold		
Withholding tax (WHT) (nonresident)	Interest = 2.5%; Royalties = 10%; Tech Serv Fees = 10%; Rent = 10%; remuneration to directors = 10%		No threshold		
Employer and Employee	5% to employee trust fund 3.5% to pension fund				
Excise /5	Tobacco: Cigarettes - B$0.26/stick; Other - B$60–B$200 per kg. Alcohol: B$55–B$250 per liter (based on alcohol content) Vehicles: 15–35 based on engine capacity				
Luxury Excise	5%–10%				
Property	12%		Only on properties located in the capital, Bandar Seri Begawan		
Stamp Duty	Fixed rate or *ad valorem* on certain business documents				
Overview of Tax Incentives	Domestic tax incentives are available for "pioneer" industries and tax credits are allowed for certain salaries and training expenditures. FDI tax incentives and customs duty exemptions apply on certain sectors, especially for non-oil investments. FDI is allowed in all sectors, except for certain fields in which local participation is required. The government has been diversifying the economy and making Brunei Darussalam into a banking center, as well as an international offshore financial center. There are no specific special economic zones, but tax and other incentives are provided for investment in certain regions. The corporate tax rate also decreased and is now among the lowest in the ASEAN countries (18.5%). Evaluation of subsidies is conducted but not published. Foreign tax credits are limited to taxes assessed at half the rate applicable in Brunei Darussalam.				

Note that Brunei Darussalam does not have local governments. /1. For fiscal year (FY) 2020, unless otherwise indicated. /2. National taxes are shown as a percentage of national tax revenue. /3. There are no personal income tax (PIT), payroll taxes, capital gains taxes, sales taxes, or value-added tax (VAT) in Brunei Darussalam. /4. Applies to approved exports. /5. Excises on alcohol and tobacco are levied at standard rates based on quantity.

Sources: IMF Art. IV reports, Deloitte Country Tax Profiles (https://www2.deloitte.com/content/dam/Deloitte/global/Documents/Tax/dttl-tax-bruneihighlights-2019.pdf), OECD Statistics, 2018 Directorate General of Taxes Annual Report.

Tax Administration Setup and Performance

Subject area	Aspect	Features and Performance	Overall Rating
Responsibilities of tax body	Main taxes collected	CIT (including oil and gas), WHT, and stamp duty	Medium – The revenue division collects around 55% of all revenue.
	Other major roles	Taxes are administered by the Revenue Division of the Ministry of Finance and Economy. The Revenue Division is the agency responsible for formulating tax policies, administration, and due collection of income tax. The Permanent Secretary of the Ministry of Finance and Economy is appointed as the Collector of Income Tax and the Division is led by the Director (Revenue).	
Tax body Autonomy	Budget flexibility, organization design	Budget and HRM appears to be conducted at the ministerial level	Low
	Human resource management (HRM)		

Digital services in tax administration	E-filing	Rate (2017)	Comments	Medium to high
	- CIT	18.5	There is no PIT or VAT but there is an excise tax administered by Customs and Excise, and stamp duties.	
	- PIT	n.a.		
	- VAT/goods and services tax (GST)	n.a.		
	E-payment	yes		
	E-services (including mobile applications)	E-services are provided via the System for Tax Administration and Revenue Services (STARS). Electronic filing and payments are accepted, and taxpayers can access their information via a portal. Mobile apps do not appear to be available.		

	Measure	Country Performance						ASEAN Ave. 2018	OECD Ave. 2018
		2014	2015	2016	2017	2018	2019		
Tax system design (refer Note 7)	Tax reliance ratio	68.6	57.0	54.0	38.9	55.8	50.7	66.9	63.8
	Tax mix	1	1	1	1	1	1	39.92	33.7
	Tax ratio	23.6	12.4	12.2	8.8	18.2	12.2	14	34.3
	CIT productivity	0.051	0.057	0.076	0.067	0.050	0.048	0.26	
	VAT productivity[2]	...	...	...	...	...	...	0.43	
	Consolidation of tax collection and administration	All taxes are raised at the national level, as Brunei Darussalam does not have local governments. Stamp duty appears to be separately administered.							
Observations	The tax mix is significantly shaped by the very high oil and gas revenues. This is reflected in the low CIT productivity. Dependence on oil and gas revenues is slowly reducing, driven by public policy. Additional revenues could be raised by broadening the tax base (administratively and via policy shifts).								

	Measure	Country Performance
Tax administration processes (refer Note 8)	Tax administration efficiency and effectiveness (Operating expenditure as a proportion of net revenue collected)	Data to complete this chart are unavailable.
	No. of labor force members/ tax body full-time equivalent staff (FTE)	
	No. of citizens/ tax body FTE	
	Proportion of staff assigned to support functions	

---

[2]   Brunei Darussalam does not currently levy any income tax on individuals and there is no sales tax or VAT.

REVENUE

	Measure	Country Performance						ASEAN Ave.	Asia and Pacific Ave.	OECD Ave. 2018
		2014	2015	2016	2017	2018	2019*			
Tax revenue collection performance *(all levels of government)* *(refer Note 9)*	Tax / GDP (%) - all	23.6	12.4	12.2	8.8	18.2	12.2	14.03	20.0	34.3
	Taxes on income and profits/GDP (%)	2	2.5	2.1	2	1.9	2.1	5.35	8.1	11.6
	Taxes on goods and services/GDP (%)	...	...	...	...	...	...	6	10.1	10.9
	Overall tax revenue trend	Tax to GDP in 2018 has been on average well above the level required to fund development, but projected figures for 2019 show a material drop, largely driven by oil and gas. Non-oil and gas growth continued to improve, underpinned by construction projects due to large investments in infrastructure projects and ramp-up of capital spending related to RKN11 (the 11th National Development Plan). The latest quarterly data show a continued recovery in the non-oil and gas sector, growing at 2.5% year-on-year in the first quarter of 2019, while the overall growth declined to -0.5% due to scheduled maintenance of oil and gas fields.								

(*) projected/provisional collections.

BROADENING THE TAX BASE

	Measure	Country Performance
Countering Tax Avoidance and Evasion *(refer Note 10)*	Effective anti-avoidance rules	There are no general or specific anti-avoidance rules, but tax authorities can disregard certain transactions or dispositions if they are satisfied that the purpose or effect of the arrangement aims at directly or indirectly reducing or avoiding liability to tax.
	Thin capitalization and controlled foreign corporation rules	No thin capitalization or controlled foreign corporation rules apply, and there are no disclosure requirements. Transfer pricing rules are limited but transactions involving related resident and nonresident entities must be conducted on an arm's length basis.
	Findings from OECD Forum on Harmful Tax Practices (FHTP)	Pioneer services companies: Regime under review by FHTP
	A focus on HNWI and professions	No
	Dealing with the shadow economy	The shadow economy in Brunei Darussalam is estimated to be in the region of 30% of GDP, which places it 3rd of 11 in the region. It is unclear if there is any administrative or policy focus on reducing shadow economy activities.

Measure		Country Status
Member of Global Forum on Transparency & Exchange of Information		Yes
Exchange of Information on Request Ratings	Round 1	Largely compliant
	Round 2	Largely compliant
Signatory to the Multilateral Convention on Mutual Assistance in Tax Matters		Yes
Commitment to Automatic Exchange of Information		Yes - 2018
Implementation of Common Reporting Standard (CRS) and Multilateral Competent Authority Agreement		No
Convention on Mutual Administrative Assistance in tax matters		Signed
Member of Base Erosion and Profit Shifting (BEPS) Inclusive Framework		Yes
Existence of harmful tax regimes (Action 5)		Under review/review scheduled
Exchange of information on tax rulings (Action 5)		Reviewed/no recommendations
CbC – Domestic law (Action 13)		Update on status pending
CbC – Information exchange network (Action 13)		CbC MCAA not signed
Effective dispute resolution (Action 14)		Stage 1 reviewed and recommendations made
Signatory to the Multilateral Convention to Implement Treaty Related Measures to Prevent BEPS (Action 6)		Reviewed in 2018 and 2019, no recommendation. 2020 review ongoing.
Network of income tax treaties for avoidance of double taxation		18

The left row-group label reads: **Countering International Tax Avoidance and Evasion and International Cooperation** *(refer Note 11)*

RESPONSIVE TAX ADMINISTRATION

% responding tax regime has become more complicated over prior 3 years	14%	
% responding tax regime has been less consistently administered over prior 3 years	8%	
% responding tax compliance and reporting rules are "complicated" or "very complicated"	3%	
Perceived fairness in tax audits	Neutral	
Perceived confidence in appeal system	Neutral	
Taxpayer relationship with authorities	Neutral	
Perceived main priority areas for reform	Timeliness and quality of tax audits, public consultation in tax policy making, adoption of BEPS recommendations, and transparency of tax statistics	

The left row-group label reads: **Important findings from Deloitte's 2017 Tax Complexity Survey** *(refer Note 12)*

Measure	Country Ranking				World Ave.	Asia and Pacific Ave.
	2017	2018	2019	2020		
Compliance/ Regulatory Burden Indicators *(as reported in the Doing Business Series)* *(refer Note 13)* — Ease of Doing Business Indicator Ranking (Ranking out of 190 countries)	56	55	55	66	–	–
Paying Taxes Indicator (Ranking out of 190 countries)	89	104	84	90	–	–
Paying Taxes – time to comply (Hours/yr.): (all)	67	64	53	53	234	192
Paying Taxes – time to comply (Hours/yr.): (CIT)	43	43	43	43	59	59
Paying Taxes – time to comply (Hours/yr.): (VAT)	n.a.	n.a.	n.a.	n.a.	90	73
Paying Taxes – time to comply (Hours/yr.): Labor taxes	24	21	10	10	85	60
Post-filing Index (VAT and CIT corrections)	0	0	0	0	61	57
Time to comply with VAT refund (hours)	n.a.	n.a.	n.a.	n.a.	14.9	19.6
Time to obtain VAT refund (weeks)	n.a.	n.a.	n.a.	n.a.	41.5	28.2
Number of payments per year	16	15	5	5	23	21
Trading Across Borders Rank	142	144	149	149	–	–

Observations	To increase transparency and strengthen corporate governance, the Company Act was amended to simplify the business climate, significantly enhancing the ease of company registration, decreasing the time required to register a limited liability company as of 2017. An Ease of Doing Business Steering Committee was also established. Despite improvements in earlier periods, the 2020 rank declined to 66th out of 190 (down 11 places). Paying taxes rank improved 20 points in 2018 following the introduction of an e-filing system, but then declined a little in 2019. According to the IMF, more reforms are needed in registering property and trading across borders. Other areas include strengthening regulatory practices such as public–private consultations and regulatory impact analysis.

	Observations
Taxpayer rights and obligations *(refer Note 14)*	Taxpayers have a right to dispute tax assessments. If rejected by a revenue body, a further review may be sought by the Income Tax Board of Review, which is an independent board under the Ministry of Finance and Economy. Public Rulings are issued by the collector of income tax.

	Observations
Corruption Perception Index Trends *(refer Note 15)*	In 2014, Brunei Darussalam's Corruption Perception Index (CPI) score was 55 out of 100 and has steadily improved to 60 in 2019. This places Brunei Darussalam at a relatively sound ranking of 35 out of 180 countries.

CAMBODIA

AT A GLANCE

	Measure	2014	2015	2016	2017	2018	2019
Demographic Overview *(refer Note 1)*	Total Population (in millions)	15.274	15.521	15.766	16.009	16.249	16.486
	Age profile (in %)						
	0–14	31.81	31.60	31.39	31.27	31.20	31.10
	15–64	64.17	64.28	64.35	64.32	64.23	64.20
	65+	4.02	4.12	4.26	4.41	4.57	4.70
	Literacy level (% of population)	78.06	80.52	…	…	…	…
	Urbanization (%)						
	Urban Population	21.80	22.19	22.58	22.98	23.39	23.80
	Rural Population	78.20	77.81	77.42	77.02	76.61	76.20
	Employment to Population	80.10	80.01	81.77	81.74	81.68	81.76
	Agriculture	46.00	42.47	37.54	35.28	33.65	32.30
	Industry	23.77	24.92	25.76	27.10	28.28	29.00
	Services	30.24	32.61	36.70	37.62	38.07	38.70

	Industrialization Indices	2012	2013	2014	ASEAN Ave.	World Ave.	
	Industrialization Intensity Index	0.24	0.24	0.24	0.54	0.65	
	Share of Medium & High Tech	0	0	0	0.44		
	Main Economic Sectors	Cambodia's two largest industries are textiles and tourism, while agricultural activities remain the main source of income for many Cambodians living in rural areas. The service sector is heavily concentrated on trading activities and catering-related services.					

	Measure	2014	2015	2016	2017	2018	2019	ASEAN Ave.
Trends in Income and Inequality *(refer Note 1)*	Income Index	0.512	0.518	0.526	0.533	0.541	…	0.734
	Inequality in Income (%)	20.3	20.3	14.3	14.3	14.3	…	20.35
	GNI per Capita	2,959	3,085	3,248	3,418	3,597	…	23,069
	Human Development Rank	146/189						

	Measure	Description
Take-up of Technology *(refer Note 2)*	E-commerce trends	Less than 4% of the population make online purchases or pay bills online.
	Internet coverage: SEA average = 66%.	Less than 50% of the population have access to the internet. Mobile Connectivity Index = 47.1/100 in 2018 (ranked 9th in SEA).
	Take-up of internet and mobile banking	Limited data is available on online banking. Around 6% have a mobile bank account.[3]
	Take-up of e-filing	E-filing has recently commenced but figures are not yet available.

---

[3] World Bank Global Financial Inclusion Data 2019.

CAMBODIA:
EMPLOYMENT BY SECTOR

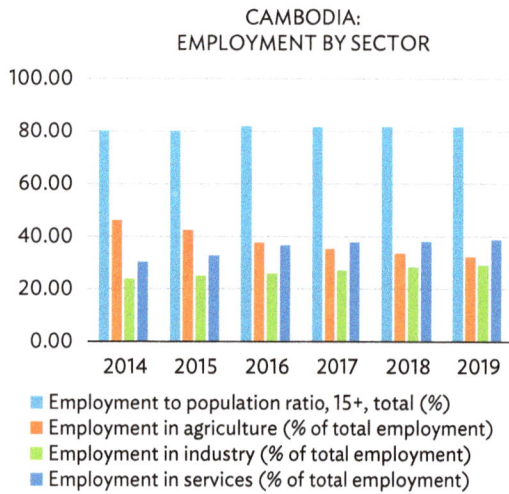

- Employment to population ratio, 15+, total (%)
- Employment in agriculture (% of total employment)
- Employment in industry (% of total employment)
- Employment in services (% of total employment)

CAMBODIA:
TAKE-UP OF TECHNOLOGY

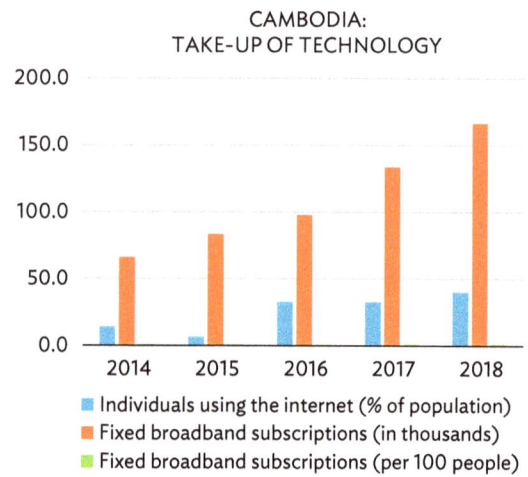

- Individuals using the internet (% of population)
- Fixed broadband subscriptions (in thousands)
- Fixed broadband subscriptions (per 100 people)

PRODUCTION STRUCTURE

		Exports ($ million)				
	Region	2014	2015	2016	2017	2018
Exports - Overall (refer Note 3)	Cambodia	9,500	10,456	11,140	12,354	13,459
	SEA	1,606,681	1,630,770	1,508,470	1,498,265	1,676,341
	US	2,273,428	2,371,704	2,266,800	2,220,609	2,356,726
Main sector 1 Clothing	Cambodia	4,832	5,339	5,938	6,651	7,188
	SEA	42,208	46,366	47,910	49,434	57,409
	US	5,861	6,103	6,120	5,712	5,728
Main sector 2 Machinery and Transport Equipment	Cambodia	618	87	663	835	823
	SEA	470,011	483,417	476,133	478,746	538,499
	US	639,053	665,625	647,286	627,333	645,863

		Imports ($ million)				
	Region	2014	2015	2016	2017	2018
Imports - Overall (refer Note 3)	Cambodia	11,192	11,939	13,238	14,219	15,536
	SEA	1,506,926	1,372,220	1,354,024	1,525,565	1,701,449
	US	2,879,362	2,786,645	2,739,415	2,932,062	3,148,464
Main sector 1 Textiles	Cambodia	3,669	3,719	4,084	4,658	5,311
	SEA			30,920		37,612
	US			28,722		31,883
Main sector 2 Machinery and Transport Equipment	Cambodia			2,659		3,548
	SEA			462,749		576,718
	US			969,943		1,103,063

Observations	Exports grew by around 8% in 2018 compared with a regional average growth of 10.1%. Imports also grew by around 8% in 2018 compared with a regional average growth of 10.3%. The top exports of Cambodia are clothing, and the top imports are gold, raw materials, and refined petroleum.

Sector	2014	2015	2016	2017	2018
Agriculture, forestry, and fishing	0.01		0.05	0.02	0.16
Mining and quarrying	0.00		0.02	0.09	0.03
Manufacturing	0.14	3.74	(11.83)	4.32	17.88
Electricity, gas, steam, and air conditioning supply	0.01		0.04	0.59	1.65
Water supply; sewerage, waste management, and remediation activities	0.00		0.16	0.04	0.26
Construction	0.04		0.20	0.08	1.20
Wholesale and retail trade; repair of motor vehicles and motorcycles	0.03	0.17	0.64	5.20	(21.44)
Transportation and storage	0.01	0.00	0.29	0.02	7.42
Accommodation and food service activities	0.02	0.00	0.13	0.04	0.59
Information and communication	0.00	0.00	0.13	0.02	0.51
Financial and insurance activities	18.95	39.25	0.19	0.29	1.21
Real estate activities	1.13	3.89	3.40	9.53	29.10
Professional, scientific, and technical activities	0.03	0.01	0.31	0.06	2.14
Administrative and support service activities	0.00		0.25	(0.04)	0.23
Education	0.00		0.02	0.01	0.09
Human health and social work activities	0.02		0.02	0.03	0.13
Arts, entertainment, and recreation	0.00		0.11	0.00	1.15
Other services activities	0.00		0.02	0.06	0.02
Unspecified activity	0.01	0.07	(1.54)	0.00	
TOTAL activities	**20.40**	**47.14**	**(7.38)**	**20.36**	**42.31**
Net FDI inflows (in percent of GDP)	11.1	10.1	12.3	12.6	13.1
Net Direct Investment (FDI) – in $ million.	...	1,735	2,398	2,675	3,088

Flows of Inward Foreign Direct Investment (FDI) to ASEAN Sourced from Cambodia, by Economic Sectors ($ million) (refer Note 4)

IMF Article IV

General Observations On FDI

FDI flowing from Cambodia into ASEAN almost doubled in 2018 driven largely by investment in real estate activities and manufacturing. There was a substantial drop in investment in the wholesale and retail trade sector.
FDI inflows into Cambodia have grown steadily both as a percentage of GDP and in absolute terms. Growth in FDI inflows in the last few years is attributed to sound macroeconomic policies, political stability, regional economic growth, and an open investment market. Cambodia recorded its highest-ever FDI in 2019, at $3.7 billion (a rise of 16% compared to $3.2 billion in 2018), mainly due to robust investments in manufacturing and services. The total stock of FDI stood at $34 billion in 2019. The construction industry attracts the largest share of foreign investors, followed by infrastructure, industry (primarily textiles), agriculture, and tourism.
New railways are under construction, ranging from Phnom Penh to Siem Reap all the way to the Viet Nam border in the other direction. This project uses PRC funding linked to Beijing's Belt and Road infrastructure program.

Component Sector	2014	2015	2016	2017	2018	ASEAN Ave.	US 2018
Gross domestic product (GDP)	100.0	100.0	100.0	100.0	100.0	100	100
Final consumption expenditure	83.0	82.2	81.3	78.5	75.6	68.04	87
Household consumption expenditure (including NPISH)	77.6	76.8	76.1	73.4	70.6	54	70
General government final consumption expenditure	5.5	5.4	5.2	5.1	4.9	14.51	17
Gross capital formation	**22.1**	**22.5**	**22.7**	**22.9**	**23.4**	**28.58**	**18**
Gross fixed capital formation	21.0	21.4	21.7	21.9	22.6	27.74	17
Changes in inventories	1.1	1.0	1.0	1.0	0.9	1.04	1
Exports of goods and services	62.6	61.7	61.3	60.7	61.6	63.65	13
Imports of goods and services	(67.0)	(66.1)	(65.7)	(64.1)	(63.3)	(61.1)	18
Total value added	100.0	100.0	100.0	100.0	100.0	100	100

Industry Structure: GDP by type of expenditure (refer Note 5)

Observations: Capital formation is a lead indicator of economic performance and is below ASEAN averages but compares favorably to US figures. Tax outcomes flowing from investment may be significantly impacted by tax incentives.

NPISH = nonprofit institutions serving households.

Component Sector	2014	2015	2016	2017	2018	ASEAN Ave.	US 2018
Agriculture, hunting, forestry, and fishing	30.7	28.2	26.3	24.9	23.5	12.11	167
Industry	27.2	29.4	31.3	32.8	34.4	38.84	1,512
Mining, manufacturing, and utilities	18.1	19.0	19.2	19.6	20.0	32	673
Manufacturing	16.3	17.0	17.0	17.2	17.4	17.29	2,321
Construction	9.1	10.4	12.1	13.2	14.5	6.99	839
Services	42.2	42.3	42.4	42.3	42.1	49.05	2,579
Wholesale, retail trade, restaurants, and hotels	15.4	15.2	15.0	15.0	14.8	16.75	2,338
Transport, storage, and communications	8.4	8.6	8.7	8.6	8.5	7.02	658
Other activities	18.3	18.6	18.6	18.7	18.8	25.28	437

Industry Structure: Value Add by kind of economic activity ($ million) (refer Note 5)

Observations: The contribution of agriculture and construction are well over ASEAN averages, while manufacturing and wholesale and retail trade are below ASEAN averages.

TAX SYSTEM AND TAX ADMINISTRATION DESIGN FEATURES

Tax Rates, Thresholds, and Overall Revenue Contribution (see Note 6)

Taxes	Rates of Tax (%) /1		Threshold		Share of All Tax Revenue (latest year)
	Basic/ Standard	Other	Local Currency	$	
CIT	20% /2	1% alternative minimum tax /3			25% (2019)
PIT (employees)	0%–20%	Paid by employer	KR150,000	$36.00	
PIT (Business)	Same as for companies				
VAT/ GST	10%	Some supplies zero rated	No threshold for companies Others - KR125 million for goods and KR60 million for services	$30,000 and $14,500	62% (2019)
WHT /4	15%	14% (nonresidents)	No threshold		
Excise /5	10%		No threshold		
Social security contributions (SSC) – Occupational risk and health care	0.8% and 2.6% of average monthly salary			Monthly cap of $2.40 and $7.80/employee	
Other taxes (subnational) /7	0.1%/yr. 2% 0.1% KR1 million	on property value on unused land on share transfers on business registration	> KR100 million /6		7.9% of general government revenue 1.2% of GDP (2016)
Overview of Tax Incentives	Cambodia has a generally open and liberal foreign investment regime. Incentives to investors include: 100% foreign ownership of companies, corporate tax holidays of up to 8 years, a 20% corporate tax rate after the incentive period ends, duty-free import of capital goods, VAT-free importation of raw materials used in manufacture of 100% exported goods, and no restrictions on capital repatriation. To facilitate foreign investment, Cambodia has created special economic zones (SEZs), which provide companies with ready access to land, infrastructure, and other services to facilitate the set up and operation of businesses. Currently there are 13 SEZs, and, according to the US Department of State, in recent years the Phnom Penh Special Economic Zone alone has attracted American companies such as Coca-Cola (which alone invested $100 million), American Liquorice, and Tiffany & Co.				

/1. For FY 2020, unless otherwise indicated. /2. Ranges from 0% to 30% depending upon type of income. Certain industries such as oil and gas and exploitation of natural resources (such as gold, timber, and precious stones) are taxed at 30%. Qualified Investment Projects are not taxed during the exemption period. /3. Alternative minimum tax is levied on turnover and applies to businesses that do not keep proper records. It is inclusive of all taxes except VAT. /4. Dividends interest, royalties, branch remittances, and technical service fees. 10%–14% WHT on rent. /5. Excise is referred to as specific tax (SPT) and applies to imported and locally produced goods. /6. Capital gains are taxed as ordinary income at a national level. /7. Other subnational taxes include tax on vehicles and accommodation taxes.

Sources: IMF Art. IV reports; Deloitte Country Tax Profiles; and OECD Statistics, 2018.

Tax Administration Setup and Performance

Subject area	Aspect	Features and Performance		Overall Rating
Responsibilities of tax body	Main taxes collected	CIT, VAT, Excise (there is no PIT)		Medium to broad – 66% of all taxes collected by the GDT
	Other major roles	General Department of Taxation (GDT) develops tax policy and drafts tax laws		
Tax body Autonomy	Budget flexibility, organization design	The General Department of Taxation is a single directorate within the Ministry of Finance with responsibility for budget and human resource (HR) decisions. The GDT is not fully autonomous.		Medium
	Human resource management			
Digital services in tax administration	E-filing	**Rate (2017)**	**Comments**	Medium to high
	- CIT	...	Cambodia has recently commenced offering e-filing and e-payment services but filing rates are not yet available.	
	- PIT	...		
	- VAT/GST	...		
	E-payment	...		
	E-services (including mobile applications)	A digital mailbox, electronic invoicing system, tools and calculators, and general information are provided online. There is no access to integrated accounts yet.		

	Measure	Country Performance						ASEAN Ave.	OECD Ave. 2018
		2014	2015	2016	2017	2018	2019		
Tax system design (refer Note 7)	Tax reliance ratio	76.4	78.8	74.7	77.2	77.3	78.7	66.9	63.8
	Tax mix	19.9	23.1	24.5	26.8	23.9	23.0	39.92	33.7
	Tax ratio	...	15.6	15.8	16.9	18.8	19.2	14	34.3
	CIT productivity	0.097	0.110	0.117	0.130	0.154	0.161	0.26	
	VAT productivity	0.435	0.503	0.496	0.510	0.528	0.564	0.43	
	Consolidation of tax collection and administration	Most taxes are raised at a national level, but stamp duties and other fees are levied at the subnational level and make up 1.2% of GDP. A Subnational Budget System Reform 2019–2025 strategy was adopted to align with the National Budget System Reform Strategy 2018–2025, aiming to improve subnational tax and to set up principles for preparation of subnational strategic plan, budget management, and report system.							
Observations	Tax reliance is a little higher than the region and the tax mix is lower. The tax ratio is at a level sufficient to support development goals and above the regional average. CIT productivity is low and is balanced by higher VAT productivity.								

	Measure	Country Performance
Tax administration processes (refer Note 8)	Tax administration efficiency and effectiveness (Operating expenditure as a proportion of net revenue collected)	In 2017, the efficiency ratio was 0.89%, increasing from 0.50% in the prior year. This increase is likely to have been driven by the expanded services and improved e-offerings. A figure around 1.0 is considered to provide the right balance between efficiency and service levels.
	No. of labor force members/tax body FTE	Over 4,500 workers per tax officer.
	No. of citizens/tax body FTE	Over 7,800 citizens per staff member, which is on the higher end of the range for the region.
	Proportion of staff assigned to support functions	43% of staff are assigned to support functions, which is the highest in the region. Regional average = 29%

REVENUE

Tax revenue collection performance (all levels of government) (refer Note 9)	Measure	Country Performance						ASEAN Ave.	Asia and Pacific Ave.	OECD Ave. 2018
		2014	2015	2016	2017	2018	2019			
	Tax/GDP (%) – all	...	15.6	15.8	16.9	18.8	19.2	14.03	20.0	34.3
	Taxes on income and profits/GDP (%)	...	3.4	3.6	4.2	4.4	4.4	5.35	8.1	11.6
	Taxes on goods and services/GDP (%)	...	9.4	9.6	10.4	10.4	12.3	6	10.1	10.9
	Overall tax revenue trend	Tax to GDP has consistently improved and is well above regional averages.								

(2019 projected/provisional collections).

BROADENING THE TAX BASE

	Measure	Country Performance
Countering Tax Avoidance and Evasion (refer Note 10)	Effective anti-avoidance rules	Cambodia has transfer pricing rules that align with the recommended standards of OECD. There are no general or specific anti-avoidance rules.
	Thin capitalization and controlled foreign corporation (CFC) rules	There are no formal rules on thin capitalization but there is a cap on interest deductions allowed. There are no con rules.
	Findings from OECD Forum on Harmful Tax Practices (FHTP)	None reported.
	A focus on HNWI and professions	Cambodia has not reported any special activities to manage HNWIs.
	Dealing with the shadow economy	The shadow economy in Cambodia is estimated to be in the region of 34% of GDP, which places it in the upper range (2/11) in the region. It is unclear whether there is any administrative or policy focus on this area.

	Measure		Country Status
Countering International Tax Avoidance and Evasion and International Cooperation (refer Note 11)	Member of Global Forum on Transparency & Exchange of Information		Yes
	Exchange of Information on Request Ratings	Round 1	Not reviewed
		Round 2	Scheduled 2022
	Signatory to the Multilateral Convention on Mutual Assistance in Tax Matters		No
	Commitment to Automatic Exchange of Information		Not committed to a specific date
	Implementation of Common Reporting Standard (CRS) and Multilateral Competent Authority Agreement		Not applicable
	Convention on Mutual Administrative Assistance in tax matters		No
	Member of Base Erosion and Profit Shifting Inclusive Framework[4]		No
	Existence of harmful tax regimes (Action 5)		n.a.
	Exchange of information on tax rulings (Action 5)		n.a.
	CbC – Domestic law (Action 13)		n.a.
	CbC – Information exchange network (Action 13)		n.a.
	Effective dispute resolution (Action 14)		n.a.
	Signatory to the Multilateral Convention to Implement Treaty Related Measures to Prevent BEPS (Action 6)		No
	Network of income tax treaties for avoidance of double taxation		6

[4]   Cambodia has not yet been required to commit to a date to commence exchanges and has not decided on the date.

RESPONSIVE TAX ADMINISTRATION

Important findings from Deloitte's 2017 Tax Complexity Survey *(refer Note 12)*	Cambodia was not included in the survey.

	Measure	Country Ranking				World Ave.	Asia and Pacific Ave.
		2017	2018	2019	2020		
Compliance/ Regulatory Burden Indicators *(as reported in the Doing Business Series)* *(refer Note 13)*	Ease of Doing Business Indicator Ranking (Ranking out of 190 countries)	135	138	138	144	–	–
	Paying Taxes Indicator (Ranking out of 190 countries)	124	136	137	138	–	–
	Paying Taxes – time to comply (Hours/yr.): (all)	173	173	173	173	234	192
	Paying Taxes – time to comply (Hours/yr.): (CIT)	23	23	23	23	59	59
	Paying Taxes – time to comply (Hours/yr.): (VAT)	66	66	66	66	90	73
	Paying Taxes – time to comply (Hours/yr.): Labor taxes	84	84	84	84	85	60
	Post Filing Index (VAT and CIT corrections)	26	26	26	26	61	57
	Time to comply with VAT Refund (hours)	21	21	21	21	14.9	19.6
	Time to obtain VAT refund (weeks)	64	64	64	64	41.5	28.2
	Number of payments per year	40	40	40	40	23	21
	Trading Across Borders Rank	102	108	115	118	–	–
Observations	The country's legal system lacks transparency, and energy supply and transportation problems remain significant obstacles to international investment. Corruption, scarcity of skilled labor, inadequate infrastructure, and high energy costs also hinder investments. The World Bank continues to draw attention to Cambodia's poor business environment, ranking the country 144th out of 190 (down by six spots compared to the previous year).						

	Observations
Taxpayer rights and obligations *(refer Note 14)*	Cambodia provides public binding rulings on tax matters free of charge. There is no private ruling system. There is a formally defined and legislated set of taxpayer rights and a formal complaints mechanism involving both internal and external bodies. Administrative and judicial reviews are available. There is a taxpayer ombudsman.

	Observations
Corruption Perception Index Trends *(refer Note 15)*	In 2014, Cambodia's CPI score was 21 out of 100, and has decreased to 20 in 2019. This places Cambodia at a ranking of 162 out of 180 countries.

INDONESIA

AT A GLANCE

Measure	2014	2015	2016	2017	2018	2019
Total Population (million)	255.12	258.38	261.55	264.64	267.663	270.62
Age profile						
0–14	27.77	27.45	27.23	26.91	26.55	26.10
15–64	66.95	67.17	67.24	67.40	67.59	67.60
65+	5.28	5.38	5.52	5.68	5.86	6.30
Literacy level (% of population)	95.1	95.2	95.4	-	95.7	-
Urbanization (%)						
Urban Population	52.64	53.31	53.99	54.66	55.33	55.80
Rural Population	47.37	46.69	46.01	45.34	44.68	44.20
Employment to Population	64.11	63.49	63.33	64.21	64.47	64.33
Agriculture	34.28	33.04	31.82	30.79	29.63	28.64
Industry	21.40	22.04	21.72	22.02	22.29	22.45
Services	44.32	44.92	46.46	47.19	48.08	48.91

Demographic Overview (refer Note 1)

Industrialization Indices	2012	2013	2014	ASEAN Ave.	World Ave.
Industrialization Intensity Index	0.59	0.58	0.59	0.54	0.65
Share of Medium & High Tech	0.43	0.41	0.43	0.44	
Main Economic Sectors	The services sector accounts for over 45% of GDP and is the largest sector followed by industry (mainly mining, manufacturing and construction). Agriculture accounts for 13% of GDP.				

Trends in Income and Inequality (refer Note 1)

Measure	2014	2015	2016	2017	2018	2019	ASEAN Ave.
Income Index	0.691	0.696	0.702	0.707	0.714	0.691	0.734
Inequality in Income (%)	17.3	17.3	17.3	24.9	20.1	...	20.35
GNI per Capita	9,679	10,029	10,419	10,811	11,256	..	23,069
Human Development Rank			111/189				99/189

Take-up of Technology (refer Note 2)

Measure	Description
E-commerce trends	Digital take-up in 2019 is 1.6 times the 2014 rate, reaching 58%, in line with the rest of Emerging Asia.[5] Around 90% of surveyed 16–64 year olds had made online purchases in 2019.
Internet coverage and availability	Almost 40% of the population use the internet, which is relatively low. Although fixed broadband subscriptions have increased from 3.4 million in 2014 to almost 9 million in 2018, with a population of over 270 million coverage is still low. Mobile and online apps are widely available. Mobile connectivity index = 61.8 (6th in the region).
Take-up of internet and mobile banking	Online banking is widely available, as is a range of other financial e-services such as loan applications. All taxes are paid online and the tax agency offers extensive e-services.
Take-up of e-filing	E-filing take-up is at one of the highest levels in Asia, according to the International Survey of Revenue Administration (ISORA).

---

[5]   According to a 2019 survey conducted by McKinsey.

INDONESIA: EMPLOYMENT BY SECTOR

Legend:
- Employment to Population (%)
- % of Total Employment in Agriculture
- % of Total Employment in Industry
- % of Total Employment in Services

INDONESIA: TAKE-UP OF TECHNOLOGY

Legend:
- Individuals using the internet (% of population)
- Fixed broadband subscriptions (in million)
- Fixed broadband subscriptions (per 100 people)

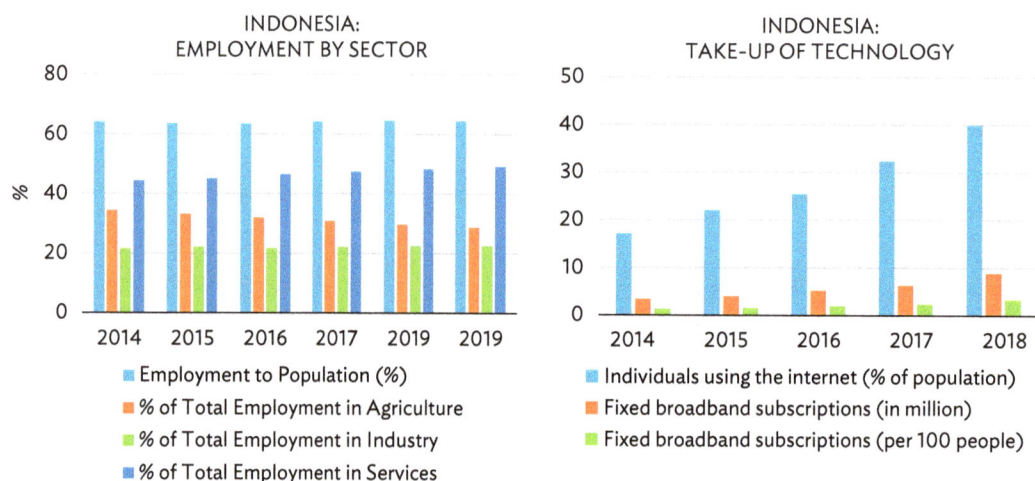

PRODUCTION STRUCTURE

	Region	Exports ($ million)				
		2014	2015	2016	2017	2018
Exports - Overall (refer Note 3)	Indonesia	218,308	210,820	182,158	177,886	204,999
	SEA	1,606,681	1,630,770	1,508,470	1,498,265	1,676,341
	US	2,273,428	2,371,704	2,266,800	2,220,609	2,356,726
Main sector 1 Fuels	Indonesia	57,396	51,126	34,649	27,871	36,865
	SEA	220,922	207,952	135,574	109,869	140,057
	US	148,866	156,185	104,639	93,753	139,261
Main sector 2 Food	Indonesia	31,939	35,389	32,256	32,188	39,136
	SEA	124,771	134,219	122,774	125,888	144,833
	US	141,891	149,139	132,962	135,280	137,279

	Region	Imports ($ million)				
		2014	2015	2016	2017	2018
Imports - Overall (refer Note 3)	Indonesia	217,485	178,864	170,835	194,699	229,861
	SEA	1,506,926	1,372,220	1,354,024	1,525,565	1,701,449
	US	2,879,362	2,786,645	2,739,415	2,932,062	3,148,464
Main sector 1 Machinery and Transport Equipment	Indonesia	51,218	45,129	43,641	48,846	59,302
	SEA	462,822	456,028	462,749	520,106	576,718
	US	956,716	989,206	969,943	1,040,707	1,103,063
Main sector 2 Fuels	Indonesia	43,929	25,028	19,241	25,433	31,580
	SEA	268,802	160,708	131,975	182,212	226,604
	US	358,193	200,458	163,065	203,934	241,513
Observations	Exports grew by 13.2% in 2018, compared with a regional average growth of 10.1%. Imports grew by 15.3% in 2018, compared with a regional average growth of 10.3%. Despite Indonesia's high oil exports, it remains a net importer of fuel, and a net importer overall. The top exports are coal briquettes, palm oil, and oil and gas. The top imports are oil and gas and vehicles.					

Sector	2014	2015	2016	2017	2018
Agriculture, forestry, and fishing	17.32	0.15	0.05	(0.02)	0.18
Mining and quarrying	44.84	408.04	38.59	204.08	304.75
Manufacturing	(177.00)	115.09	7.48	(24.13)	(11.29)
Electricity, gas, steam, and air conditioning supply	0.23	1.38	0.45	4.91	2.05
Water supply; sewerage, waste management and remediation activities	0.06	0.01	0.25	0.29	0.33
Construction	(1.45)	2.75	(0.39)	1.02	2.43
Wholesale and retail trade; repair of motor vehicles and motorcycles	57.63	(101.71)	26.39	302.19	553.44
Transportation and storage	8.58	0.10	3.60	(9.50)	24.18
Accommodation and food service activities	0.55	0.18	0.21	0.26	0.73
Information and communication	3.36	(0.85)	(0.34)	2.06	0.47
Financial and insurance activities	(225.30)	(230.95)	1,637.45	644.43	587.28
Real estate activities	1,525.66	680.43	672.23	346.63	(313.68)
Professional, scientific, and technical activities	1.96	(0.56)	(7.88)	6.89	2.09
Administrative and support service activities	0.01	0.03	0.08	0.38	0.28
Education	0.08	0.01	0.03	0.06	0.11
Human health and social work activities	0.43	0.01	0.03	1.14	(2.13)
Arts, entertainment, and recreation	(0.09)	0.30	0.17	0.02	1.43
Other services activities	(134.24)	(23.02)	82.07	171.25	(6.01)
Unspecified activity	0.71	0.61	2.31	0.00	
TOTAL activities	**1,173.45**	**838.13**	**2,462.77**	**1,651.97**	**1,146.64**
Net FDI inflows (in percent of GDP)	1.7	1.2	1.7	1.8	1.4
Net Direct Investment in Indonesia (FDI) – in $ billion	21.8	16.6	3.9	20.6	22.0

Flows of Inward Foreign Direct Investment (FDI) to ASEAN Sourced from Indonesia, by Economic Sectors ($ million) (refer Note 4)

IMF Article IV

General Observations on FDI

Indonesia's FDI patterns are influenced by regulations restricting and, in some cases, prohibiting, FDI in a wide range of sectors. For example, FDI into construction and transport and storage are limited, and the information and communications sector is largely a state-owned monopoly. As reported by the IMF, the authorities have been implementing growth-enhancing structural reforms including efforts to streamline regulations, expand infrastructure, and open some sectors to more FDI. The low level of net FDI inflows, based on worldwide sources, is considered a vulnerability by the IMF.

After peaking in 2016, largely driven by a massive spike in net outflows in the financial and insurance sector, Indonesia has since seen declining overall net outflows of FDI (into the ASEAN region) through 2018. This trend may have been driven in part by the changes in insurance regulations, which were announced in 2014 and took effect in 2016. Real estate activities have shown material declines in net outflows, with 2018 recording a net inflow of FDI into Indonesia in this sector.

Sectors with high net outflows, such as mining, wholesale and retail trade, and financial and insurance, may require closer study to identify potential tax planning (including avoidance) practices enabled by FDI through offshore hubs.

FDI developments in 2016 may have reflected some one-off transactions associated with the tax amnesty program.

Component Sector	2014	2015	2016	2017	2018	ASEAN Ave.	US 2018
Gross domestic product (GDP)	100	100	100	100	100	100	100
Final consumption expenditure	66.6	67.2	67.4	66.4	65.9	68.04	87
Household consumption expenditure (including NPISH)	57.1	57.5	57.8	57.3	57.0	54	70
General government final consumption expenditure	9.4	9.7	9.5	9.1	9.0	14.51	17
Gross capital formation	**34.6**	**34.1**	**33.9**	**33.7**	**34.6**	**28.58**	**18**
Gross fixed capital formation	32.5	32.8	32.6	32.2	32.3	27.74	17
Changes in inventories	2.1	1.3	1.3	1.6	2.3	1.04	1
Exports of goods and services	23.7	21.2	19.1	20.2	21.0	63.65	13
Imports of goods and services	(24.4)	(20.8)	(18.3)	(19.2)	(22.1)	(61.1)	18
Total value added	**100**	**100**	**100**	**100**	**100**	**100**	**100**

Industry Structure: GDP by type of expenditure (refer Note 5)

Observations: Capital formation is a lead indicator of economic performance and compares favorably with US figures. Tax outcomes flowing from investments may be significantly impacted by tax incentives.

NPISH = nonprofit institutions serving households.

Component Sector	2014	2015	2016	2017	2018	ASEAN Ave.	US 2018
Agriculture, hunting, forestry, and fishing	13.7	13.9	14.0	13.7	13.3	12.11	167
Industry	43.0	41.4	40.8	41.0	41.4	38.84	1,512
Mining, manufacturing, and utilities	32.9	30.8	30.0	30.2	30.4	32	673
Manufacturing	21.6	21.7	21.3	21.0	20.7	17.29	2,321
Construction	10.1	10.5	10.8	10.8	11.0	6.99	839
Services	43.3	44.7	45.3	45.4	45.2	49.05	2,579
Wholesale, retail trade, restaurants, and hotels	16.9	16.8	16.7	16.5	16.5	16.75	2,338
Transport, storage, and communications	8.1	8.8	9.1	9.6	9.5	7.02	658
Other activities	18.3	19.1	19.4	19.3	19.2	25.28	437

Industry Structure: Value Add by kind of economic activity ($ million) (refer Note 5)

Observations: There is a heavy reliance on services and industry, particularly mining. Tax compliance strategies for these sectors should be considered as part of the broader large business compliance approach. The high level of outbound FDI (ASEAN) in mining should be factored into this thinking.

TAX SYSTEM AND TAX ADMINISTRATION DESIGN FEATURES
Tax Rates, Thresholds, and Overall Revenue Contribution (see Note 6)

Taxes	Rates of Tax (%) /1		Threshold			Share of All Tax Revenue (latest year)
	Basic/Standard	Other	Type	Local Currency	$	
CIT	22% on net income /2		Levying tax	> Rp4.8 billion	$343,000	42% (2019)
	0.5% of gross income /3		Levying tax	< Rp4.8 billion	$343,000	
PIT	5%, 15%, 25%, 30% on net income		Personal allowance	Rp54 million	$3,800	
	0.5% of gross income /3		Levying tax	< Rp4.8 billion	$343,000	
WHT /4	20% (nonresident) 15% (resident) on gross income		Levying tax			
WHT /5	2%, 10% on gross income		Levying tax			
VAT/GST /6	10% (includes digital services), 0		Registration	> Rp4.8 billion	$343,000	32% (2019)
Sales	(Up to 100 on certain luxury goods)					
Excise	Varies by product		-	-	-	9% (2019)
SSC /7	11.74 (employers), employees also contribute		Levying SSC			4% (2019
Property	2.5%, 1%, 0% (for sellers), 5% (for buyers)					1.5% (2018)
*Subnational taxes	n.a.		-	-	-	13% (2019) 8.1% (2016)

Overview of Tax Incentives	Resident entity taxpayers, with gross income of Rp50 billion, receive 50% reduced rate imposed on taxable income from the part of gross revenue of Rp4.8 billion. Tax incentives include 30% or 60% investment allowance (spread over 6 years), accelerated depreciation, extended carry forward losses, and reduced WHT on dividends paid to nonresidents. These incentives are available to entities with capital investment in certain sectors or operating in certain regions (subject to conditions). An alternative tax holiday regime is offered for new or increased investment in specific sectors and includes a CIT holiday for qualifying investments. A super deduction tax is provided to a maximum of 200% of costs incurred for apprenticeships, internships, and/or teaching activities conducted by the taxpayer's employees, or 300% of costs incurred on certain research and development activities. A public company with at least 40% of paid-up shares traded on the Indonesian Stock Exchange and meeting certain associate tests receives a 5% discount on the standard CIT rate.

* Indonesia has three levels of government and almost 89,000 subnational governments. /1. For FY 2020, unless otherwise indicated. Excises are collected by Customs and Excise, not the main tax body. /2. Headline rate reducing to 20% in 2022. /3. These taxing regimes apply to certain individuals and corporate taxpayers deriving business income and are a final tax. /4. Applied to interest, dividends, royalties, and other specific income. Withholding is an advance payment of tax withheld by withholding agents. /5. Rate of 2% applied to technical, management, and consulting services, and rentals other than land and buildings that are subject to a 10% withholding levied as a final tax. /6. In May 2020, Indonesia introduced a digital services tax commencing 1 July 2020 on nonresident companies with a "significant economic presence" in Indonesia. The tax is levied at 10% and expands the range of intangible goods and services subject to VAT to include e-books, apps, games, software, movies, and music, among others (https://www.aseanbriefing.com/news/indonesia-issues-regulation-taxing-digital-services/#:~:text=Indonesia%20introduced%20Reg%2048%2F2020,VAT)%20on%20digital%20service%20providers.&text=Intangible%20goods%20and%20services%20subject,%2C%20and%20music%2C%20among%20others). This law is in addition to the law on e-commerce introduced in 2019 to clarify tax obligations of domestic and international e-commerce businesses. /7. Two schemes (manpower and health insurance). Employer contributions of 0.24%–1.74% for work accidents; 0.3% for death insurance; 3.7% for old age savings; 2% (with income cap) for pension; and 4% (with income cap) for health insurance.

Sources: IMF Art. IV reports; Deloitte Country Tax Profiles; OECD Statistics; 2018 Directorate General of Taxes Annual Report; OECD Economics Department Working Papers No. 1534 *Raising More Public Revenue in Indonesia in a Growth- and Equity-Friendly Way*; Christine Lewis, 2019.

Tax Administration Setup and Performance

Subject Area	Aspect	Features and Performance	Overall Rating
Responsibilities of tax body	Main taxes collected	CIT, PIT, VAT, Tax on luxury goods, and stamp duty	Broad – DGT collects around 77% of all revenue
	Other major roles	Formulation of tax policy	
Tax body Autonomy	Budget flexibility, organization design	The DGT is a single directorate within the Ministry of Finance with authority to set performance targets and issue binding rulings. DGT does not have authority to determine structure or allocate budget but has broad authority on HRM matters.	Medium
	Human resource management (HRM)		

Subject Area	Aspect	Rate (2017)	Comments	Overall Rating
Digital services in tax administration	E-filing		In addition to the VAT, there is a Sales Tax on Luxury Goods	High
	– CIT	74		
	– PIT	85		
	– VAT/GST	99		
	E-payment	100		
	E-services (including mobile applications)	A comprehensive range, including access to integrated accounts and e-invoicing for businesses		

	Measure	Country Performance						ASEAN Ave.	OECD Ave. 2018
		2014	2015	2016	2017	2018	2019		
Tax system design *(refer Note 7)*	Tax reliance ratio	72.46	79.64	80.28	78.25	78.23	79.4	66.9	63.8
	Tax mix	44.0	46.4	51.1	46.1	47.1	48.1	39.92	33.7
	Tax ratio	16.8	15.1	14.5	14.3	14.8	10.7	14	34.3
	CIT productivity	0.195	0.218	0.232	0.200	0.209	0.232	0.26	
	VAT productivity	0.390	0.370	0.330	0.350	0.360	0.410	0.43	
	Consolidation of tax collection and administration	90% of tax revenues are raised at the national level, while the remaining 10% are mainly collected at the provincial level, with very limited collections at the local level.							
Observations	Subnational taxes, including property taxes, are low in comparison to OECD averages. Legislation introduced in 2000 increased taxing powers of subnational levels of government, but these were partially unwound in 2009. With three levels of government and almost 89,000 subnational agencies, administrative capacity is likely to vary. Additional revenue could be raised by subnational governments to strengthen local responsibility and accountability, taking into account administrative constraints.[6] Subnational tax administration taxing capacity is considered weak according to OECD reports, perhaps explaining the unwinding in 2009.[7]								

	Measure	Country Performance
Tax administration processes *(refer Note 8)*	Tax administration efficiency and effectiveness (Operating expenditure as a proportion of net revenue collected)	In 2017, Indonesia reported a cost of collection of 1.25%, which is relatively high. Revenue bodies typically aim for a figure between 0.5% and 1%. This may in part be influenced by the high proportion of staff allocated to support functions.
	No. of labor force members/tax body FTE	Over 2,900 workers per tax officer
	No. of citizens/tax body FTE	Over 6,000 citizens per tax officer
	Proportion of staff assigned to support functions	40 % Regional average = 29%

6   OECD. 2016. OECD Economic Surveys: Indonesia 2016, OECD Publishing, Paris, https://www.oecd-ilibrary.org/economics/oecd-economic-surveys-indonesia-2016_eco_surveys-idn-2016-en.

7   OECD. 2019. Economics Department Working Papers No. 1534 *Raising More Public Revenue in Indonesia in a Growth- and Equity-Friendly Way*, Christine Lewis, 2019.

REVENUE

	Measure	Country Performance						ASEAN Ave.	Asia and Pacific Ave.	OECD Ave. 2018
		2014	2015	2016	2017	2018	2019*			
Tax revenue collection performance *(all levels of government)* *(refer Note 9)*	Tax /GDP (%) - all	10.0	10.3	10.1	9.5	9.8	10.7	14.03	20.0	34.3
	Taxes on income & profits/GDP (%)	10.0	10.3	10.1	9.5	9.8	10.7	5.35	8.1	11.6
	Taxes on goods & services/GDP (%)	6.3	6.2	5.5	5.7	5.8	4.1	6	10.1	10.9
	Overall tax revenue trend									

(*) projected/provisional collections.

BROADENING THE TAX BASE

	Measure	Country Performance
Countering Tax Avoidance and Evasion *(refer Note 10)*	Effective anti-avoidance rules	There is no General Anti-Avoidance Rule (GAAR) or Seasonally Adjusted Annual Rate (SAAR) in Indonesia.
	Thin capitalization and controlled foreign corporation rules	Indonesia has a CFC regime. Where a "special relationship" exists between parties, interest may be disallowed as a deduction where such charges are considered excessive, such as interest rates in excess of commercial rates. The law allows the tax authority to issue a decree defining the maximum ratio of debt to equity in determining deductible interest. Special rules on tax deductibility of interest apply in the mining, and oil and gas sectors in accordance with the contracts.
	Findings from OECD Forum on Harmful Tax Practices (FHTP)	Public/listed company regime, investment allowance regime, special economic zone regime, and tax holiday regime, were all reviewed and found to be out of scope, with no benefits for income from geographically mobile activities.
	A focus on HNWI and professions	A focus on wealthy Indonesians, including high income earners, commenced in 2019 as part of the midterm revenue strategy (MTRS).
	Dealing with the shadow economy	The shadow economy in Indonesia is estimated to be in the region of 22% of GDP. Indonesia is ranked 7th out of 11 in the region. A focus on shadow economy and VAT commenced in 2019 as part of the MTRS.

	Measure		Country Status
Countering International Tax Avoidance and Evasion and International Cooperation *(refer Note 11)*	Member of Global Forum on Transparency & Exchange of Information		Yes
	Exchange of Information on Request Ratings	Round 1	Partially compliant
		Round 2	Largely compliant
	Signatory to the Multilateral Convention on Mutual Assistance in Tax Matters		Yes
	Commitment to Automatic Exchange of Information		Yes - 2018
	Implementation of Common Reporting Standard (CRS) and Multilateral Competent Authority Agreement		Signed
	Convention on Mutual Administrative Assistance in tax matters		Signed
	Member of Base Erosion and Profit Shifting Inclusive Framework		Yes
	Existence of harmful tax regimes (Action 5)		Not harmful - no harmful regimes exist
	Exchange of information on tax rulings (Action 5)		Reviewed – no recommendations
	CbC – Domestic law (Action 13)		Legal framework in place
	CbC – Information exchange network (Action 13)		Activated
	Effective dispute resolution (Action 14)		Stage 1 reviewed and recommendations made
	Signatory to the Multilateral Convention to Implement Treaty Related Measures to Prevent BEPS (Action 6)		Yes – Reviewed in 2018 and 2019, with no recommendations. 2020 review underway.
	Network of income tax treaties for avoidance of double taxation		71 treaties in 2019

RESPONSIVE TAX ADMINISTRATION

Important findings from Deloitte's 2017 Tax Complexity Survey *(refer Note 12)*	% responding tax regime has become more complicated over prior 3 years	45%
	% responding tax regime has been less consistently administered over prior 3 years	37%
	% responding tax compliance and reporting rules are "complicated" or "very complicated"	52%
	Perceived fairness in tax audits	Low
	Perceived confidence in appeal system	Low
	Taxpayer relationship with authorities	Poor
	Perceived main priority areas for reform	Tax officer training, time and quality of audits

	Measure	Country Ranking				World Ave.	Asia and Pacific Ave.
		2017	2018	2019	2020		
Compliance/ Regulatory Burden Indicators (as reported in the Doing Business Series) *(refer Note 13)*	Ease of Doing Business Indicator Ranking (Ranking out of 190 countries)	72	73	73	73	–	–
	Paying Taxes Indicator (Ranking out of 190 countries)	104	114	112	81	–	–
	Paying Taxes – time to comply (Hours/yr.): (all)	221	208	208	191	234	192
	Paying Taxes – time to comply (Hours/yr.): (CIT)	75	74	74	69	59	59
	Paying Taxes – time to comply (Hours/yr.): (VAT)	90	78	78	66	90	73
	Paying Taxes – time to comply (Hours/yr.): Labor taxes	56	56	56	56	85	60
	Post Filing Index (VAT and CIT corrections)	68.8	68.8	68.8	68.8	61	57
	Time to comply with VAT refund (hours)	18	18	18	18	14.9	19.6
	Time to obtain VAT refund (weeks)	48	48	48	48	41.5	28.2
	Number of payments per year	42	42	42	26	23	21
	Trading Across Borders Rank	108	112	116	116	–	–
Observations	According to the IMF, the adoption of a transparent minimum wage formula, simplification of the land acquisition process, and the partial liberalization of FDI regime were major factors in the notable rise in Indonesia's Doing Business ranking, from 106th in 2016 to 73rd in 2019. The target is to reach a rank of 50th over the next 3 years. If this is to be achieved, significant reforms will be required, as there has been little movement in this indicator since the big jumps seen between 2016 and 2017. Businesses report concerns about the time it takes to process a VAT refund, which has shown no improvement, requiring 18 hours to prepare (compared with a world-best figure of 3 hours) and 48 weeks to process, placing Indonesia among the world's worst economies on this measure (55 weeks). The post-filing index, which assesses a range of processes for post-filing adjustments, has also showed no movement in recent years. The improvement in paying taxes in 2020 follows the introduction of e-filing.						

Taxpayer rights and obligations *(refer Note 14)*	**Observations**
	Indonesia provides both public and private binding rulings on tax matters free of charge. There is a formally defined and legislated set of taxpayer rights and a formal complaints mechanism involving both internal and external bodies. Administrative and judicial reviews are available. There is no taxpayer ombudsman.

Corruption Perception Index Trends *(refer Note 15)*	**Observations**
	In 2014, Indonesia's CPI score out of 100 was 34 and has steadily improved to 40 in 2019. This places Indonesia at a ranking of 85th out of 180 countries.

LAO PEOPLE'S DEMOCRATIC REPUBLIC

AT A GLANCE

	Measure	2014	2015	2016	2017	2018	2019
Demographic Overview *(refer Note 1)*	Total Population (million)	6.639	6.741	6.845	6.953	7.061	7.1695
	Age profile						
	0–14	34.04	33.61	33.21	32.88	32.60	32.30
	15–64	62.16	62.55	62.88	63.13	63.32	63.53
	65+	3.79	3.84	3.91	3.99	4.08	4.16
	Literacy level (% of population)	...	84.66	...	...	...	...
	Urbanization (%)						
	Urban Population	32.49	33.11	33.74	34.37	35.00	31.50
	Rural Population	67.51	66.89	66.26	65.63	65.00	68.50
	Employment to Population	77.87	77.94	77.93	77.93	77.92	77.98
	Agriculture	66.91	65.87	65.03	64.16	63.24	62.42
	Industry	10.17	10.59	10.90	11.26	11.61	11.89
	Services	22.92	23.54	24.07	24.58	25.15	25.68

Industrialization Indices	2012	2013	2014	ASEAN Ave.	World Ave.
Industrialization Intensity Index	...	...	...	0.54	0.65
Share of Medium & High Tech	...	...	...	0.44	
Main Economic Sectors	Agriculture, dominated by rice cultivation in lowland areas, accounts for about 18% of GDP but 63% of total employment in 2019. Industry, dominated by mining, accounts for 32% of GDP. The Lao PDR has underdeveloped infrastructure, particularly in rural areas, with a basic, but improving, road system, and limited external and internal landline telecommunications. Electricity is available to 83% of the population.				

	Measure	2014	2015	2016	2017	2018	2019	ASEAN Ave.
Trends in Income and Inequality *(refer Note 1)*	Income Index	0.596	0.604	0.612	0.618	0.626	...	0.734
	Inequality in Income (%)	20.3	20.3	20.3	20.3	20.3	...	20.35
	GNI per Capita	5,166	5,460	5,748	5,985	6,317	...	23,069
	Human Development Rank	140/189						

	Measure	Description
Take-up of Technology *(refer Note 2)*	E-commerce trends	Around 7% made an online purchase or paid bills online.
	Internet coverage and availability	Around 40% of the population has internet access and uses social media. Internet usage increased by 13% in 2019. Mobile Connectivity Index = 43.9 (Ranked 10th in SEA). Internet speed is low but, increased by 100% in 2019.
	Take-up of internet and mobile banking	Mobile banking data are not available.
	Take-up of e-filing	Electronic filing figures are not available.

LAO PDR: EMPLOYMENT BY SECTOR

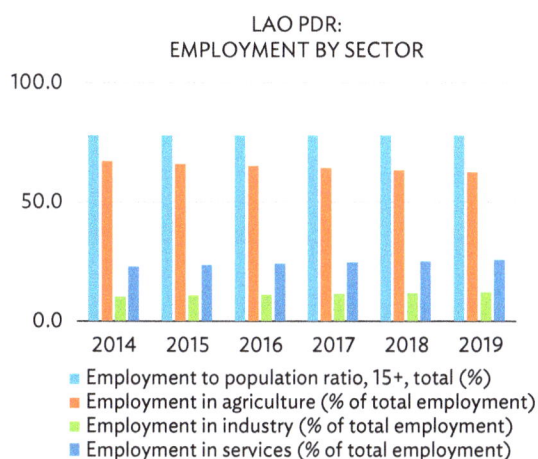

- Employment to population ratio, 15+, total (%)
- Employment in agriculture (% of total employment)
- Employment in industry (% of total employment)
- Employment in services (% of total employment)

LAO PDR: TAKE-UP OF TECHNOLOGY

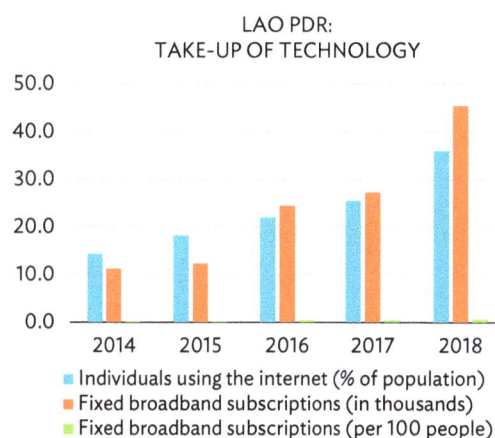

- Individuals using the internet (% of population)
- Fixed broadband subscriptions (in thousands)
- Fixed broadband subscriptions (per 100 people)

PRODUCTION STRUCTURE

	Region	Exports ($ million)				
		2014	2015	2016	2017	2018
Exports – Overall (refer Note 3)	Lao PDR	4,559	5,408	4,886	5,249	5,408
	SEA	1,606,681	1,630,770	1,508,470	1,498,265	1,676,341
	US	2,273,428	2,371,704	2,266,800	2,220,609	2,356,726
Main sector 1 Food	Lao PDR	423	446	629	917	953
	SEA	124,771	134,219	122,774	125,888	144,833
	US	141,891	149,139	132,962	135,280	137,279
Main sector 2 Fuels	Lao PDR	18	1	607	628	726
	SEA	220,922	207,952	135,574	109,869	140,057
	US	148,866	156,185	104,639	93,753	139,261
	Region	Imports ($ million)				
		2014	2015	2016	2017	2018
Imports – Overall (refer Note 3)	Lao PDR	7,736	7,461	6,620	5,667	6,315
	SEA	1,506,926	1,372,220	1,354,024	1,525,565	1,701,449
	US	2,879,362	2,786,645	2,739,415	2,932,062	3,148,464
Main sector 1 Machinery and Transport Equipment	Lao PDR	1,899	1,572	1,711	1,913	1,705
	SEA	462,822	456,028	462,749	520,106	576,718
	US	956,716	989,206	969,943	1,040,707	1,103,063
Main sector 2 Fuels	Lao PDR	696	760	615	689	877
	SEA	268,802	160,708	131,975	182,212	226,604
	US	358,193	200,458	163,065	203,934	241,513
Observations	Exports grew by 6.1% in 2017, compared with a regional average growth of 10.1%. Imports declined by 12.7% in 2016, compared with a regional average growth of 10.3%. Lao People's Democratic Republic (Lao PDR) exports are dominated by food and fuels, with the top exports being hydroelectricity, copper ore, and refined copper. The top imports are petroleum and cars.					

	Sector	2014	2015	2016	2017	2018
Flows of Inward Foreign Direct Investment (FDI) to ASEAN Sourced from Lao PDR, by Economic Sectors ($ million) (refer Note 4)	Agriculture, forestry, and fishing		0.02	0.03	0.00	0.00
	Mining and quarrying		0.00	0.02	0.01	0.00
	Manufacturing	(0.08)	1.29	4.69	0.27	0.26
	Electricity, gas, steam, and air conditioning supply		0.16	0.04	0.04	0.02
	Water supply; sewerage, waste management and remediation activities		0.00	0.14	0.00	0.00
	Construction	0.00	0.04	0.18	0.00	0.03
	Wholesale and retail trade; repair of motor vehicles and motorcycles	0.00	0.03	0.56	0.01	0.05
	Transportation and storage	0.00	0.01	0.26	0.00	0.01
	Accommodation and food service activities		0.01	0.12	0.00	0.01
	Information and communication	(0.04)	(0.09)	0.23	(0.01)	(0.15)
	Financial and insurance activities	(0.03)	0.02	14.74	0.36	24.31
	Real estate activities	1.93	0.73	2.25	5.70	4.60
	Professional, scientific, and technical activities	0.00	0.02	0.27	0.00	0.03
	Administrative and support service activities		0.00	0.05	0.00	0.00
	Education		0.00	0.02	0.00	0.00
	Human health and social work activities		0.00	0.02	0.00	0.00
	Arts, entertainment, and recreation		0.00	0.10	0.00	0.01
	Other services activities		0.00	0.15	0.31	0.29
	Unspecified activity	0.06	0.00	0.00	0.00	
	TOTAL activities	**1.85**	**2.24**	**23.86**	**6.70**	**29.47**
IMF Article IV[8]	Net FDI inflows (in percent of GDP)	7.49	5.92	10.46	7.35	7.6
	Net direct investment in Lao PDR (FDI) – in $ million	1,078	1,076	1,693	1,420	1,459
General Observations on FDI	The main sources of FDI into the Lao PDR are the PRC, Thailand, and Viet Nam, with the PRC accounting for the vast bulk of FDI. Overall FDI has declined markedly since 2014, both in dollar terms and as a percentage of GDP. FDI inflows to the Lao PDR decreased further in 2019, despite the introduction of an investment law and a policy of FDI promotion and the start of new electricity and service projects. These amendments allow foreigners to invest in any sector or business, unless it would cause a threat to national security, health, or national traditions, or if it may negatively impact the environment. Ongoing barriers to FDI include the lengthy procedure to obtain authorizations, overlapping of jurisdictions between the different ministries, inequalities in terms of tax benefits, high tariff costs, and the poor quality infrastructure. Hydroelectricity and mining represent around 80% of the foreign investment accumulated over the last 10 years. Transportation infrastructure, tourism, and large agro forestry projects are also attracting new investors. The government is aiming at integrating the Lao PDR into regional supply chains by developing a light manufacturing industry to make the country a low-cost export base. According to the IMF, the medium-term outlook for FDI and external financing remains stable. FDI inflows remain around 7.8% of GDP. Several infrastructure projects are expected to wind down by 2021; however, some new investments are also expected.					

8   Also sourced from the World Bank: https://data.worldbank.org/indicator/BX.KLT.DINV.CD.WD?display=graph&locations=LA.

	Component Sector	2014	2015	2016	2017	2018	ASEAN Ave.	US 2018
Industry Structure: GDP by type of expenditure (refer Note 5)	Gross domestic product (GDP)	100.0	100.0	100.0	100.0	100.0	100	100
	Final consumption expenditure	87.7	86.3	79.7	78.1	81.4	68.04	87
	Household consumption expenditure (including NPISH)	72.6	71.2	65.7	65.2	67.4	54	70
	General government final consumption expenditure	15.2	15.1	14.0	12.9	14.0	14.51	17
	Gross capital formation	**29.8**	**31.6**	**29.0**	**29.0**	**29.9**	**28.58**	**18**
	Gross fixed capital formation	29.8	31.6	29.0	29.0	29.9	27.74	17
	Changes in inventories	..	..	..	..	..	1.04	1
	Exports of goods and services	40.8	34.0	33.2	34.3	33.8	63.65	13
	Imports of goods and services	(58.3)	(51.8)	(41.9)	(41.5)	(45.1)	(61.12)	18
	Total value added	**100.0**	**100.0**	**100.0**	**100.0**	**100.0**	**100**	**100**
Observations	Capital formation is a lead indicator of economic performance and is on par with regional averages. Tax outcomes flowing from investment may be significantly impacted by tax incentives.							

NPISH = nonprofit institutions serving households.

	Component Sector	2014	2015	2016	2017	2018	ASEAN Ave.	US 2018
Industry Structure: Value Add by kind of economic activity ($ million) (refer Note 5)	Agriculture, hunting, forestry, and fishing	19.7	19.7	19.5	18.3	17.7	12.11	167
	Industry	31.7	31.0	32.5	34.9	35.5	38.84	1,512
	Mining, manufacturing, and utilities	26.1	24.7	26.2	28.0	27.6	32	673
	Manufacturing	9.3	9.2	8.8	8.4	8.4	17.29	2,321
	Construction	5.6	6.3	6.3	6.8	7.8	6.99	839
	Services	48.6	49.4	48.0	46.8	46.8	49.05	2,579
	Wholesale, retail trade, restaurants, and hotels	16.7	17.0	16.1	15.9	16.7	16.75	2,338
	Transport, storage, and communications	3.3	3.4	3.4	3.3	3.3	7.02	658
	Other activities	28.7	29.0	28.5	27.7	26.8	25.28	437
Observations	The contributions of agriculture and mining are well above regional averages, while those of manufacturing and transport are below the averages for the region.							

TAX SYSTEM AND TAX ADMINISTRATION DESIGN FEATURES

Tax Rates, Thresholds, and Overall Revenue Contribution (see Note 6)

| Taxes | Rates of Tax (%) /1 | | Threshold | | Share of All Tax Revenue (latest year) |
	Basic/ Standard	Other	Local Currency	$	
CIT /2	20%	20% - Branch Tax	KN50 million	$5,400	
PIT /3		0%–25%	KN130,000	$140	21.4% (2019)
PIT - Capital gains tax (CGT)		1%–3% on Business Income 5%–25% on S&W 2% of selling price of land & shares	KN2,220,000	$240	
VAT/GST		10%	KN400 million	$50,000	30.4% (2019)
CGT /4		2%			
WHT /5	10%	5% - Royalties			
WHT	1%–3%	Nonresident technical service fees			
Excise		3%–100% (environmental tax)			
SSC		6% (+ 5.5% by employee)	<KN270,000/month	$30.00	
Property					
*Subnational taxes	Tax on land and various rates	Applies to individuals and corporates			
Overview of Tax Incentives	Profit tax exemptions or deductions are allowed for investment in certain sectors in certain geographic areas. The IMF estimates that 80% of the corporate tax base is exempt. Compared to other countries in the region, the Lao PDR's profit tax revenues and productivity are the lowest, while its profit tax rate is relatively high. The Law on Investment Promotion provides tax holidays ranging between 7–15 years, depending on the business activity and location of the business. The duration of the tax holidays offered in special economic zones is negotiable. Additional investment incentives include exemptions from import duties for the importation of raw material, equipment, spare parts, and vehicles directly used for production and exemptions from export duties for general goods and products.				

The Lao PDR has 18 subnational bodies across four levels of government.

/1. For FY 2020, unless otherwise indicated. /2. Other rates of CIT include 5% for health and education, 1%–3% for micro and small enterprises, 22% for tobacco, and 35% for mining. /3. The employer withholds the tax and remits monthly. No deductions or allowances are available to individuals. 4/. Sale of shares listed on the stock exchange are excluded. /5. Applies to interest, dividends paid to residents and nonresidents.

Sources: IMF Art. IV reports; Deloitte Country Tax Profiles; OECD Statistics.

Tax Administration Setup and Performance

Subject Area	Aspect	Features and Performance	Overall Rating
Responsibilities of tax body	Main taxes collected	CIT, PIT, VAT, and excise	Medium – collect a little over 50% of revenue
	Other major roles	The GDT is a single directorate within the Ministry of Finance.	
Tax body Autonomy	Budget flexibility, organization design	The GDT has limited autonomy.	low
	Human resource management		

Digital services in tax administration	E-filing	Rate (2017)	Comments	low
	- CIT	...	E-filing appears to be offered but no data were provided on filing rates. E-payment does not appear to be offered.	
	- PIT	...		
	- VAT/GST	...		
	E-payment	n.a.		
	E-services (including mobile applications)	Online calculators, frequently asked questions, and other resources are available.		

		Country Performance						ASEAN Ave.	OECD Ave. 2018
	Measure	2014	2015	2016	2017	2018	2019		
Tax system design *(refer Note 7)*	Tax reliance ratio	66.00	68.87	77.98	74.82	72.4	71.1	66.9	63.8
	Tax mix	19.6	20.5	19.95	20.35	21.6	21.0	39.92	33.7
	Tax ratio	13.8	13.9	12.5	12.0	11.2	11.2	14	34.3
	CIT productivity	0.042	0.042	0.054	0.050	0.046	0.042	0.26	
	VAT productivity	0.400	0.430	0.350	0.370	0.340	0.35	0.43	
	Consolidation of tax collection and administration	Most taxes are raised at a national level, with stamp duties and fees levied at a municipal level. Loans to subnational governments are required to supplement revenue raised.							
Observations	Tax reliance is higher than regional figures and CIT productivity is very low.								

	Measure	Country Performance
Tax administration processes *(refer Note 8)*	Tax administration efficiency and effectiveness (Operating expenditure as a proportion of net revenue collected)	Not available
	No. of labor force members/tax body FTE	1,415
	No. of citizens/tax body FTE	2,633
	Proportion of staff assigned to support functions	Not available

REVENUE

Tax revenue collection performance (all levels of government) (refer Note 9)	Measure	Country Performance						ASEAN Ave.	Asia and Pacific Ave.	OECD Ave. 2018
		2014	2015	2016	2017	2018	2019*			
	Tax/GDP (%) - all	13.8	13.9	12.5	12.0	11.2	11.2	14.03	20.0	34.3
	Taxes on income and profits/GDP (%)	3.2	2.9	2.6	2.4	2.4	2.4	5.35	8.1	11.6
	Taxes on goods and services/GDP (%)	6.8	4.3	3.5	3.7	3.4	3.5	6	10.1	10.9
	Overall tax revenue trend	Tax revenue is flat and well below levels required for sustainable development (15%).								

(*) projected/provisional collections.

BROADENING THE TAX BASE

	Measure	Country Performance
Countering Tax Avoidance and Evasion (refer Note 10)	Effective anti-avoidance rules	No general or specific anti-avoidance rules apply and there are no transfer pricing rules.
	Thin capitalization and controlled foreign corporation rules	There are no limits on interest deductions, no CFC rules, no rules on hybrids or on economic substance, and no disclosure requirements.
	Findings from OECD Forum on Harmful Tax Practices (FHTP)	No findings reported.
	A focus on HNWI and professions	No focus reported.
	Dealing with the shadow economy	The shadow economy is estimated to be around 25% of GDP, which is in the midrange for the region. The Lao PDR is ranked 6th out of 11 in SEA.

	Measure	Country Status
Countering International Tax Avoidance and Evasion and International Cooperation (refer Note 11)	Member of Global Forum on Transparency & Exchange of Information	The Lao PDR is not a member country and has not implemented any measures to combat international tax avoidance. No credits are allowed for foreign taxes except where there is a specific treaty.
	Exchange of Information on Request Ratings	
	Signatory to the Multilateral Convention on Mutual Assistance in Tax Matters	
	Commitment to Automatic Exchange of Information	
	Implementation of Common Reporting Standard (CRS) and Multilateral Competent Authority Agreement	
	Convention on Mutual Administrative Assistance in tax matters	
	Member of Base Erosion and Profit Shifting Inclusive Framework	
	Existence of harmful tax regimes (Action 5)	
	Exchange of information on tax rulings (Action 5)	
	CbC – Domestic law (Action 13)	
	CbC – Information exchange network (Action 13)	
	Effective dispute resolution (Action 14)	
	Signatory to the Multilateral Convention to Implement Treaty Related Measures to Prevent BEPS (Action 6)	
	Network of income tax treaties for avoidance of double taxation	12

RESPONSIVE TAX ADMINISTRATION

Important findings from Deloitte's 2017 Tax Complexity Survey *(see Note 12)*	The Lao PDR was not included in the survey.

	Measure	Country Ranking				World Ave.	Asia and Pacific Ave.
		2017	2018	2019	2020		
Compliance/ Regulatory Burden Indicators *(as reported in the Doing Business Series)* *(refer Note 13)*	Ease of Doing Business Indicator Ranking (Ranking out of 190 countries)	141	154	154	154	–	–
	Paying Taxes Indicator (Ranking out of 190 countries)	146	156	155	157	–	–
	Paying Taxes – time to comply (Hours/yr.): (all)	362	362	362	362	234	192
	Paying Taxes – time to comply (Hours/yr.): (CIT)	138	138	138	138	59	59
	Paying Taxes – time to comply (Hours/yr.): (VAT)	182	182	182	182	90	73
	Paying Taxes – time to comply (Hours/yr.): Labor taxes	42	42	42	42	85	60
	Post Filing Index (VAT and CIT corrections)	18.6	18.6	18.6	18.6	61	57
	Time to comply with VAT refund (hours)	n.a.	n.a.	n.a.	n.a.	14.9	19.6
	Time to obtain VAT refund (weeks)	n.a.	n.a.	n.a.	n.a.	41.5	28.2
	Number of Payments per year	35	35	35	35	23	21
	Trading Across Borders Rank	120	124	76	78	–	–
Observations	The ranking of 154th out of 190 is stable compared to the previous year. In relation to the procedures to start a business, the Lao PDR ranks 181st, placing it among the worst countries in the world. Significant improvements have been made in cross-border trading measures, as a result of the introduction of streamlined customs clearances. VAT refunds are only available to international traders, and were not included in the World Bank case study.						

	Observations
Taxpayer rights and obligations *(refer Note 14)*	Taxpayers' rights are formally defined in law. Taxpayers have a right to challenge assessments both administratively and in courts. Private binding rulings are available to individuals and corporates. No public rulings are provided. There is a tax ombudsman.

	Observations
Corruption Perception Index Trends *(refer Note 15)*	In 2014, the Lao PDR's CPI score out of 100 was 25 and has steadily improved to 29 in 2019. This places the Lao PDR at a ranking of 130th out of 180 countries, meaning that corruption is still widespread.

MALAYSIA

AT A GLANCE

Measure	2014	2015	2016	2017	2018	2019
Total Population (million)	29.866	30.270	30.684	31.105	31.528	**32.680**
Age profile						
0–14	25.60	25.09	24.72	24.34	24.00	23.10
15–64	68.65	68.93	69.08	69.22	69.33	70.07
65+	5.75	5.98	6.20	6.43	6.67	6.82
Literacy level (% of population)	...	...	93.73	95.08	94.85	...
Urbanization (%)						
Urban Population	73.58	74.21	74.84	75.45	76.04	76.60
Rural Population	26.42	25.79	25.16	24.55	23.96	23.40
Employment to Population	62.42	62.44	62.08	62.04	62.04	62.15
Agriculture	12.23	12.47	11.37	10.99	10.66	10.36
Industry	28.02	27.52	27.49	27.40	27.15	27.00
Services	59.75	60.01	61.14	61.61	62.18	62.64

Industrialization Indices	2012	2013	2014	ASEAN Ave.	World Ave.
Industrialization Intensity Index	0.62	0.61	0.62	0.54	0.65
Share of Medium & High Tech	0.5	0.49	0.52	0.44	

Main Economic Sectors — In 2019, the share of agriculture in Malaysia's gross domestic product was around 10.36%, industry contributed approximately 27%, and the services sector contributed about 62.64%.

Demographic Overview *(refer Note 1)*

Measure	2014	2015	2016	2017	2018	2019	ASEAN Ave.
Income Index	0.826	0.832	0.836	0.843	0.847	...	0.734
Inequality in Income (%)	...	...	...	...	..	...	20.35
GNI per Capita	23,686	24,703	25,394	26,555	27,227	...	23,069
Human Development Rank			61/189				

Trends in Income and Inequality *(refer Note 1)*

Measure	Description
E-commerce trends	88% have visited online stores and 75% have made online purchases.
Internet coverage and availability	Around 80% of the population uses the internet and almost 80% use social media. Mobile connectivity index = 67.4 (Ranked 3rd in SEA). Fixed internet speed increased by almost 200% in 2019.
Take-up of internet and mobile banking	66% use mobile banking and 42% have made mobile payments.
Take-up of e-filing	CIT e-filing is mandatory. 97% of PIT returns are filed electronically.

Take-up of Technology *(refer Note 2)*

MALAYSIA: EMPLOYMENT BY SECTOR

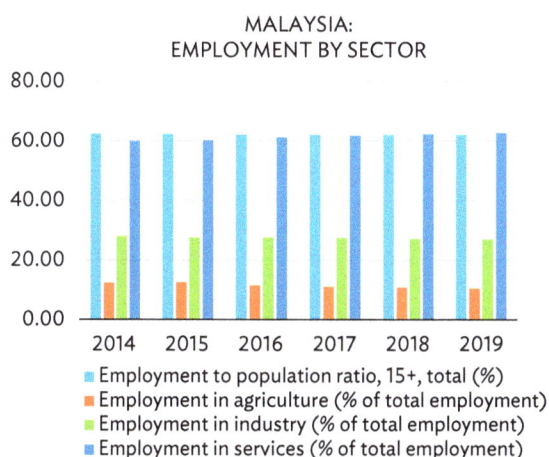

- Employment to population ratio, 15+, total (%)
- Employment in agriculture (% of total employment)
- Employment in industry (% of total employment)
- Employment in services (% of total employment)

MALAYSIA: TAKE-UP OF TECHNOLOGY

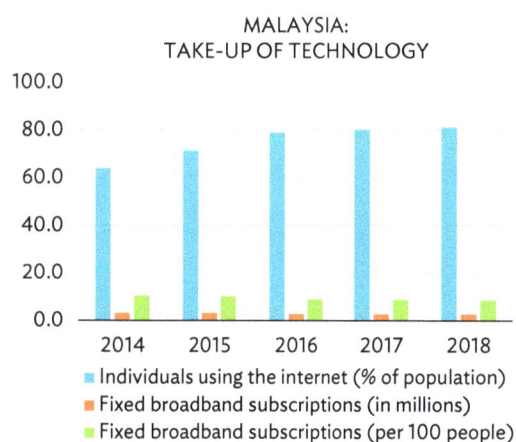

- Individuals using the internet (% of population)
- Fixed broadband subscriptions (in millions)
- Fixed broadband subscriptions (per 100 people)

PRODUCTION STRUCTURE

	Region	Exports ($ million)				
		2014	2015	2016	2017	2018
Exports - Overall (refer Note 3)	Malaysia	244,491	249,468	209,287	201,165	223,416
	SEA	1,606,681	1,630,770	1,508,470	1,498,265	1,676,341
	US	2,273,428	2,371,704	2,266,800	2,220,609	2,356,726
Main sector 1 Machinery and Transport Equipment	Malaysia	86,917	90,823	83,848	81,802	95,825
	SEA	470,011	483,417	476,133	478,746	538,499
	US	639,053	665,625	647,286	627,333	645,863
Main sector 2 Office and Telecom Equipment	Malaysia	63,187	65,721	59,201	57,617	69,483
	SEA	284,959	293,811	291,494	289,701	325,385
	US	140,971	145,946	142,274	140,473	145,475

	Region	Imports ($ million)				
		2014	2015	2016	2017	2018
Imports - Overall (refer Note 3)	Malaysia	218,113	186,603	181,126	201,498	221,408
	SEA	1,506,926	1,372,220	1,354,024	1,525,565	1,701,449
	US	2,879,362	2,786,645	2,739,415	2,932,062	3,148,464
Main sector 1 Machinery and Transport Equipment	Malaysia	87,398	76,383	76,340	87,200	95,000
	SEA	462,822	456,028	462,749	520,106	576,718
	US	956,716	989,206	969,943	1,040,707	1,103,063
Main sector 2 Office and Telecom Equipment	Malaysia	46,987	41,269	40,238	48,032	53,162
	SEA	220,691	218,183	220,271	257,966	287,275
	US	314,209	321,039	316,947	350,850	362,342
Observations	Exports grew by 9.9% in 2018, compared with a regional average growth of 10.1%. Imports grew by 17.1% in 2018, compared with a regional average growth of 10.3%. The top exports are integrated circuits, refined and unrefined petroleum gas, and crude and palm oil. The top imports are integrated circuits, refined and crude petroleum, and office machine parts. Malaysia is a net importer of refined petroleum and a net exporter of crude petroleum.					

	Sector	2014	2015	2016	2017	2018
Flows of Inward Foreign Direct Investment (FDI) to ASEAN Sourced from Malaysia, by Economic Sectors ($ million) (refer Note 4)	Agriculture, forestry, and fishing	160.54	313.59	272.59	25.35	88.11
	Mining and quarrying	495.92	434.28	280.86	210.33	270.45
	Manufacturing	347.67	950.80	404.60	380.60	773.53
	Electricity, gas, steam, and air conditioning supply	(2.13)	170.26	1.07	29.36	15.55
	Water supply; sewerage, waste management and remediation activities	2.98	2.61	14.44	1.96	1.71
	Construction	109.34	131.96	6.02	525.76	35.67
	Wholesale and retail trade; repair of motor vehicles and motorcycles	139.27	313.62	74.42	124.69	180.20
	Transportation and storage	209.92	178.99	20.75	35.32	(153.00)
	Accommodation and food service activities	3.71	6.91	8.00	(11.46)	(19.64)
	Information and communication	518.64	180.38	123.04	0.46	13.81
	Financial and insurance activities	(377.18)	(268.24)	1,184.10	486.86	167.98
	Real estate activities	1,507.20	1,406.86	1,332.43	1,356.53	316.47
	Professional, scientific, and technical activities	4.61	11.95	19.83	2.27	13.58
	Administrative and support service activities	3.95	10.24	6.43	2.74	9.22
	Education	0.58	1.34	1.18	0.39	0.53
	Human health and social work activities	3.14	0.77	1.42	1.37	1.17
	Arts, entertainment, and recreation	(0.63)	0.16	6.41	0.09	6.10
	Other services activities	(1,419.55)	(110.73)	485.86	596.56	(30.47)
	Unspecified activity	(60.86)	7.81	87.90	0.00	
	TOTAL activities	1,647.11	3,743.55	4,331.33	3,769.19	1,690.95
IMF Article IV	Net FDI inflows (in percent of GDP)	3.1	3.3	4.5	2.9	2.4
	Net Direct Investment (FDI) – in $ billion	(5.5)	(0.5)	3.3	3.8	4.1
General Observations on FDI	FDI inflows decreased during the last 2 years. Multinationals involved in mergers and acquisitions, such as those in the health and mining sectors (e.g., the acquisition of a stake in IHH Healthcare by Mitsui & Co, Japan and in Seb Upstream by OMV, Austria) have been major contributors to investment. Based on the data from the Malaysian Investment Development Authority, most investments came from the PRC, Singapore, Japan, and the US.					

	Component Sector	2014	2015	2016	2017	2018	ASEAN Ave.	US 2018
	Gross domestic product (GDP)	100.0	100.0	100.0	100.0	100.0	100	100
	Final consumption expenditure	65.7	67.0	67.4	67.6	69.4	68.04	87
	Household consumption expenditure (including NPISH)	52.4	54.0	54.8	55.4	57.4	54	70
Industry Structure: GDP by type of expenditure (refer Note 5)	General government final consumption expenditure	13.3	13.1	12.6	12.2	12.0	14.51	17
	Gross capital formation	**25.0**	**25.4**	**26.0**	**25.6**	**23.6**	**28.58**	**18**
	Gross fixed capital formation	26.0	25.9	25.5	25.1	24.2	27.74	17
	Changes in inventories	(1.0)	(0.4)	0.5	0.5	(0.6)	1.04	1
	Exports of goods and services	73.8	69.4	66.8	70.0	68.8	63.65	13
	Imports of goods and services	(64.5)	(61.9)	(60.1)	(63.2)	(61.7)	(61.12)	18
	Total value added	**100.0**	**100.0**	**100.0**	**100.0**	**100.0**		**100**
Observations	Capital formation is a lead indicator of economic performance and is below regional averages. Tax outcomes flowing from investment may be significantly impacted by tax incentives.							

NPISH = nonprofit institutions serving households.

	Component Sector	2014	2015	2016	2017	2018	ASEAN Ave.	US 2018
	Agriculture, hunting, forestry, and fishing	9.0	8.4	8.6	8.7	7.6	12.11	167
	Industry	40.4	38.9	38.2	38.7	38.8	38.84	1,512
Industry Structure: Value Add by kind of economic activity ($ million) (refer Note 5)	Mining, manufacturing, and utilities	35.9	34.2	33.2	33.8	33.9	32	673
	Manufacturing	23.1	22.6	22.1	22.2	21.8	17.29	2,321
	Construction	4.4	4.8	5.0	4.9	4.9	6.99	839
	Services	50.7	52.7	53.2	52.6	53.6	49.05	2,579
	Wholesale, retail trade, restaurants, and hotels	18.1	18.9	19.3	19.4	20.1	16.75	2,338
	Transport, storage, and communications	8.6	9.0	9.2	9.1	9.3	7.02	658
	Other activities	24.1	24.7	24.8	24.1	24.2	25.28	437
Observations	Malaysia's largest value add is driven by the retail and services sectors. Agriculture is steadily declining, and the heavy reliance on the palm oil trade poses some risks in this sector.							

TAX SYSTEM AND TAX ADMINISTRATION DESIGN FEATURES

Tax Rates, Thresholds, and Overall Revenue Contribution (see Note 6)

| Taxes | Rates of Tax (%) /1 | | Thresholds | | Share of All Tax Revenue (latest year) |
	Basic/ Standard	Other	Local Currency	$	
CIT /2	24%	24% - Branch tax			76.7% (2019)
CIT - SME	17%	24% for income > threshold	< RM600,000	$140,000	
PIT		1%–30%	RM5,000	$1,150	
Sales and Services Tax /3	6% - Services (including Digital Services), 10% - Sales				23.3% (2019) (Excludes Excise)
PAYE WHT	1%–30%	Withheld by employer	RM5,000	$1,150	
WHT	0%–15%	Nonresidents /4			
Excise	7.4%–33.5% - Alcohol; 7.5%–22% -Tobacco; 10%–105% - Motor Vehicles /7				
SSC	1.75/12/0.2% /6				
Property	0%–35% (Capital Gains Tax) /5				
Subnational taxes	1%–4% Based on Engine Capacity	Stamp duty on property and share transfers Motor vehicle license fee			13.4% of general government revenue and 2.9% of GDP (2016)
Overview of Tax Incentives	The authorities seek to position Malaysia as a gateway to the ASEAN market by offering various incentives to foreign companies, such tax reductions for approved pioneer companies and other investments. The government has a discretionary power for authorizing investment projects and uses it to obtain the maximum benefits from foreign participation and by requiring the transfer of technologies or creation of joint ventures. There are two major tax incentives for the manufacturing and services sectors: 1. Pioneer Status - Income tax exemption of 70%–100% of statutory income for 5 to 10 years. Unabsorbed capital allowances and accumulated losses incurred during the pioneer period can be carried forward and deducted from the post pioneer status of the company. 2. Investment Tax Allowance - An allowance of 60%–100% on qualifying capital expenditure (factory, plant, machinery, or other equipment used for the approved project) incurred within 5 to 10 years from the date the first qualifying capital expenditure is incurred.				

* Malaysia has 167 subnational agencies across two levels of subnational government.

/1. For FY 2020, unless otherwise indicated. /2. Labuan companies conducting local business are taxed at 3% of audited accounting profits. /3. In July 2019, the Government of Malaysia passed amendments to the Sales and Services Tax that expands the scope of services included in the 6% band. The expanded tax became effective 1 January 2020. It requires foreign service providers to file quarterly tax returns for services provided to Malaysian consumers. The tax covers services delivered over digital platforms that are delivered to consumers in Malaysia, and includes streaming services and app store purchases (https://taxfoundation.org/different-approach-taxing-digital-services-malaysia/). /4. Real property and shares only. Rates vary according to how long the property has been held and the residence status of the owner. /5. Nonresident – dividends, interest, royalties, and certain services fees. Rates may be reduced under a treaty. Domestic dividends are exempt. /6. Social security, employee provident fund, and employment insurance contributions required. Employees also contribute. /7. Standard rates are generally applied to tobacco and alcohol. Ad valorem rates apply to other goods.

Sources: IMF Art. IV reports; Deloitte Country Tax Profiles; OECD Statistics.

Tax Administration Setup and Performance

Subject Area	Aspect	Features and Performance		Overall Rating
Responsibilities of tax body	Main taxes collected	PIT & CIT – IRBM Sales tax & Excise = RMCD		Low/Medium collect around 67% of revenue
	Other major roles	Separate bodies are responsible for direct and indirect tax (including sales tax and excises) administration.		
Tax body Autonomy	Budget flexibility, organization design	The Inland Revenue Board of Malaysia (IRBM) is responsible for direct taxes and is largely autonomous, reporting to a board of directors comprising external officials. The Royal Malaysia Customs Department is responsible for indirect taxes and operates as a normal government department reporting to the minister.		High
	Human resource management			
Digital services in tax administration	E-filing	**Rate (2017)**	**Comments**	High
	– CIT	100%	CIT e-filing is compulsory. PIT e-filing is not compulsory; nevertheless, the rates are very high.	
	– PIT	97%		
	– VAT/GST	n.a.		
	E-payment	31%		
	E-services (including mobile applications)	Mobile payment services are offered through the MyPay app, which is part of the Malaysian government's MyGov service. Extensive e-services are offered, but the IRBM does not offer tax specific apps.		

		Country Performance						ASEAN Ave.	OECD Ave. 2018
	Measure	2014	2015	2016	2017	2018	2019		
Tax system design (refer Note 7)	Tax reliance ratio	74.43	75.51	79.72	80.61	74.7	67.3	66.9	63.8
	Tax mix	77.20	67.60	64.73	65.50	66.60	77.3	39.92	33.7
	Tax ratio	14.63	14.06	13.55	12.95	12.03	11.6	14	34.3
	CIT productivity	0.433	0.360	0.332	0.319	0.343	0.371	0.26	
	VAT productivity	0.293	0.424	0.492	0.460	0.313	0.27	0.43	
	Consolidation of tax collection and administration	Subnational taxes account for 2.9% of GDP (2016). Taxes are administered at national and subnational levels and tax administration is also split at a national level between two agencies.							
Observations	There is a heavy reliance on CIT, which may represent future risk as CIT bases are eroding in many jurisdictions. The tax ratio is low compared with regional averages.								

	Measure	Country Performance
Tax administration processes (refer Note 8)	Tax administration efficiency and effectiveness (Operating expenditure as a proportion of net revenue collected)	1.93% - Calculated on direct taxes only. Efficient administrations aim for a figure between 0.5% and 1%.
	No. of labor force members/ tax body FTE	1,102
	No. of citizens/ tax body FTE	2,366
	Proportion of staff assigned to support functions	38% of staff are assigned to support functions. Regional average = 29%

REVENUE

	Measure	Country Performance						ASEAN Ave.	Asia and Pacific Ave.	OECD Ave. 2018
		2014	2015	2016	2017	2018	2019*			
Tax revenue collection performance *(all levels of government)* *(refer Note 9)*	Tax/GDP (%) - all	14.63	14.06	13.55	12.95	12.03	11.6	14.03	20.0	34.3
	Taxes on income and profits/GDP (%)	10.39	8.63	7.97	7.67	8.24	8.9	5.35	8.1	11.6
	Taxes on goods and services/GDP (%)	2.93	4.24	4.92	4.60	3.13	2.7	6	10.1	10.9
	Overall tax revenue trend	At just below 12% of GDP in 2019, tax revenue in Malaysia is low compared to peers and OECD countries, and is declining.								

(*) projected/provisional collections.

BROADENING THE TAX BASE

	Measure	Country Performance
Countering Tax Avoidance and Evasion *(refer Note 10)*	Effective anti-avoidance rules	Malaysia has a general anti-avoidance rule, and economic substance requirements, as well as disclosure rules on foreign transactions. There is a comprehensive transfer pricing regime.
	Thin capitalization and controlled foreign corporation rules	Thin capitalization rules apply but there are no rules on CFCs or hybrids.
	Findings from OECD Forum on Harmful Tax Practices (FHTP)	Principal hub regime was reviewed and found to be not harmful (amended) - Ring-fencing removed. Substance requirements (non-IP) in place. No grandfathering provided. International currency business unit (abolished) was reviewed. Grandfathering was in accordance with FHTP timelines.
	A focus on HNWI and professions	IRBM has an administrative focus on HNWI (within the Large Taxpayer Unit).
	Dealing with the shadow economy	The shadow economy is estimated to be around 26% of GDP, which is in the midrange for the region. Malaysia is ranked 5th of 11 in SEA.

	Measure		Country Status
Countering International Tax Avoidance and Evasion and International Cooperation *(refer Note 11)*	Member of Global Forum on Transparency & Exchange of Information		Yes
	Exchange of Information on Request Ratings	Round 1	Largely compliant
		Round 2	Largely compliant
	Signatory to the Multilateral Convention on Mutual Assistance in Tax Matters		In force
	Commitment to Automatic Exchange of Information		2018
	Implementation of Common Reporting Standard (CRS) and Multilateral Competent Authority Agreement		Yes
	Convention on Mutual Administrative Assistance in tax matters		In force
	Member of Base Erosion and Profit Shifting Inclusive Framework		Yes
	Existence of harmful tax regimes (Action 5)		Not harmful (no harmful regime exists)
	Exchange of information on tax rulings (Action 5)		Reviewed/recommendations made
	CbC – Domestic law (Action 13)		Legal framework in place
	CbC – Information exchange network (Action 13)		Activated
	Effective dispute resolution (Action 14)		Review to be scheduled/deferred
	Signatory to the Multilateral Convention to Implement Treaty Related Measures to Prevent BEPS (Action 6)		Reviewed in 2018 and 2019, no recommendation. 2020 Review ongoing.
	Network of income tax treaties for avoidance of double taxation		Over 70

RESPONSIVE TAX ADMINISTRATION

Important findings from Deloitte's 2017 Tax Complexity Survey *(refer Note 12)*	% responding tax regime has become more complicated over prior 3 years	45%
	% responding tax regime has been less consistently administered over prior 3 years	22%
	% responding tax compliance and reporting rules are "complicated" or "very complicated"	44%
	Perceived fairness in tax audits	Neutral
	Perceived confidence in appeal system	Neutral
	Taxpayer relationship with authorities	Neutral
	Perceived main priority areas for reform	Tax officer training and adoption of the BEPS mechanisms

	Measure	Country Ranking				World Ave.	Asia and Pacific Ave.
		2017	2018	2019	2020		
Compliance/ Regulatory Burden Indicators *(as reported in the Doing Business Series)* *(refer Note 13)*	Ease of Doing Business Indicator Ranking (Ranking out of 190 countries)	24	15	15	12	-	-
	Paying Taxes Indicator (Ranking out of 190 countries)	61	73	72	80	-	-
	Paying Taxes- time to comply (Hours/yr.): (all)	164	188	188	174	234	192
	Paying Taxes- time to comply (Hours/yr.): (CIT)	26	26	26	26	59	59
	Paying Taxes- time to comply (Hours/yr.): (VAT)	88	112	112	95	90	73
	Paying Taxes- time to comply (Hours/yr.): Labor taxes	50	50	50	53	85	60
	Post Filing Index (VAT and CIT corrections)	41.1	52.6	52.6	51	61	57
	Time to comply with VAT refund (hours)	n.a.	22	22	n.a.	14.9	19.6
	Time to obtain VAT refund (weeks)	n.a.	18	18	n.a.	41.5	28.2
	Number of payments per year	9	8	8	9	23	21
	Trading Across Borders Rank	60	61	48	49	-	-
Observations	To ensure the coordination of efforts across agencies, Malaysia has formed a regulatory reform committee. The committee uses the Doing Business indicators as one input to inform their programs for improving the business environment. The Malaysia Investment Development Authority also offers assistance to investors, including with relevant agencies at both the federal and state levels. Help is provided in securing infrastructural facilities, including land, factory sites, electricity and water supplies, telecommunication and others, and expediting approvals relating to Building Plans, Certificate of Fitness and Business Licenses, and other necessary approvals for projects until they are operational. The Doing Business rank is among the world's best, but the trading across borders and the paying taxes ranks are somewhat lower by comparison. There was no VAT in 2017, and VAT was again abolished in 2018–2019.						

	Observations
Taxpayer rights and obligations *(refer Note 14)*	Malaysia has a formally defined set of taxpayer rights (not legislated) and both internal and external complaint mechanism. Surprisingly, no complaints were reported in 2017. Taxpayers have a right to challenge assessments and there are both internal and external review bodies. Alternative dispute resolution mechanisms are available. There is no tax ombudsman.

	Observations
Corruption Perception Index Trends *(refer Note 15)*	In 2014, Malaysia's CPI score was 52 out of 100 and has improved slightly to 53 in 2019. This places Malaysia at a ranking of 51st out of 180 countries, indicating moderate corruption concerns. The new government has launched multiple initiatives to address governance weaknesses and corruption.

PHILIPPINES

AT A GLANCE

Measure	2014	2015	2016	2017	2018	2019
Total Population (million)	100.513	102.113	103.663	105.173	106.651	108.116
Age profile						
0–14	32.65	32.28	31.92	31.47	30.96	30.48
15–64	62.86	63.12	63.32	63.59	63.91	64.21
65+	4.49	4.60	4.76	4.94	5.12	5.31
Literacy level (% of population)	...	98.18	...	...	...	...
Urbanization (%)						
Urban Population	46.09	46.28	46.48	46.68	46.91	47.10
Rural Population	53.91	53.72	53.53	53.32	53.09	52.90
Employment to Population	60.54	60.30	60.47	58.15	58.18	58.34
Agriculture	30.42	29.19	27.03	25.44	24.29	23.41
Industry	15.94	16.19	17.45	18.27	19.06	19.44
Services	53.65	54.62	55.52	56.29	56.64	57.16

Demographic Overview *(refer Note 1)*

Industrialization Indices	2012	2013	2014	ASEAN Ave.	World Ave.
Industrialization Intensity Index	0.64	0.66	0.68	0.54	0.65
Share of Medium & High Tech	0.64	0.64	0.68	0.44	
Main Economic Sectors	The Philippine economy is based on food processing; production of cement, iron, and steel; and telecommunications, among others. The agriculture sector in 2019 employs 23.41% of the labor force but contributes only 9.3% of GDP.				

Trends in Income and Inequality *(refer Note 1)*

Measure	2014	2015	2016	2017	2018	2019	ASEAN Ave.
Income Index	0.661	0.667	0.675	0.682	0.689	...	0.734
Inequality in Income (%)	26.8	26.8	26.8	26.8	28.1	...	20.35
GNI per Capita	7,947	8,290	8,701	9,133	9,540	...	23,069
Human Development Rank	106/189						

Take-up of Technology *(refer Note 2)*

Measure	Description
E-commerce trends	92% visited an online store and 70% made an online purchase. E-commerce sales increased by 22% in 2019.
Internet coverage and availability	71% use the internet and 71% also use social media. Internet connection speeds increased by 25% in 2019. Mobile connectivity Index – 61.6 (7th in the region).
Take-up of internet and mobile banking	54% use mobile banking and 40% make mobile payments.
Take-up of e-filing	E-filing data was not supplied.

PHILIPPINES:
EMPLOYMENT BY SECTOR

- Employment to population ratio, 15+, total (%)
- Employment in agriculture (% of total employment)
- Employment in industry (% of total employment)
- Employment in services (% of total employment)

PHILIPPINES:
TAKE-UP OF TECHNOLOGY

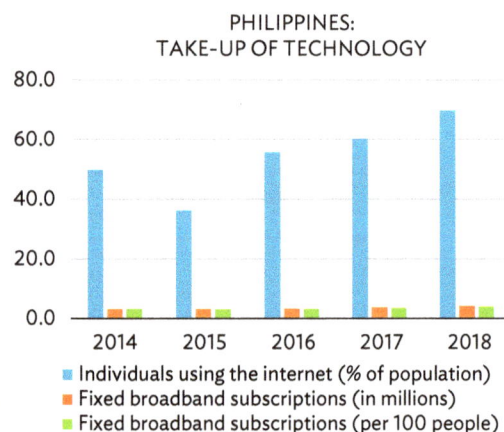

- Individuals using the internet (% of population)
- Fixed broadband subscriptions (in millions)
- Fixed broadband subscriptions (per 100 people)

PRODUCTION STRUCTURE

	Region	Exports ($ million)				
		2014	2015	2016	2017	2018
Exports - Overall (refer Note 3)	Philippines	76,162	82,281	83,135	85,681	97,295
	SEA	1,269,978	1,296,847	1,167,083	1,145,109	1,316,080
	US	2,273,428	2,371,704	2,266,800	2,220,609	2,356,726
Main sector 1 Machinery and Transport Equipment	Philippines	31,574	35,579	37,871	36,321	45,161
	SEA	470,011	483,417	476,133	478,746	538,499
	US	639,053	665,625	647,286	627,333	645,863
Main sector 2 Office and Telecom Equipment	Philippines	20,520	23,179	25,674	25,383	25,417
	SEA	284,959	293,811	291,494	289,701	325,385
	US	140,971	145,946	142,274	140,473	145,475
	Region	Imports ($ million)				
		2014	2015	2016	2017	2018
Imports - Overall (refer Note 3)	Philippines	92,658	100,405	114,042	128,185	146,841
	SEA	1,506,926	1,372,220	1,354,024	1,525,565	1,701,449
	US	2,879,362	2,786,645	2,739,415	2,932,062	3,148,464
Main sector 1 Machinery and Transport Equipment	Philippines	27,598	34,356	42,064	47,271	53,052
	SEA	462,822	456,028	462,749	520,106	576,718
	US	956,716	989,206	969,943	1,040,707	1,103,063
Main sector 2 Office and Telecom Equipment	Philippines	14,013	19,290	20,436	22,625	26,087
	SEA	220,691	218,183	220,271	257,966	287,275
	US	314,209	321,039	316,947	350,850	362,342
Observations	Exports grew by 11.9% in 2018, compared with a regional average growth of 10.1%. Imports grew by 0.1% in 2018, compared with a regional average growth of 10.3%. The top exports are integrated circuits, office machine parts, and computers. The top imports are integrated circuits, refined and crude petroleum, and cars.					

	Sector	2014	2015	2016	2017	2018
Flows of Inward Foreign Direct Investment (FDI) to ASEAN Sourced from the Philippines, by Economic Sectors ($ million) (refer Note 4)	Agriculture, forestry, and fishing	0.10	0.04	0.13	0.10	3.03
	Mining and quarrying	2.83	0.93	0.08	1.36	0.12
	Manufacturing	(46.70)	88.98	79.48	71.47	50.99
	Electricity, gas, steam, and air conditioning supply	0.06	0.35	0.15	2.79	1.06
	Water supply; sewerage, waste management and remediation activities	0.02	(0.02)	0.60	0.20	0.17
	Construction	0.20	(0.13)	3.69	5.13	178.08
	Wholesale and retail trade; repair of motor vehicles and motorcycles	32.55	(34.07)	13.80	59.09	(30.26)
	Transportation and storage	0.04	2.62	18.46	2.22	(1.07)
	Accommodation and food service activities	0.13	0.02	0.47	0.17	21.68
	Information and communication	0.03	(0.09)	0.27	0.29	0.47
	Financial and insurance activities	(0.18)	806.15	143.35	(52.67)	780.05
	Real estate activities	(46.42)	(59.33)	9.83	1.57	7.91
	Professional, scientific, and technical activities	0.63	0.41	1.91	(0.05)	1.23
	Administrative and support service activities	0.00	0.01	0.19	(0.02)	0.25
	Education	0.02	0.00	0.07	0.04	0.06
	Human health and social work activities	0.11	0.00	0.06	0.13	0.09
	Arts, entertainment, and recreation	(0.02)	0.00	0.38	0.01	0.74
	Other services activities	47.36	51.30	10.95	(2.45)	(11.23)
	Unspecified activity	0.01	0.00	0.00	0.00	
	TOTAL activities	**334.15**	**904.95**	**400.07**	**353.38**	**1,235.56**
IMF Article IV	Net FDI inflows (in percent of GDP)	2	1.9	2.7	3.3	3
	Net Direct Investment (FDI) – in $ billion	(0.1)	(5.9)	(7)	(5.9)	(5.3)
General Observations on FDI	FDI to the Philippines fell in 2019 and remains below the full-year target of $8 billion set by the Central Bank of the Philippines. Inflows are concentrated in manufacturing and real estate. Nevertheless, the PRC overtook Japan and Singapore as the largest investor in the Philippines in 2018. This was mainly due to the construction of an iron and steel plant by the PRC's Hesteel Group (HBIS) in the southern Philippines. Last year, the country eased the obligation of local employment for foreign investor workers. Despite this, the Philippines trails regional peers, in part because the Philippines' constitution limits foreign investment, and in part due to the threat of terrorism in some parts of the country. The government also favors subcontracting agreements between foreign companies and local enterprises rather than FDI. Factors such as corruption, inadequate infrastructure, high power costs, tax regulations, and foreign ownership restrictions discourage investment.					

	Component Sector	2014	2015	2016	2017	2018	ASEAN Ave.	US 2018
Industry Structure: GDP by type of expenditure *(refer Note 5)*	Gross domestic product (GDP)	100.0	100.0	100.0	100.0	100.0	100	100
	Final consumption expenditure	83.1	84.7	84.9	84.7	85.8	68.04	87
	Household consumption expenditure (including NPISH)	72.5	73.8	73.7	73.5	73.8	54	70
	General government final consumption expenditure	10.6	10.9	11.2	11.2	11.9	14.51	17
	Gross capital formation	**20.6**	**21.2**	**24.4**	**25.1**	**26.9**	**28.58**	**18**
	Gross fixed capital formation	20.7	22.0	24.6	25.0	26.8	27.74	17
	Changes in inventories	(0.1)	(0.8)	(0.2)	0.1	0.2	1.04	1
	Exports of goods and services	28.9	28.4	28.1	31.0	31.7	63.65	13
	Imports of goods and services	(32.6)	(34.3)	(37.4)	(40.9)	(44.4)	(61.12)	18
	Total value added	**100.0**	**100.0**	**100.0**	**100.0**	**100.0**	**100**	**100**
Observations	Capital formation is a lead indicator of economic performance and is slightly below regional averages. Tax outcomes flowing from investment may be significantly impacted by tax incentives.							

NPISH = nonprofit institutions serving households.

	Component Sector	2014	2015	2016	2017	2018	ASEAN Ave.	US 2018
Industry Structure: Value Add by kind of economic activity ($ million) *(refer Note 5)*	Agriculture, hunting, forestry, and fishing	11.3	10.3	9.7	9.7	9.3	12.11	167
	Industry	31.4	30.9	30.8	30.5	30.8	38.84	1,512
	Mining, manufacturing, and utilities	25.0	24.1	23.6	23.4	23.1	32	673
	Manufacturing	20.6	20.0	19.7	19.5	19.1	17.29	2,321
	Construction	6.4	6.8	7.1	7.0	7.7	6.99	839
	Services	57.3	58.8	59.6	59.9	59.9	49.05	2,579
	Wholesale, retail trade, restaurants, and hotels	19.5	19.9	20.1	20.3	20.4	16.75	2,338
	Transport, storage, and communications	6.2	6.4	6.3	6.1	5.9	7.02	658
	Other activities	31.6	32.5	33.2	33.5	33.6	25.28	437
Observations	The contributions of agriculture and industry are below regional averages and services are well above the regional average.							

TAX SYSTEM AND TAX ADMINISTRATION DESIGN FEATURES

Tax Rates, Thresholds, and Overall Revenue Contribution (see Note 6)

Taxes	Rates of Tax (%) /1		Threshold			Share (%) of Total Taxes (latest year)
	Basic/ Standard	Other	Type	Local Currency	$ (approx.)	
CIT	30%	/2	-	-	-	20% (2019)
PIT	20%, 25%, 30%, 32%, 35%		Levying tax	P250,000	$5,000	13% (2019)
Withholding /3	10	5				
Withholding /4	20	10				
VAT/GST /5	12	12% - Digital Services	Registration	P1.9 million	$38,000	22% (2019)
Excise	(Varies by product type)		-	-	-	20% (2019)
SSC /6	3.63%		-	Employees: 1,450 Employers: 2,280	-	13% (2019)
Property	-	-	-	-	-	<3% (2019)
*Subnational taxes	-	-	-	-	-	20.1% of general government revenue and 3.8% of GDP (2016)

Overview of Tax Incentives	The Philippine tax system, principally the corporate income tax, features an array of tax incentives that are currently the subject of legislative reform proposals before Congress. Under existing laws, domestic and foreign enterprises registered with the Board of Investments under the 1987 Omnibus Investments Code are eligible for an income tax holiday and exemption from certain other taxes and duties. Enterprises located in special economic zones that are registered with the Philippine Economic Zone Authority can also be granted an income tax holiday or a special tax regime under which a 5% tax is imposed on gross income instead of all national and local taxes.[9] According to the Department of Finance,[10] the incentives regime is overly generous to a few companies at the expense of the majority. By way of illustration, it notes that, in 2017, the incentives granted to only 3,150 companies, including some on the elite list of top 1,000 corporations, cost the equivalent of PHP441 billion (or 2.8% of GDP) in foregone tax revenues. These companies pay an effective discounted corporate income tax rate of between 6% to 13% while, under the current corporate taxation system, firms with no incentives, which include almost all of the country's 90,000 SMEs, pay the regular CIT rate of 30% of their net taxable income, the highest statutory rate in the region. Modernization of various investment tax incentives is planned and is intended to make incentives more performance-based, targeted, time-bound, and transparent.

* The Philippines has close to 44,000 subnational government bodies across three levels of subnational government.

/1. For FY 2019, unless otherwise indicated. /2. An alternative minimum tax of 2% of gross income applied to corporations that fall within specific criteria. /3. Professional fees paid to individuals are subject to a 5% or 10% creditable withholding, based on annual income. /4. For resident individuals, final withholding applies to basic interest income (20%) and dividends (10%). /5. On 19 May 2020, the government introduced a bill (The Digital Economy Taxation Act) which will, once enacted, expand the VAT to cover digital advertising services, subscription-based services, and transactions made on e-commerce platforms. Providers of services must establish a resident agent or representative office to act as a withholding agent in the Philippines (https://www.pwc.com/ph/en/taxwise-or-otherwise/2020/are-we-ready-for-a-tax-on-digital-services.html). /6. The total maximum monthly contributions to three separate funds—social security, health, and home development. Voluntary contributions are also allowed.

Sources: IMF Art. IV reports; Deloitte Philippines Country Tax Profiles; Ernst and Young Worldwide Personal Tax and Immigration Guide, 2019–20.

[9]   Ernst and Young. 2019. *World-wide Corporate Tax Guide 2019,* Page 1,311 https://www.ey.com/Publication/vwLUAssets/ey-worldwide-corporate-tax-guide-2019/$FILE/ey-worldwide-corporate-tax-guide-2019.pdf.
[10]   Government of the Philippines, Department of Finance. Package 2: Corporate Recovery and Tax Incentives for Enterprises (CREATE) Act. https://taxreform.dof.gov.ph/tax-reform-packages/p2-corporate-recovery-and-tax-incentives-for-enterprises-act/.

Tax Administration Setup and Performance

Subject Area	Aspect	Features and Performance	Overall Rating
Responsibilities of tax body	Main taxes collected	CIT, PIT, VAT, Excise, Percentages Taxes	Broad – collect 76% of all taxes
	Other major roles	-	
Tax body Autonomy	Budget flexibility, organization design	The Bureau of Internal Revenue (BIR) has very broad autonomy, reporting that it has discretion around budget and organization design matters, as well as most aspects of HRM.	Good
	Human resource management		

Digital services in tax administration	E-filing	Rate (2017)	Comments	
	- CIT	No data	BIR administers a range of e-filing and e-payment services but does not appear able to readily report usage by tax type.	Insufficient data to assess on e-filing and e-payment usage. Scope for enhancements in other areas.
	- PIT	No data		
	- VAT/GST	No data		
	E-payment	No data		
	E-services (including mobile applications)	ISORA response indicates very limited array of modern e-services in 2017.		

	Measure	Country Performance						ASEAN Ave.	OECD Ave. 2018
		2014	2015	2016	2017	2018	2019		
Tax system design (refer Note 7)	Tax reliance ratio	90.2	88.7	90.2	91.0	90.5	90.1	66.9	63.8
	Tax mix	46.0	46.6	46.5	45.6	40.4	40.0	39.92	33.7
	Tax ratio	13.6	13.6	13.7	14.2	14.7	15.0	14	34.3
	CIT productivity	0.213	0.213	0.217	0.197	0.200	0.200	0.26	
	VAT productivity	0.350	0.350	0.367	0.367	0.342	0.358	0.43	
	VAT revenue ratio								
	Consolidation of tax collection and administration	Subnational governments collect taxes comprising 3.8% of GDP. There is a relatively high reliance on the national tax body for tax collections, with 76% of all taxes collected by BIR.							
Observations	Tax reliance levels are extremely high by regional comparison. Other measures of system design are on a par with regional comparators.								

	Measure	Country Performance
Tax administration processes (refer Note 8)	Tax administration efficiency and effectiveness (Operating expenditure as a proportion of net revenue collected)	0.57% - A figure under 1% is considered efficient, however low figures (below 0.5%) may indicate under resourcing.
	No. of labor force members/tax body FTE	Over 4,000 workers for every staff member.
	No. of citizens/tax body FTE	There are around 9,800 citizens per tax officer.
	Proportion of staff assigned to support functions	32% are assigned to support and IT functions. Regional average = 29%

REVENUE

<table>
<tr><th rowspan="2"></th><th rowspan="2">Measure</th><th colspan="6">Country Performance</th><th rowspan="2">ASEAN Ave.</th><th rowspan="2">Asia and Pacific Ave.</th><th rowspan="2">OECD Ave. 2018</th></tr>
<tr><th>2014</th><th>2015</th><th>2016</th><th>2017</th><th>2018</th><th>2019*</th></tr>
<tr><td rowspan="4">**Tax revenue collection performance** *(all levels of government)* *(refer Note 9)*</td><td>Tax/GDP (%) - all</td><td>13.61</td><td>13.63</td><td>13.68</td><td>14.24</td><td>14.73</td><td>15.0</td><td>14.03</td><td>20.0</td><td>34.3</td></tr>
<tr><td>Taxes on income and profits/GDP (%)</td><td>6.40</td><td>6.40</td><td>6.50</td><td>5.90</td><td>6.00</td><td>6.0</td><td>5.35</td><td>8.1</td><td>11.6</td></tr>
<tr><td>Taxes on goods & services/GDP (%)</td><td>6.60</td><td>6.60</td><td>7.10</td><td>7.80</td><td>7.70</td><td>8.0</td><td>6</td><td>10.1</td><td>10.9</td></tr>
<tr><td>Overall tax revenue trend</td><td colspan="9">Tax-to-GDP rate has been trending upward and has now reached a level considered sufficient to fund sustainable development. Taxes on income and profits are trending downward, which may be an indication of potential design and/or administration gaps.</td></tr>
</table>

(*) projected/provisional collections.

BROADENING THE TAX BASE

<table>
<tr><th></th><th>Measure</th><th>Country Performance</th></tr>
<tr><td rowspan="5">**Countering Tax Avoidance and Evasion** *(refer Note 10)*</td><td>Effective anti-avoidance rules</td><td>There is no general or specific anti-avoidance rule. The transfer pricing rules are consistent with OECD guidance.</td></tr>
<tr><td>Thin capitalization and controlled foreign corporation rules</td><td>There are no thin cap or anti-hybrid rules, and no disclosure requirements for related party dealings.</td></tr>
<tr><td>Findings from OECD Forum on Harmful Tax Practices (FHTP)</td><td>Regional or area headquarters regime was out of scope with no benefits for income from geographically mobile activities. Regional operating headquarters regime is in the process of being eliminated. The review found potentially harmful features to be addressed.</td></tr>
<tr><td>A focus on HNWI and professions</td><td>None reported.</td></tr>
<tr><td>Dealing with the shadow economy</td><td>The shadow economy in the Philippines is estimated to be around 28% of GDP, placing it at 4th in the region.</td></tr>
</table>

<table>
<tr><th></th><th>Measure</th><th></th><th>Country Status</th></tr>
<tr><td rowspan="16">**Countering International Tax Avoidance and Evasion and International Cooperation** *(refer Note 11)*</td><td colspan="2">Member of Global Forum on Transparency & Exchange of Information</td><td>Yes</td></tr>
<tr><td rowspan="2">Exchange of Information on Request Ratings</td><td>Round 1</td><td>Largely compliant</td></tr>
<tr><td>Round 2</td><td>Largely compliant</td></tr>
<tr><td colspan="2">Signatory to the Multilateral Convention on Mutual Assistance in Tax Matters</td><td>Signed</td></tr>
<tr><td colspan="2">Commitment to Automatic Exchange of Information</td><td>Not committed to a specific date</td></tr>
<tr><td colspan="2">Implementation of Common Reporting Standard (CRS) and Multilateral Competent Authority Agreement</td><td>Not applicable</td></tr>
<tr><td colspan="2">Convention on Mutual Administrative Assistance in tax matters</td><td>Signed</td></tr>
<tr><td colspan="2">Member of Base Erosion and Profit Shifting Inclusive Framework</td><td>No</td></tr>
<tr><td colspan="2">Existence of harmful tax regimes (Action 5)</td><td>In the process of being amended/eliminated</td></tr>
<tr><td colspan="2">Exchange of information on tax rulings (Action 5)</td><td>Reviewed/recommendations made</td></tr>
<tr><td colspan="2">CbC – Domestic law (Action 13)</td><td>Not applicable</td></tr>
<tr><td colspan="2">CbC – Information exchange network (Action 13)</td><td>Cbc mcaa not signed</td></tr>
<tr><td colspan="2">Effective dispute resolution (Action 14)</td><td>Not applicable</td></tr>
<tr><td colspan="2">Signatory to the Multilateral Convention to Implement Treaty Related Measures to Prevent BEPS (Action 6)</td><td>No</td></tr>
<tr><td colspan="2">Network of income tax treaties for avoidance of double taxation</td><td>48</td></tr>
</table>

RESPONSIVE TAX ADMINISTRATION

Important findings from Deloitte's 2017 Tax Complexity Survey *(refer Note 12)*	% responding tax regime has become more complicated over prior 3 years	31%
	% responding tax regime has been less consistently administered over prior 3 years	22%
	% responding tax compliance and reporting rules are "complicated" or "very complicated"	31.3%
	Perceived fairness in tax audits	Low
	Perceived confidence in appeal system	Low
	Taxpayer relationship with authorities	Low
	Perceived main priority areas for reform	Tax officer training and adoption of BEPS recommendations

	Measure	Country Ranking				World Ave.	Asia and Pacific Ave.
		2017	2018	2019	2020		
Compliance/ Regulatory Burden Indicators *(as reported in the Doing Business Series)* *(refer Note 13)*	Ease of Doing Business Indicator Ranking (Ranking out of 190 countries)	113	124	95	95	–	–
	Paying Taxes Indicator (Ranking out of 190 countries)	115	105	124	95	–	–
	Paying Taxes – time to comply (Hours/yr.): (all)	186	182	181	171	234	192
	Paying Taxes – time to comply (Hours/yr.): (CIT)	39	38	38	33	59	59
	Paying Taxes – time to comply (Hours/yr.): (VAT)	110	108	108	108	90	73
	Paying Taxes – time to comply (Hours/yr.): Labor taxes	37	36	35	30	85	60
	Post Filing Index (VAT and CIT corrections)	50	50	50	50	61	57
	Time to comply with VAT refund (hours)	n.a.	n.a.	n.a.	n.a.	14.9	19.6
	Time to obtain VAT refund (weeks)	n.a.	n.a.	n.a.	n.a.	41.5	28.2
	Number of payments per year	27	19	13	13	23	21
	Trading Across Borders Rank	95	99	104	113	–	–
Observations	The Philippines substantially improved its business climate in 2019: starting a business is now easier due to the abolishment of the minimum capital requirement for domestic companies; dealing with construction permits has been improved (improvement of coordination, standardization of the process for obtaining an occupancy certificate); and minority investor protection has also been strengthened. These changes have been credited with the significant improvement in 2019. Despite this improvement, the cross-border trading ranking continues to decline. Refunds are restricted to international traders. Tax reforms announced in 2018 may have contributed to the improved rank.						

Taxpayer rights and obligations *(refer Note 14)*	**Observations**
	The Philippines has a formally defined and legislated set of taxpayer rights including internal and external dispute mechanisms. Taxpayers may challenge assessments and seek administrative and/or judicial reviews. BIR issues private rulings at the taxpayer's request. There is no tax ombudsman.

Corruption Perception Index Trends *(refer Note 15)*	**Observations**
	In 2014, the Philippines' CPI score was 38 out of 100 and has decreased to 34 in 2019. This places the Philippines at a relatively low ranking of 113th out of 180 countries.

SINGAPORE

AT A GLANCE

Measure	2014	2015	2016	2017	2018	2019
Total Population (million)	5.469	5/535	5.607	5.612	5.638	5.804
Age profile						
0–14	12.91	12.63	12.29	12.21	12.28	12.33
15–64	78.37	78.32	77.94	77.21	76.26	75.28
65+	8.72	9.05	9.77	10.58	11.46	12.39
Literacy level (% of population)	...	96.72	96.83	97.05	97.2	97.34
Urbanization (%)						
Urban Population	100.00	100.00	100.00	100.00	100.00	100.00
Rural Population	-	-	-	-	-	-
Employment to Population	67.98	68.68	68.19	68.00	67.79	67.64
Agriculture	0.81	0.80	0.78	0.76	0.74	0.73
Industry	17.55	17.30	16.89	16.30	15.81	15.47
Services	81.64	81.90	82.33	82.94	83.45	83.80

Demographic Overview (refer Note 1)

Industrialization Indices	2012	2013	2014	ASEAN Ave.	World Ave.	
Industrialization Intensity Index	0.81	0.8	0.79	0.54	0.65	
Share of Medium & High Tech	1	1	1	0.44		
Main Economic Sectors	Singapore's largest industry by far is the manufacturing sector, which contributes 21% of the country's annual GDP in 2018. Key manufacturing clusters in Singapore include electronics, chemicals, biomedical sciences, logistics, and transport engineering.					

Trends in Income and Inequality (refer Note 1)

Measure	2014	2015	2016	2017	2018	2019	ASEAN Ave.
Income Index	1	1	1	1	1		0.734
Inequality in Income (%)	...	...	...	25	25		20.35
GNI per Capita	79,236	77,686	78,759	81,500	83,793		23,069
Human Development Rank				9/189			

Take-up of Technology (refer Note 2)

Measure	Description
E-commerce trends	87% visited an online store and 73% made online purchases.
Internet coverage and availability	84% use the internet and 79% use social media. Internet speeds increased by 18% in 2019. Mobile Connectivity Index + 86.6 (1st in the region). Singapore is the only country in SEA with 100% 3G (or higher) coverage.
Take-up of internet and mobile banking	64% use mobile banking and 36% make mobile payments.
Take-up of e-filing	E-filing has been well accepted by businesses.

SINGAPORE: EMPLOYMENT BY SECTOR

- Employment to population ratio, 15+, total (%)
- Employment in agriculture (% of total employment)
- Employment in industry (% of total employment)
- Employment in services (% of total employment)

SINGAPORE: TAKE-UP OF TECHNOLOGY

- Individuals using the internet (% of population)
- Fixed broadband subscriptions (in millions)
- Fixed broadband subscriptions (per 100 people)

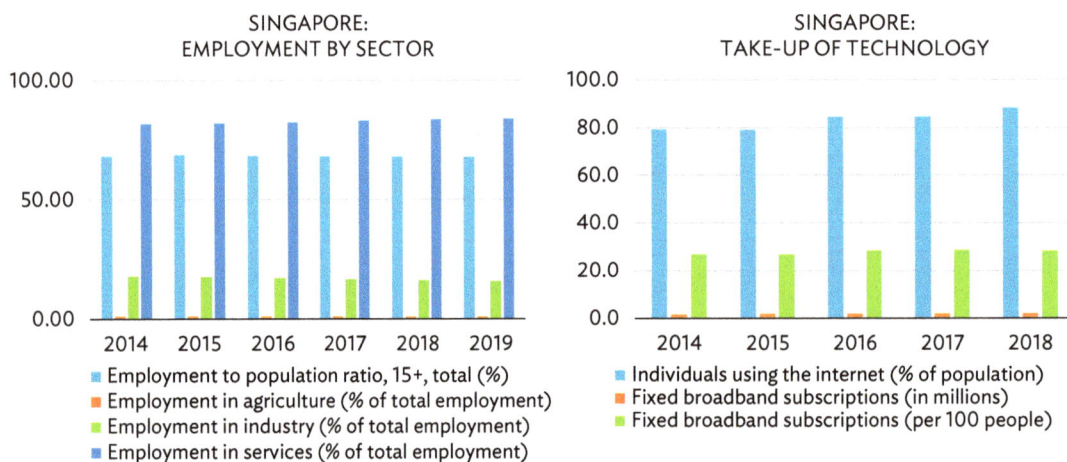

PRODUCTION STRUCTURE

	Region	Exports ($ million)				
		2014	2015	2016	2017	2018
Exports - Overall (refer Note 3)	Singapore	549,432	526,580	580,099	526,580	580,099
	SEA	1,606,681	1,630,770	1,508,470	1,498,265	1,676,341
	US	2,273,428	2,371,704	2,266,800	2,220,609	2,356,726
Main sector 1 Machinery and Transport Equipment	Singapore	190,318	187,620	177,532	170,992	182,840
	SEA	470,011	483,417	476,133	478,746	538,499
	US	639,053	665,625	647,286	627,333	645,863
Main sector 2 Office and Telecom Equipment	Singapore	126,995	125,849	118,621	112,467	120,695
	SEA	284,959	293,811	291,494	289,701	325,385
	US	140,971	145,946	142,274	140,473	145,475
	Region	Imports ($ million)				
		2014	2015	2016	2017	2018
Imports - Overall (refer Note 3)	Singapore	530,568	465,354	441,870	495,467	545,565
	SEA	1,506,926	1,372,220	1,354,024	1,525,565	1,701,449
	US	2,879,362	2,786,645	2,739,415	2,932,062	3,148,464
Main sector 1 Machinery and Transport Equipment	Singapore	151,387	141,154	139,453	150,533	172,466
	SEA	462,822	456,028	462,749	520,106	576,718
	US	956,716	989,206	969,943	1,040,707	1,103,063
Main sector 2 Office and Telecom Equipment	Singapore	90,785	84,291	83,045	91,910	101,646
	SEA	220,691	218,183	220,271	257,966	287,275
	US	314,209	321,039	316,947	350,850	362,342
Observations	Exports grew by 9.2% in 2018, compared with a regional average growth of 10.1%. Imports grew by 9.2% in 2018, compared with a regional average growth of 10.3%. The top exports are integrated circuits, refined petroleum, and gold. The top imports are refined and crude petroleum, integrated circuits, and gold. Singapore is a net exporter of refined petroleum.					

	Sector	2014	2015	2016	2017	2018
Flows of Inward Foreign Direct Investment (FDI) to ASEAN Sourced from Singapore, by Economic Sectors ($ million) (refer Note 4)	Agriculture, forestry, and fishing	3,750.21	3,618.97	2,326.22	3,634.75	3,188.72
	Mining and quarrying	477.25	60.12	320.32	(242.14)	(1,383.16)
	Manufacturing	5,526.82	3,071.07	5,375.46	6,317.20	6,423.47
	Electricity, gas, steam, and air conditioning supply	(54.14)	263.35	95.38	708.50	135.24
	Water supply; sewerage, waste management, and remediation activities	5.43	25.73	62.65	29.56	24.38
	Construction	48.80	129.57	92.38	57.45	149.93
	Wholesale and retail trade; repair of motor vehicles and motorcycles	1,250.98	980.55	1,238.23	2,384.87	3,111.60
	Transportation and storage	27.78	190.74	118.51	148.44	212.00
	Accommodation and food service activities	(39.71)	30.10	206.38	70.98	86.28
	Information and communication	(302.26)	547.70	142.89	1,203.12	665.99
	Financial and insurance activities	2,902.41	2,370.97	1,690.37	1,415.38	1,478.80
	Real estate activities	1,473.52	789.89	1,229.83	1,191.52	1,476.40
	Professional, scientific, and technical activities	36.46	(43.68)	108.84	156.70	115.14
	Administrative and support service activities	43.76	9.66	39.28	34.14	118.38
	Public administration and defense; compulsory social security			6.35	0.24	0.10
	Education	7.46	1.77	12.85	13.01	11.71
	Human health and social work activities	34.12	15.38	42.11	68.39	47.51
	Arts, entertainment, and recreation	1.43	(19.18)	(3.27)	2.61	70.70
	Other services activities	(165.03)	224.78	543.38	291.87	89.67
	Unspecified activity	695.94	1,434.73	1,811.36	0.03	
	TOTAL activities	**15,721.23**	**13,702.22**	**15,459.52**	**17,486.61**	**16,022.88**
IMF Article IV	Net FDI inflows (in percent of GDP)	21.8	22.7	22.2	28.9	25
	Net Direct Investment (FDI) – in $ billion	(16.2)	(24.6)	(33.8)	(51.1)	(45.7)

General Observations on FDI

FDI inflows rose in 2019. Singapore is the fifth-largest recipient of FDI inflows in the world, after the US; the PRC; the Netherlands, and Hong Kong, China. Singapore is also a major investor abroad and has sought to diversify its investments beyond traditional target markets in Asia. The main investors in Singapore are the US, British Virgin Islands, Cayman Islands, the Netherlands, Japan, and the UK. Financial and insurance activities are by far the main recipient of foreign investment, accounting for 54.5% of all FDI stock. Singapore has based its economic development on a proactive strategy to attract FDI using its trade openness. Being conducive for lending to foreign investors, a sound regulatory system, stable tax regime, well-developed infrastructure, political stability, a skilled workforce, and the absence of corruption make Singapore an attractive destination for investment.

	Component Sector	2014	2015	2016	2017	2018	ASEAN Ave.	US 2018
Industry Structure: GDP by Type of Expenditure (refer Note 5)	Gross domestic product (GDP)	100.0	100.0	100.0	100.0	100.0	100	100
	Final consumption expenditure	46.9	47.0	46.3	45.5	44.8	68.04	87
	Household consumption expenditure (including NPISH)	37.0	36.6	35.7	34.9	34.1	54	70
	General government final consumption expenditure	9.9	10.4	10.6	10.6	10.7	14.51	17
	Gross capital formation	**30.1**	**26.5**	**27.0**	**28.5**	**27.0**	**28.58**	**18**
	Gross fixed capital formation	28.3	27.5	26.5	26.4	24.5	27.74	17
	Changes in inventories	1.8	(1.0)	0.5	2.0	2.5	1.04	1
	Exports of goods and services	190.5	176.7	164.7	170.1	175.8	63.65	13
	Imports of goods and services	(167.0)	(149.5)	(138.3)	(145.6)	(149.6)	(61.12)	18
	Total value added	**100.0**	**100.0**	**100.0**	**100.0**	**100.0**	**100**	**100**
Observations	Capital formation is a lead indicator of economic performance and is close to regional averages.							

NPISH = nonprofit institutions serving households.

	Component Sector	2014	2015	2016	2017	2018	ASEAN Ave.	US 2018
Industry Structure: Value Add by kind of economic activity ($ million) (refer Note 5)	Agriculture, hunting, forestry, and fishing	0.04	0.03	0.03	0.03	0.02	12.11	167
	Industry	25.26	25.62	24.78	24.75	26.11	38.84	1,512
	Mining, manufacturing, and utilities	20.12	20.45	19.96	20.85	22.58	32	673
	Manufacturing	18.67	18.98	18.59	19.60	21.36	17.29	2,321
	Construction	5.14	5.17	4.82	3.90	3.53	6.99	839
	Services	74.70	74.35	75.19	75.22	73.86	49.05	2,579
	Wholesale, retail trade, restaurants, and hotels	19.68	18.78	20.30	20.63	20.11	16.75	2,338
	Transport, storage, and communications	11.49	11.56	10.94	11.36	11.03	7.02	658
	Other activities	43.53	44.01	43.95	43.23	42.71	25.28	437
Observations	Services is the dominant sector, with financial services featuring prominently. Manufacturing also trends above regional averages. Due to the nature of the Singapore geography and economy, it is unsurprising that agriculture has a very small footprint.							

TAX SYSTEM AND TAX ADMINISTRATION DESIGN FEATURES

Tax Rates, Thresholds, and Overall Revenue Contribution (see Note 6)

Taxes	Rates of Tax (%) /1 Basic/ Standard	Other	Thresholds Local Currency	$	Share (%) of Total Taxes (latest year)
CIT /2	17%	17% - Branch tax	S$10,000/190,000	$7,170/136,000	54% (2019)
PIT	2%–22%	15% flat rate or progressive rate for nonresidents /3	S$20,000	$14,300	
VAT/ GST	7%	Zero rate for certain G&S /5	S$1 million	$717,000	21% (2019)
WHT /4	15%	Interest			3% (2019)
WHT /4	10%	Royalties			
WHT /4	17%	Fees for technical services			
Excise /6	12%/20% Specific Rates	Motorcycles, private cars, taxis Alcohol, tobacco, and fuels,			
SSC/7	17%/20%	Employers/employees			
Property /8	0%–16% 10%–20% 10%	Owner-occupied Non-owner-occupied Commercial	S$8,000 Annual Value for owner-occupied residential properties only.	$5,736	9% (2019)
Stamp Duty /9	Up to 4% (buyers) Up to 3% (buyers) 0.4%	Shares/Residential property Nonresidential property Leases	If annual rent exceeds S$1,000	$717.00	8% (2019)
Overview of Tax Incentives	For FY 2020 onward, qualifying start-up companies receive tax exemption of 75% on the first S$100,000 and 50% on the next S$100,000 of chargeable income for the first 3 consecutive years of operation. Otherwise, partial tax exemption is provided to companies: for FY 2020 onward, 75% of the first S$10,000 and 50% of the next S$190,000 of chargeable income is exempt from tax. For FY 2020, CIT rebate is provided at 25% of tax payable, capped at S$15,000.				

Note that Singapore does not have subnational governments.

/1. For FY 2020, unless otherwise indicated. /2. For the year of assessment 2020 onward, partial tax exemption is provided for companies based on the following parameters: 75% of the first S$10,000 and 50% of the next S$190,000 of chargeable income is exempt from tax. /3. For employment income, the rate is either 15% flat or progressive, whichever is higher; for nonemployment income, the rate is 22%. /4. Nonresidents only. Residents and nonresidents are not taxed on dividends and there is no WHT for residents on other categories of income. /5. Zero rate applies to international services and exports. Specified financial services and the sale and lease of residential properties and import and local supply of investment precious metals are exempt. A separate overseas vendor tax (OVT) regime applies to foreign companies providing digital services and online trading. The OVT applies to foreign companies with global turnover> S$1 million and local sales> S$100,000 (https://www.iras.gov.sg/irashome/News-and-Events/Newsroom/Media-Releases-and-Speeches/Media-Releases/2019/GST-payable-on-overseas-digital-services-from-1-Jan-2020/). /6. There are four categories of dutiable goods: Intoxicating liquors, tobacco products, motor vehicles, and petroleum products and biodiesel blends. A carbon tax at S$5 per ton of greenhouse gas (GHG) came into effect in January 2019, targeting direct emissions from large emitters, without exemption for any sector. /7. Known as the Central Provident Fund (CPF). The CPF is not a tax but rather a mandatory social security savings scheme funded by contributions by employers and employees. /8. Progressive rates apply depending upon value. There is no CGT in Singapore. /9. Additional buyers stamp duty and sellers stamp duty may apply in certain circumstances, such as where properties are held for a short period. These additional stamp duties may be phased out, as they were introduced to dampen the property market. Other Stamp duties apply to Mortgages (0.4% – capped at S$500) and Shares (0.2%).

Sources: IMF Art. IV reports; Deloitte Country Tax Profiles; OECD Statistics.

Tax Administration Setup and Performance

Subject Area	Aspect	Features and Performance	Overall Rating
Responsibilities of tax body	Main taxes collected	CIT, PIT and VAT/GST	Broad – collect around 70% of Government revenue
	Other major roles	Drafts legislation and provides advice on property valuations	
Tax body Autonomy	Budget flexibility, organization design	The Inland Revenue Authority of Singapore (IRAS) is a unified semiautonomous body with a board composed of external officials. IRAS has budget flexibility in the allocation of resources and has control over staffing and recruitment	High
	Human resource management		

Digital services in tax administration	E-filing	Rate (2017)[11]	Comments	High
	– CIT	69%	Most VAT/GST and 60% of PIT returns are pre-populated. Online payment was not offered in 2017.	
	– PIT	39%		
	– VAT/GST	99%		
	E-payment	1%		
	E-services (including mobile applications)	IRAS offers e-services designed to be optimized on desktop/tablet and mobile devices. A wide range of e-services are available via the myTax Portal and e-Stamping Portal where individuals and businesses/companies can access and perform personal and/or corporate transactions.		

	Measure	Country Performance						ASEAN Ave.	OECD Ave. 2018
		2014	2015	2016	2017	2018	2019*		
Tax system design (refer Note 7)	Tax reliance ratio	77.7	75.5	70.3	73.3	73.4	74.0	66.9	63.8
	Tax mix	52.3	52.7	52.4	55.0	53.6	53.5	39.92	33.7
	Tax ratio	13.56	13.14	13.33	14.06	13.15	13.37	14	34.3
	CIT productivity	0.197	0.192	0.182	0.186	0.187	0.194	0.26	
	VAT productivity	0.366	0.349	0.360	0.332	0.316	0.315	0.43	
	Consolidation of tax collection and administration	Reliance on taxes is a little over the regional and OECD averages.							
Observations	Although the tax-to-GDP ratio is relatively low, Singapore's net investment returns on government assets are high and supplement the lower tax to GDP.								

* projected/provisional collections.

	Measure	Country Performance
Tax administration processes (refer Note 8)	Tax administration efficiency and effectiveness (Operating expenditure as a proportion of net revenue collected)	2018 - 0.84% 2019 - 0.78% - A figure between 0.5% and 1% is considered efficient.
	No. of labor force members/tax body FTE	Around 1,200 workers per tax officer.
	No. of citizens/tax body FTE	Around 1,800 citizens per tax officer.
	Proportion of staff assigned to support functions	25% of staff are assigned to support functions. Regional average = 29%

[11] Note that more recent figures are available but for comparison purposes 2017 data are retained. 2019 figures are: CIT – 76%, PIT – 97%, VAT/GST – 100%. E-payment – 98% (based on number of payments received).

REVENUE

Tax revenue collection performance *(all levels of government)* *(refer Note 9)*	Measure	Country Performance						ASEAN Ave.	Asia and Pacific Ave.	OECD Ave. 2018
		2014	2015	2016	2017	2018	2019*			
	Tax/GDP (%) - all	13.56	13.14	13.33	14.06	13.15	13.37	14.03	20.0	34.3
	Taxes on income and profits/GDP (%)	6.00	5.88	5.99	6.79	6.12	6.39	5.35	8.1	11.6
	Taxes on goods and services/GDP (%)	2.56	2.44	2.52	2.32	2.21	2.20	6	10.1	10.9
	Overall tax revenue trend									

(*) projected/provisional collections.

BROADENING THE TAX BASE

	Measure	Country Performance
Countering Tax Avoidance and Evasion *(refer Note 10)*	Effective anti-avoidance rules	Singapore has a general anti-avoidance rule and transfer pricing rules that are consistent with the OECD model. A 5% additional tax is applied to transfer pricing adjustments.
	Thin capitalization and controlled foreign corporation rules	There are no thin capitalization, CFC, or anti-hybrid rules in Singapore. Singapore has implemented the country-by-country reporting requirements under the BEPS minimum standards.
	Findings from OECD Forum on Harmful Tax Practices (FHTP)	Singapore's preferential regimes were reviewed and found to be not harmful (compliant).
	A focus on HNWI and professions	None reported.
	Dealing with the shadow economy	The shadow economy in Singapore is estimated to be 9.2% of GDP, placing it at the lowest in the region.

	Measure		Country Status
Countering International Tax Avoidance and Evasion and International Cooperation *(refer Note 11)*	Member of Global Forum on Transparency & Exchange of Information		Yes
	Exchange of Information on Request Ratings	Round 1	Largely compliant
		Round 2	Compliant
	Signatory to the Multilateral Convention on Mutual Assistance in Tax Matters		In force
	Commitment to Automatic Exchange of Information		2018
	Implementation of Common Reporting Standard (CRS) and Multilateral Competent Authority Agreement		Yes
	Convention on Mutual Administrative Assistance in tax matters		In force
	Member of Base Erosion and Profit Shifting Inclusive Framework		Yes
	Existence of harmful tax regimes (Action 5)		Not harmful (no harmful regime exists)
	Exchange of information on tax rulings (Action 5)		Reviewed/no recommendations
	CbC – Domestic law (Action 13)		Legal framework in place
	CbC – Information exchange network (Action 13)		Activated
	Effective dispute resolution (Action 14)		Stage 2 reviewed and recommendations made
	Signatory to the Multilateral Convention to Implement Treaty Related Measures to Prevent BEPS (Action 6)		Reviewed in 2018 and 2019, no recommendation. 2020 review ongoing.
	Network of income tax treaties for avoidance of double taxation		Over 90

RESPONSIVE TAX ADMINISTRATION

Important findings from Deloitte's 2017 Tax Complexity Survey *(refer Note 12)*	% responding tax regime has become more complicated over prior 3 years	20%
	% responding tax regime has been less consistently administered over prior 3 years	4%
	% responding tax compliance and reporting rules are "complicated" or "very complicated"	20%
	Perceived fairness in tax audits	High
	Perceived confidence in appeal system	High
	Taxpayer relationship with authorities	Good
	Perceived main priority areas for reform	Adoption of BEPS recommendations and transparency in taxation statistics

	Measure	Country Ranking				World Ave.	Asia and Pacific Ave.
		2017	2018	2019	2020		
Compliance/ Regulatory Burden Indicators *(as reported in the Doing Business Series) (refer Note 13)*	Ease of Doing Business Indicator Ranking (Ranking out of 190 countries)	2	2	2	2	–	–
	Paying Taxes Indicator (Ranking out of 190 countries)	8	7	8	7	–	–
	Paying Taxes – time to comply (Hours/yr.): (all)	67	64	64	64	234	192
	Paying Taxes – time to comply (Hours/yr.): (CIT)	24	24	24	24	59	59
	Paying Taxes – time to comply (Hours/yr.): (VAT)	30	30	30	30	90	73
	Paying Taxes – time to comply (Hours/yr.): Labor taxes	13	10	10	10	85	60
	Post-Filing Index (VAT and CIT corrections)	72	72	72	72	61	57
	Time to comply with VAT refund (hours)	5	5	5	5	14.9	19.6
	Time to obtain VAT refund (weeks)	21	21	21	21	41.5	28.2
	Number of payments per year	5	5	5	5	23	21
	Trading Across Borders Rank	41	42	45	47	–	–

Observations	Singapore has one of the best regulatory systems in the world for paying taxes and for enforcing contracts. In 2019, dealing with construction permits was facilitated (improvement of the risk-based approach to inspections, improvement of the public access to soil information, and rationalization of the process of obtaining a building permit). Improvements to the paying taxes rank are attributed to the introduction of an online payment and filing system.

	Observations
Taxpayer rights and obligations *(refer Note 14)*	IRAS does not have a formally defined set of taxpayers' rights, but does publish service levels. IRAS also has internal and external complaints channels. Complaint levels are very low. An advance ruling system is available, but public binding rulings are not issued. Taxpayers have the right to challenge assessments, with internal administrative and judicial review mechanisms, but no alternative dispute resolution or taxpayer ombudsman.

	Observations
Corruption Perception Index Trends *(refer Note 15)*	In 2014, Singapore's CPI score was 84 out of 100, improving to 85 in 2019. This places Singapore at a ranking of 4th out of 180 countries.

THAILAND

AT A GLANCE

Measure	2014	2015	2016	2017	2018	2019
Total Population (million)	68.438	68.714	68.971	69.209	69.428	69.625
Age profile						
0–14	18.23	17.97	17.65	17.35	17.09	16.82
15–64	71.57	71.42	71.35	71.21	71.01	70.77
65+	10.21	10.60	11.01	11.44	11.90	12.41
Literacy level (% of population)		...	92.87	...	...	93.77
Urbanization (%)						
Urban Population	46.94	47.69	48.45	49.20	49.95	50.70
Rural Population	53.06	52.31	51.55	50.80	50.05	49.30
Employment to Population	69.28	68.63	67.60	66.73	67.07	66.82
Agriculture	33.44	32.28	31.16	31.46	32.14	31.61
Industry	23.52	23.68	23.68	22.85	22.81	22.63
Services	43.04	44.04	45.16	45.69	45.06	45.75

Demographic Overview *(refer Note 1)*

Industrialization Indices	2012	2013	2014	ASEAN Ave.	World Ave.
Industrialization Intensity Index	0.69	0.68	0.68	0.54	0.65
Share of Medium & High Tech	0.47	0.47	0.5	0.44	
Main Economic Sectors	Thailand's economy is heavily based on agriculture, which contributes 8.1% of the GDP and employs 30.4% of the active population. The country is the largest producer of rubber in the world and one of the leading producers and exporters of rice; it also grows sugar, corn, jute, cotton, and tobacco as major crops.				

Trends in Income and Inequality *(refer Note 1)*

Measure	2014	2015	2016	2017	2018	2019	ASEAN Ave.
Income Index	0.748	0.751	0.757	0.762	0.768	...	0.734
Inequality in Income (%)	34	34	23.8	23.8	23.8	...	20.35
GNI per Capita	14,101	14,466	14,966	15,548	16,129	...	23,069
Human Development Rank	77/189						

Take-up of Technology *(refer Note 2)*

Measure	Description
E-commerce trends	85% visited an online store and 80% made a purchase.
Internet coverage and availability	82% use internet and 74% use social media. Internet speeds increased by over 40% in 2019. Mobile Connectivity Index = 68.3 (2nd in the region).
Take-up of internet and mobile banking	74% have mobile banking and 47% made mobile payments.
Take-up of e-filing	40% of CIT returns and 77% of PIT returns are filed electronically.

THAILAND:
EMPLOYMENT BY SECTOR

- Employment to population ratio, 15+, total (%)
- Employment in agriculture (% of total employment)
- Employment in industry (% of total employment)
- Employment in services (% of total employment)

THAILAND:
TAKE-UP OF TECHNOLOGY

- Individuals using the internet (% of population)
- Fixed broadband subscriptions (in millions)
- Fixed broadband subscriptions (per 100 people)

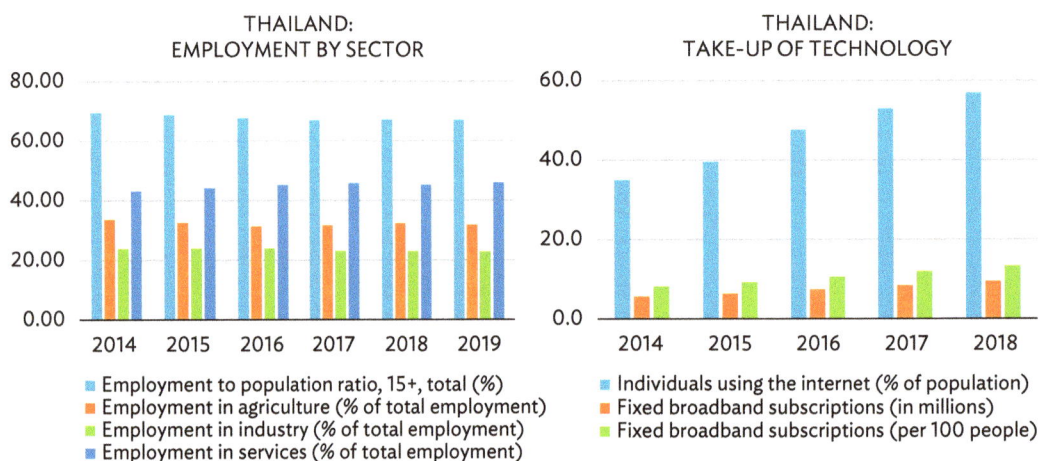

PRODUCTION STRUCTURE

	Region	Exports ($ million)				
		2014	2015	2016	2017	2018
Exports - Overall (refer Note 3)	Thailand	286,315	282,181	275,776	282,022	310,394
	SEA	1,606,681	1,630,770	1,508,470	1,498,265	1,676,341
	US	2,273,428	2,371,704	2,266,800	2,220,609	2,356,726
Main sector 1 Machinery and Transport Equipment	Thailand	95,396	97,868	94,587	96,711	105,565
	SEA	470,011	483,417	476,133	478,746	538,499
	US	639,053	665,625	647,286	627,333	645,863
Main sector 2 Office and Telecom Equipment	Thailand	35,176	35,836	34,620	33,450	37,302
	SEA	284,959	293,811	291,494	289,701	325,385
	US	140,971	145,946	142,274	140,473	145,475
	Region	Imports ($ million)				
		2014	2015	2016	2017	2018
Imports - Overall (refer Note 3)	Thailand	254,633	229,553	221,169	247,430	285,262
	SEA	1,506,926	1,372,220	1,354,024	1,525,565	1,701,449
	US	2,879,362	2,786,645	2,739,415	2,932,062	3,148,464
Main sector 1 Machinery and Transport Equipment	Thailand	79,709	76,282	76,275	82,504	86,629
	SEA	462,822	456,028	462,749	520,106	576,718
	US	956,716	989,206	969,943	1,040,707	1,103,063
Main sector 2 Fuels	Thailand	48,079	30,181	24,609	31,045	42,041
	SEA	268,802	160,708	131,975	182,212	226,604
	US	358,193	200,458	163,065	203,934	241,513
Observations	Exports grew by 9.1% in 2018, compared with a regional average growth of 10.1%. Imports grew by 13.3% in 2018, compared with a regional average growth of 10.3%. The top exports are office machine parts, cars, integrated circuits, delivery trucks, and vehicle parts. The top imports are crude petroleum, integrated circuits, gold, petroleum gas, and vehicle parts.					

	Sector	2014	2015	2016	2017	2018
Flows of Inward Foreign Direct Investment (FDI) to ASEAN Sourced from Thailand, by Economic Sectors ($ million) (refer Note 4)	Agriculture, forestry, and fishing	10.73	29.02	27.32	47.46	29.78
	Mining and quarrying	201.39	269.84	547.58	466.77	166.64
	Manufacturing	244.47	110.96	567.05	524.08	635.02
	Electricity, gas, steam, and air conditioning supply	4.27	26.49	15.77	170.50	78.79
	Water supply; sewerage, waste management and remediation activities	0.28	0.11	7.36	7.93	2.18
	Construction	3.99	11.64	11.44	18.32	42.96
	Wholesale and retail trade; repair of motor vehicles and motorcycles	(190.27)	61.47	329.13	432.40	541.55
	Transportation and storage	63.78	69.12	75.88	37.47	8.72
	Accommodation and food service activities	4.83	5.34	12.02	49.23	8.52
	Information and communication	(0.62)	0.12	7.52	11.11	30.02
	Financial and insurance activities	3,052.80	(96.74)	660.62	(164.92)	623.87
	Real estate activities	12.72	12.46	26.11	46.46	160.71
	Professional, scientific, and technical activities	0.66	6.12	10.36	(2.01)	23.31
	Administrative and support service activities	1.37	0.52	2.63	0.88	5.04
	Education	0.40	1.96	2.14	0.91	0.85
	Human health and social work activities	1.87	8.74	12.00	42.32	55.83
	Arts, entertainment, and recreation	(0.38)	0.02	4.94	0.29	10.65
	Other services activities	68.15	(10.69)	43.28	5.82	109.54
	Unspecified activity	83.42	552.07	99.56	0.00	
	TOTAL activities	**3,598.46**	**1,084.66**	**2,574.09**	**1,712.64**	**2,547.87**
IMF Article IV	Net FDI inflows (in percent of GDP)	1.2	2.2	0.7	1.8	2.6
	Net Direct Investment (FDI) – in $ billion	(0.8)	3.9	(10.6)	(7.3)	(6.6)

General Observations on FDI	Thailand is one of the major FDI destinations in SEA, but FDI decreased in 2019. This was, in part, the result of a general drop in investment in ASEAN member states. However, despite a large export sector, Thailand's competitiveness has deteriorated due to low productivity growth and high wages relative to the region. As a result, multinational Thai firms have increased investment abroad, particularly in Cambodia, the Lao PDR, and Viet Nam, to take advantage of lower labor costs and access to global supply chains. The profitability of small firms and their willingness to invest domestically have declined in the face of increasing global competition. These factors have offset robust FDI inflows. Japan and Singapore are the largest investors and account for slightly more than half of FDI inflows. Hong Kong, China; the Netherlands; Germany; Mauritius; and the UK are also among the major investors. Manufacturing and financial and insurance activities attract nearly 70% of all FDI inflows. Investments in real estate, commerce, and information and communication technology are also important. Thailand offers incentives to invest in advanced technologies, innovative activities and research and development through the Investment Promotion Act, and the Eastern Economic Corridor (EEC) Act, which offers tax subsidies, right to land ownership, and ease of issuing of visas to investors in this zone.

	Component Sector	2014	2015	2016	2017	2018	ASEAN Ave.	US 2018
Industry Structure: GDP by type of expenditure (refer Note 5)	Gross domestic product (GDP)	100.0	100.0	100.0	100.0	100.0	100	100
	Final consumption expenditure	69.3	68.1	66.8	65.1	64.9	68.04	87
	Household consumption expenditure (including NPISH)	52.4	51.0	49.8	48.7	48.7	54	70
	General government final consumption expenditure	16.9	17.1	16.9	16.4	16.2	14.51	17
	Gross capital formation	**23.9**	**22.4**	**20.9**	**22.8**	**25.0**	**28.58**	**18**
	Gross fixed capital formation	24.7	24.5	23.8	23.2	22.8	27.74	17
	Changes in inventories	(0.7)	(2.2)	(2.8)	(0.3)	2.2	1.04	1
	Exports of goods and services	69.3	68.7	68.4	68.2	66.8	63.65	13
	Imports of goods and services	(62.5)	(57.2)	(53.6)	(54.3)	(56.5)	(61.12)	18
	Total value added	**100.0**	**100.0**	**100.0**	**100.0**	**100.0**	**100**	**100**
Observations	Capital formation is a lead indicator of economic performance and is below regional averages. Tax outcomes flowing from investment may be significantly impacted by tax incentives.							

NPISH = nonprofit institutions serving households.

	Component Sector	2014	2015	2016	2017	2018	ASEAN Ave.	US 2018
Industry Structure: Value Add by kind of economic activity ($ million) (refer Note 5)	Agriculture, hunting, forestry, and fishing	10.1	8.9	8.4	8.3	8.3	12.11	167
	Industry	36.8	36.2	35.7	35.2	35.6	38.84	1,512
	Mining, manufacturing, and utilities	34.2	33.4	32.9	32.7	33.0	32	673
	Manufacturing	27.6	27.4	27.2	27.2	27.4	17.29	2,321
	Construction	2.5	2.8	2.8	2.6	2.6	6.99	839
	Services	53.1	54.9	55.9	56.5	56.1	49.05	2,579
	Wholesale, retail trade, restaurants, and hotels	17.5	18.7	19.8	20.8	22.5	16.75	2,338
	Transport, storage, and communications	7.7	8.1	8.0	8.0	7.6	7.02	658
	Other activities	27.9	28.2	28.0	27.6	26.0	25.28	437
Observations	Manufacturing and services sectors are well above the regional averages.							

TAX SYSTEM AND TAX ADMINISTRATION DESIGN FEATURES

Tax Rates, Thresholds, and Overall Revenue Contribution (see Note 6)

| Taxes | Rates of Tax (%) /1 | | Thresholds | | Share (%) of Total Taxes (latest year) |
	Basic/ Standard	Other	Local Currency	$	
CIT /2	20%	20% - Branch Profits Tax			35.3%
PIT /3	5%–35%	Capital gains taxed at marginal rate	B300,000	$3,200	
VAT/ GST /4	7/10%	0% on exported Goods & Services	B1.8 million	$57,700	
WHT - Div	10/10/10%	Company/Individual/Nonresident			56.9%
WHT - Int	1/15/15%	Company/Individual/Nonresident			
WHT - Roy	3/5–35/15%	Company/Individual/Nonresident			
WHT-Ser Fee	3/5–35/15%	Company/Individual/Nonresident			
Inheritance	10%	5% on gifts	> B100,000	> $1,000	
SBT /5	3%				
Excise	Specific Rates/ Ad Valorem	Alcohol and tobacco/Petroleum products & vehicles.			
SSC	5%	Paid by both employee and employer	Capped		
CGT /6	20%	Taxed as ordinary income/loss			
*Subnational taxes / 7	0.01–0.1% 0.02–0.1% 0.3–0.7%	Agricultural land Residential land Commercial land			19.3% of general government revenue and 4.1% of GDP (2016)
Overview of Tax Incentives	Tax holidays of 3–8 years are available for business activities promoted by the board of investment. Reduced corporate tax rates apply to International Business Centers receiving certain qualifying income (such as management, technical support, and financial management services), qualifying royalties (on R&D and innovation) received from associated entities.				

* Thailand has over 2,500 government bodies across two levels of subnational government.

/1. For FY 2020, unless otherwise indicated. /2. Small and medium-sized limited companies are subject to lower progressive rates. /3. Withheld by employer. /4. Reduced to 7% until September 2020. In July 2020, Thailand introduced a bill to impose VAT on foreign suppliers of digital services at a rate of 7%. The tax will apply to foreign companies that earn > B1.8 million per year from provision of services in Thailand (https://www.reuters.com/article/us-thailand-tax-digital/thailand-proposes-to-tax-foreign-internet-companies-idUSKBN23G1K0#:~:text=The%20Thai%20bill%2C%20which%20still,spokeswoman%20Ratchada%20Thanadirek%20told%20reporters). /5. Special Business Tax applies to individuals and companies on banking and similar transactions, transfer of property, and some other business income. /6. Capital losses may be offset against ordinary income. /7. Subnational taxes are administered by provincial, district, and local governments, but the rates are set at a national level. The Land Construction Act prescribes rates and specifies exemptions.

Sources: IMF Art. IV reports; Deloitte Country Tax Profiles; OECD Statistics.

Tax Administration Setup and Performance

Subject Area	Aspect	Features and Performance		Overall Rating
Responsibilities of tax body	Main taxes collected	PIT, CIT, and VAT/GST		Extensive – collect over 80% of revenue
	Other major roles	The Thai Revenue Department (TRD) is a single directorate within the ministry. Provides advice and proposes tax policies to the minister. The Fiscal Policy Office also proposes tax policy.		
Tax body Autonomy	Budget flexibility, organization design	Has some level of budget and human resource management flexibility but must work within the ministry and public service wide framework.		Medium
	Human resource management			
Digital services in tax administration	E-filing	**Rate (2017)**	**Comments**	Medium to high
	– CIT	39%	CIT e-filing is relatively low by regional standards. E-payment is made online. No mobile payment app was available in 2017. PIT may now be paid via mobile app. using an e-invoice QR code provided by TRD.	
	– PIT	77%		
	– VAT/GST	50%		
	E-payment	50%		
	E-services (including mobile applications)	TRD provides a wide range of e-services, including tools and calculators, access to an integrated taxpayer account, a digital mailbox, and a mobile app.		

	Measure	Country Performance						ASEAN Ave.	OECD Ave. 2018
		2014	2015	2016	2017	2018	2019		
Tax system design *(refer Note 7)*	Tax reliance ratio	86.7	85.2	84.7	84.9	84.5	78.0	66.9	63.8
	Tax mix	43.9	42.3	40.9	39.9	40.8	35.3	39.92	33.7
	Tax ratio	17.2	17.7	17.2	16.6	16.7	16.7	14	34.3
	CIT productivity	0.244	0.228	0.210	0.200	0.213	0.295	0.26	
	VAT productivity	0.5	0.512	0.500	0.492	0.485	0.499	0.43	
	Consolidation of tax collection and administration	Subnational revenue accounts for 4.1% of GDP. The tax reliance ratio remains relatively high by regional standards, despite a sustained decline in recent years.							
Observations	Legislation introduced in late 2019 increased and rationalized the taxing powers of subnational governments. Additional revenue should be generated from this broadening of the subnational tax base, but implementation capacities are unknown. In addition, Thailand has a rather complex local government structure with 76 provinces, and 878 districts and local governments so consistent implementation is likely to be a challenge.								

	Measure	Country Performance
Tax administration processes *(refer Note 8)*	Tax administration efficiency and effectiveness (Operating expenditure as a proportion of net revenue collected)	0.90% (in 2015) - A figure between 0.5% and 1% is considered efficient.
	No. of labor force members/ tax body FTE	Around 2,200 workers per tax officer.
	No. of citizens/ tax body FTE	Almost 4,000 citizens per tax officer.
	Proportion of staff assigned to support functions	16% of staff are assigned to support functions. Regional average = 29%

REVENUE

	Measure	Country Performance						ASEAN Ave.	Asia and Pacific Ave.	OECD Ave. 2018
		2014	2015	2016	2017	2018	2019*			
Tax revenue collection performance *(all levels of government)* *(refer Note 9)*	Tax/GDP (%) - all	17.2	17.7	17.2	16.6	16.7	16.7	14.03	20.0	34.3
	Taxes on income & profits/GDP (%)	6.7	6.6	6.2	5.9	5.9	5.9	5.35	8.1	11.6
	Taxes on goods and services/GDP (%)	9.3	10.0	9.9	9.5	9.4	9.5	6	10.1	10.9
	Overall tax revenue trend	Tax-to-GDP ratio is healthy by regional standards, although authorities and the IMF have highlighted a need to lift tax to GDP to support growing social welfare demands. There may be scope to strengthen VAT to raise ratios closer to regional levels.								

(*) projected/provisional collections.

BROADENING THE TAX BASE

	Measure	Country Performance
Countering Tax Avoidance and Evasion *(refer Note 10)*	Effective anti-avoidance rules	Transfer pricing and reporting rules apply and are consistent with the OECD guidance. There are no specific or general anti-avoidance rules and no economic substance test, although economic substance may be a factor considered by authorities.
	Thin capitalization and controlled foreign corporation rules	There are no specific thin capitalization rules, but interest may be disallowed if it is not charged at an arms-length rate, is not for a profit-making purpose, or does not relate to a business operation.
	Findings from OECD Forum on Harmful Tax Practices (FHTP)	International headquarters and treasury center were reviewed: Non-IP: Abolished; IP: Abolished. No grandfathering provided. Regional operating headquarters 1 was reviewed: IP: Abolished. No grandfathering provided. Regional operating headquarters 2 was reviewed: Non-IP: Abolished IP: Abolished. No grandfathering provided. International trade center was abolished. No grandfathering provided. International business center was reviewed: Non-IP: Not harmful IP: Not harmful. New regime, designed in compliance with FHTP standards.
	A focus on HNWI and professions	None reported.
	Dealing with the shadow economy	The shadow economy in Thailand is estimated to be around 43% of GDP, which is the highest in the region.

Measure		Country Status
Member of Global Forum on Transparency & Exchange of Information		Yes
Exchange of Information on Request Ratings	Round 1	Not reviewed
	Round 2	Scheduled 2021
Signatory to the Multilateral Convention on Mutual Assistance in Tax Matters		Yes
Commitment to Automatic Exchange of Information		2023
Implementation of Common Reporting Standard (CRS) and Multilateral Competent Authority Agreement		Not applicable
Convention on Mutual Administrative Assistance in tax matters		No
Member of Base Erosion and Profit Shifting Inclusive Framework		Yes
Existence of harmful tax regimes (Action 5)		Not harmful (no harmful regime exists)
Exchange of information on tax rulings (Action 5)		Reviewed/recommendations made
CbC – Domestic law (Action 13)		Update on status pending
CbC – Information exchange network (Action 13)		CbC MCAA not signed
Effective dispute resolution (Action 14)		Review scheduled
Signatory to the Multilateral Convention to Implement Treaty Related Measures to Prevent BEPS (Action 6)		Reviewed in 2018 and 2019, no recommendation. 2020 review ongoing.
Network of income tax treaties for avoidance of double taxation		61

The left spanning cell reads: **Countering International Tax Avoidance and Evasion and International Cooperation** *(refer Note 11)*

RESPONSIVE TAX ADMINISTRATION

Measure	Country Status
% responding tax regime has become more complicated over prior 3 years	19%
% responding tax regime has been less consistently administered over prior 3 years	17%
% responding tax compliance and reporting rules are "complicated" or "very complicated"	32.6%
Perceived fairness in tax audits	Neutral
Perceived confidence in appeal system	Low
Taxpayer relationship with authorities	Neutral
Perceived main priority areas for reform	Tax officer training and adoption of the BEPS recommendations

The left spanning cell reads: **Important findings from Deloitte's 2017 Tax Complexity Survey** *(refer Note 12)*

	Measure	Country Ranking				World Ave.	Asia and Pacific Ave.
		2017	2018	2019	2020		
Compliance/ Regulatory Burden Indicators *(as reported in the Doing Business Series)* *(refer Note 13)*	Ease of Doing Business Indicator Ranking (Ranking out of 190 countries)	26	27	27	21	–	–
	Paying Taxes Indicator (Ranking out of 190 countries)	109	67	59	68	–	–
	Paying Taxes – time to comply (Hours/yr.): (all)	262	262	229	229	234	192
	Paying Taxes – time to comply (Hours/yr.): (CIT)	156	156	123	123	59	59
	Paying Taxes – time to comply (Hours/yr.): (VAT)	58	58	58	58	90	73
	Paying Taxes – time to comply (Hours/yr.): Labor taxes	48	48	48	48	85	60
	Post-Filing Index (VAT and CIT corrections)	42.6	73.4	73.4	73.4	61	57
	Time to comply with VAT refund (hours)	16	16	16	16	14.9	19.6
	Time to obtain VAT refund (weeks)	33	33	33	33	41.5	28.2
	Number of payments per year	21	21	21	21	23	21
	Trading Across Borders Rank	56	57	59	62	–	–
Observations	Thailand is among the countries with the most reforms in business regulation over the past few years, which have facilitated the setting-up processes and reduced the time to start a business from 29 days to 6 days. The rights of borrowers and creditors have been strengthened as well as the system of land administration. The country has taken steps to clarify corporate governance, ownership, and control structures by enacting legislation requiring companies to appoint independent members of the board of directors and to establish an audit committee.						

	Observations
Taxpayer rights and obligations *(refer Note 14)*	Thailand has a formally defined set of taxpayer rights (not legislated) and an internal complaints mechanism. Taxpayers may challenge assessments and seek internal, administrative, and judicial reviews. An alternative dispute resolution mechanism is also available. There is no taxpayer ombudsman.

	Observations
Corruption Perception Index Trends *(refer Note 15)*	In 2014, Thailand's CPI score was 36 out of 100 and has remained the same through 2019. This ranks Thailand at 101st out of 180 countries. Thailand recently approved a new law covering all stages of the procurement cycle. This provides a good framework for controlling costs in public investment projects, and is strong on governance and anti-corruption, including an integrity pact. The IMF recommends strengthening the operational aspects of the procurement law, including limiting common members across various subcommittees and strengthening the complaints process to include both actual and potential bidders. The authorities emphasized that their anti-corruption framework has been strengthened in recent years. Their overarching goals are: create a society that does not tolerate corruption; promote political will to fight corruption; deter corruption in public policy; develop proactive corruption prevention systems; reform corruption suppression mechanisms and processes; and improve Thailand's corruption perception index (CPI). The Organic Act on Anti-Corruption that was adopted in 2018 aims to improve the capacity and effectiveness of Thailand's anti-corruption agency to counter corruption; comply with Thailand's mandatory international obligations as a state party to the United Nations Convention against Corruption; and comply with international standards and best practices (OECD Anti-Bribery Convention).

TIMOR-LESTE

AT A GLANCE

Measure	2014	2015	2016	2017	2018	2019
Total Population (million)	1,174,331	1,196,302	1,219,288	1,243,261	1,267,972	...
Age profile						
0–14	40.08	39.48	38.86	38.30	37.78	...
15–64	55.54	56.12	56.74	57.33	57.90	...
65+	4.36	4.38	4.39	4.35	4.31	...
Literacy level (% of population)	...	...	...	...	68.07	
Urbanization (%)						
Urban Population	29.13	29.49	29.85	30.21	30.58	...
Rural Population	70.87	70.51	70.15	69.79	69.42	...
Employment to Population	64.57	63.61	63.58	64.28	64.37	64.27
Agriculture	49.25	47.42	46.96	46.45	45.47	44.48
Industry	8.39	10.02	9.85	9.36	9.49	9.66
Services	42.35	42.55	43.17	44.18	45.02	45.85

Industrialization Indices	2012	2013	2014	ASEAN Ave.	World Ave.
Industrialization Intensity Index	...	...	...	0.54	0.65
Share of Medium & High Tech	...	...	...	0.44	
Main Economic Sectors	Timor-Leste's economy is dependent on the extraction of oil reserves from the Timor Sea which accounts for 80% of GDP. These funds have enabled significant investment in core services and infrastructure, especially related to roads and electricity. However, oil revenue from active fields are expected to end in 2022, although other deposits are available for development.				

Demographic Overview *(refer Note 1)*

Measure	2014	2015	2016	2017	2018	2019	ASEAN Ave.
Income Index	0.61	0.667	0.668	0.651	0.653		0.734
Inequality in Income (%)	17.8	17.8	17.8	13.6	13.6		20.35
GNI per Capita	5,666	8,284	8,350	7,434	7,527		23,069
Human Development Rank	131/189						

Trends in Income and Inequality *(refer Note 1)*

Measure	Description
E-commerce trends	No data available.
Internet coverage and availability	42% use the internet and use social media. Internet usage increased by 37% in 2019. Mobile Connectivity Index = 37.4 (Ranking 11th in the region)
Take-up of internet and mobile banking	The first electronic banking system was introduced in 2018 and is expected to be integrated with other regional payment systems in the near future.
Take-up of e-filing	No data available.

Take-up of Technology *(refer Note 2)*

TIMOR-LESTE:
EMPLOYMENT BY SECTOR

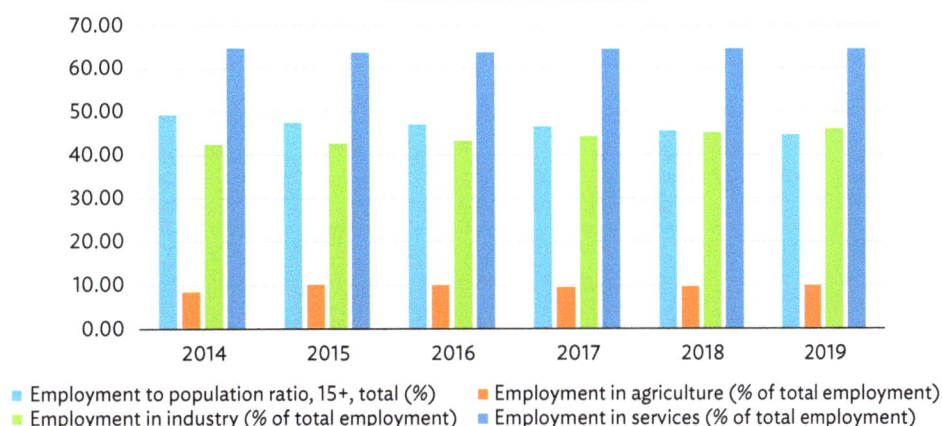

- Employment to population ratio, 15+, total (%)
- Employment in agriculture (% of total employment)
- Employment in industry (% of total employment)
- Employment in services (% of total employment)

PRODUCTION STRUCTURE

		Exports ($ million)				
	Region	2014	2015	2016	2017	2018
Exports - Overall (refer Note 3)	Timor-Leste	78	66	49	52	38
	SEA	1,606,681	1,630,770	1,508,470	1,498,265	1,676,341
	US	2,273,428	2,371,704	2,266,800	2,220,609	2,356,726
Main sector 1 Fuels	Timor-Leste	...	...	...	...	39.8
	SEA	220,922	207,952	135,574	109,869	140,057
	US	148,866	156,185	104,639	93,753	139,261
Main sector 2 Machinery and Food	Timor-Leste	...	...	...	...	20.47
	SEA	124,771	134,219	122,774	125,888	144,833
	US	141,891	149,139	132,962	135,280	137,279
		Imports ($ million)				
	Region	2014	2015	2016	2017	2018
Imports - Overall (refer Note 3)	Timor-Leste	1,131	907	938	871	945
	SEA	1,506,926	1,372,220	1,354,024	1,525,565	1,701,449
	US	2,879,362	2,786,645	2,739,415	2,932,062	3,148,464
Main sector 1 Food	Timor-Leste	...	...	151	178	191
	SEA	83,402	80,109	85,591	92,665	98,492
	US	133,230	134,912	137,511	146,441	155,557
Main sector 2 Machinery and Transport Equipment	Timor-Leste	...	...	181	145	131
	SEA	462,822	456,028	462,749	520,106	576,718
	US	956,716	989,206	969,943	1,040,707	1,103,063
Observations	Exports declined by 36.8% in 2018, compared with a regional average growth of 10.1%. Imports grew by 7.8% in 2018, compared with a regional average growth of 10.3%. The top exports are crude petroleum, coffee, and raw materials for food manufacture. The top imports are rice, special-purpose ships, cars, and cement.					

	Sector	2014	2015	2016	2017	2018
IMF Article IV (refer Note 4)	Net FDI inflows (in percent of GDP)	2.3	2.7	0.3	0.4	3.1
	Net Direct Investment (FDI) – in $ million	...	30	7	7	30
General Observations on FDI	In 2016–2017, FDI hit the lowest level in 10 years, having all but dried up (against a backdrop of political and economic uncertainty). Some projects that were slow to get started in 2017, such as the new Tibar Bay container port development, picked up in 2018, while other projects, such as the new Hilton hotel, continued. Together with ongoing smaller-scale investments, particularly in the Dili area, this means that inward investment levels recovered.					

	Component Sector	2014	2015	2016	2017	2018	ASEAN Ave.	US 2018
Industry Structure: GDP by type of expenditure (refer Note 5)	Gross domestic product (GDP)	100.0	100.0	100.0	100.0	100.0	100	100
	Final consumption expenditure	46.7	60.4	76.6	76.3	71.1	68.04	87
	Household consumption expenditure (including NPISH)	23.2	30.1	40.2	41.2	37.1	54	70
	General government final consumption expenditure	23.5	30.3	36.4	35.2	34.0	14.51	17
	Gross capital formation	**16.5**	**19.2**	**26.3**	**22.5**	**22.7**	**28.58**	**18**
	Gross fixed capital formation	15.8	18.5	25.3	21.4	21.7	27.74	17
	Changes in inventories	0.7	0.7	1.0	1.0	0.9	1.04	1
	Exports of goods and services	96.3	75.1	57.9	61.1	64.7	63.65	13
	Imports of goods and services	(59.5)	(54.7)	(60.8)	(59.9)	(58.5)	(61.12)	18
	Total value added	**100.0**	**100.0**	**100.0**	**100.0**	**100.0**	**100**	**100**
Observations	Capital formation is a lead indicator of economic performance and is well below regional averages. Tax outcomes flowing from investment may be significantly impacted by tax incentives.							

	Component Sector	2014	2015	2016	2017	2018	ASEAN Ave.	US 2018
Industry Structure: Value Add by kind of economic activity ($ million) (refer Note 5)	Agriculture, hunting, forestry, and fishing	7.3	8.9	10.8	10.4	10.0	12.11	167
	Industry	69.9	57.9	45.4	45.6	49.6	38.84	1,512
	Mining, manufacturing, and utilities	64.2	48.9	33.6	36.7	39.7	32	673
	Manufacturing	0.3	0.5	0.7	1.0	0.7	17.29	2,321
	Construction	5.7	9.0	11.9	8.9	9.9	6.99	839
	Services	22.7	33.2	43.8	44.0	40.3	49.05	2,579
	Wholesale, retail trade, restaurants, and hotels	6.2	9.5	12.9	11.8	11.4	16.75	2,338
	Transport, storage, and communications	0.5	1.2	1.7	1.6	1.5	7.02	658
	Other activities	16.0	22.5	29.2	30.6	27.4	25.28	437
Observations	Timor-Leste is one of the most oil-dependent economies in the world, so declining value add from this sector raises material concerns, particularly as other sectors are relatively flat.							

TAX SYSTEM AND TAX ADMINISTRATION DESIGN FEATURES

Tax Rates, Thresholds, and Overall Revenue Contribution (see Note 6)

| Taxes | Rates of Tax (%) /1 | | Thresholds | | Share (%) of Total Taxes (latest year) |
	Basic/ Standard	Other	Local Currency	$	
CIT /2	10%	10% – Branch Tax			
PIT /3	10%	On wages	$500/month	$500/month	
PIT	10%	Other than wages	$6,000 per annum	$6,000 per annum	
Sales Tax /3	2.5%	On Imported goods			
Sales Tax /4	5%	On certain services	$500/month	$500/month	
WHT /5	10%	Royalties and rent-land/buildings			
WHT	2%	Construction and building	No threshold		
WHT	4%	Construction consulting	No threshold		
WHT	2.64%	Air and sea transport	No threshold		
WHT	4.5%	Mining and mining support	No threshold		
WHT	10%	Payments to nonresidents	No threshold		
Excise	Various rates on imported and domestically manufactured goods				
SSC	6/4%	Employer/employee			
CGT	10%				
Overview of Tax Incentives	A company investing in Timor-Leste may be eligible to apply for a private investor certificate under the private investor laws. This investor certificate provides exemption from income tax and indirect taxes for the first 5/8/10 years, depending on the location of the investment.				

Note that Timor-Leste has 455 government bodies across two levels of subnational government. Figures are not available on revenue share.

/1. For FY 2020, unless otherwise indicated. /2. Petroleum operations are subject to different tax rules under four specific petroleum tax regimes. /3. and /4. No VAT/GST. Services subject to Sales Tax include certain hotels, restaurants, bars, and telecommunications. /5. The obligation for wage income tax rests with the employer. /4. Certain income items subject to final WHT are excluded from taxable income.

Sources: IMF Art. IV reports; Deloitte Country Tax Profiles; OECD Statistics.

Tax Administration Setup and Performance

Subject Area	Aspect	Features and Performance	Overall Rating
Responsibilities of tax body	Main taxes collected	Customs, petroleum revenues, and domestic revenues	Broad – responsible for all government revenues.
	Other major roles	Revenues, customs, and excises	
Tax body Autonomy	Budget flexibility, organization design	Directorate General of Revenue and Customs (DGRC) is a single directorate within the Ministry of Finance. The mission of the DGRC is to ensure general guidance and integrated coordination for all Ministry services in Revenue and Customs.	Low to Medium – Limited autonomy for structure and HRM
	Human resource management		

Digital services in tax administration	E-filing	Rate (2017)	Comments	
	- CIT		E-payments can be made via Electronic Funds Transfer (EFT) only. E-filing does not appear to be offered.	Low
	- PIT			
	- VAT/GST			
	E-payment			
	E-services (including mobile applications)		An informative website is available for each of the revenue streams administered.	

	Measure	Country Performance						ASEAN Ave.	OECD Ave. 2018
		2014	2015	2016	2017	2018	2019		
Tax system design (refer Note 7)	Tax reliance ratio	36.3	38.8	35.5	26.2	32.5	31.7	66.9	63.8
	Tax mix	90.9	88.6	81.3	64.9	73.4	76.9	39.92	33.7
	Tax ratio	23.24	22.49	18.60	9.89	12.89	14.31	14	34.3
	CIT productivity	...	0.020	0.027	0.572	0.869	1.036	0.26	
	VAT productivity	...	0.036	0.044	0.077	0.083	0.097	0.43	
	Consolidation of tax collection and administration	High level of consolidation with all government revenue streams administered within a single directorate of the Ministry of Finance (figures cited above only relate to the domestic taxes branch of DGRC).							
Observations	Direct taxes dominate as limited indirect taxes are imposed. The planned VAT will rebalance this position once introduced.								

	Measure	Country Performance
Tax administration processes (refer Note 8)	Tax administration efficiency and effectiveness (Operating expenditure as a proportion of net revenue collected)	Data are not available for Timor-Leste.
	No. of labor force members/ tax body FTE	
	No. of citizens/ tax body FTE	
	Proportion of staff assigned to support functions	

REVENUE

<table>
<tr><td rowspan="2" colspan="2"></td><td colspan="7">Country Performance</td><td rowspan="2">ASEAN Ave.</td><td rowspan="2">Asia and Pacific Ave.</td><td rowspan="2">OECD Ave. 2018</td></tr>
<tr><td>Measure</td><td>2014</td><td>2015</td><td>2016</td><td>2017</td><td>2018</td><td>2019*</td></tr>
<tr><td rowspan="4">Tax revenue collection performance (all levels of government) (refer Note 9)</td><td>Tax/GDP (%) - all</td><td>23.24</td><td>22.49</td><td>18.60</td><td>9.89</td><td>12.89</td><td>14.31</td><td>14.03</td><td>20.0</td><td>34.3</td></tr>
<tr><td>Taxes on income & profits/GDP (%)</td><td>23.24</td><td>22.49</td><td>18.60</td><td>9.89</td><td>12.89</td><td>14.31</td><td>5.35</td><td>8.1</td><td>11.6</td></tr>
<tr><td>Taxes on goods & services/GDP (%)</td><td>1.19</td><td>2.23</td><td>3.06</td><td>2.90</td><td>2.77</td><td>2.56</td><td>6</td><td>10.1</td><td>10.9</td></tr>
<tr><td>Overall tax revenue trend</td><td colspan="9">Tax-to-GDP ratio is declining due to reduced oil and gas revenue and reduced domestic taxes resulting from recent political and economic instability.</td></tr>
</table>

(*) projected/provisional collections.

BROADENING THE TAX BASE

Measure	Country Performance
Effective anti-avoidance rules	There are no general or specific anti-avoidance rules and no transfer pricing regime.
Thin capitalization and controlled foreign corporation rules	There are not thin capitalization rules, interest deduction limitations, anti-hybrid, or CFC rules.
Findings from OECD Forum on Harmful Tax Practices (FHTP)	None reported.
A focus on HNWI and professions	None reported.
Dealing with the shadow economy	No data available.

Countering Tax Avoidance and Evasion (refer Note 10)

Measure	Country Status
Member of Global Forum on Transparency & Exchange of Information	Timor-Leste is not a signatory.
Exchange of Information on Request Ratings	
Signatory to the Multilateral Convention on Mutual Assistance in Tax Matters	
Commitment to Automatic Exchange of Information	
Implementation of Common Reporting Standard (CRS) and Multilateral Competent Authority Agreement	
Convention on Mutual Administrative Assistance in tax matters	
Member of Base Erosion and Profit Shifting Inclusive Framework	
Existence of harmful tax regimes (Action 5)	
Exchange of information on tax rulings (Action 5)	
CbC – Domestic law (Action 13)	
CbC – Information exchange network (Action 13)	
Effective dispute resolution (Action 14)	
Signatory to the Multilateral Convention to Implement Treaty Related Measures to Prevent BEPS (Action 6)	
Network of income tax treaties for avoidance of double taxation	1 – with Portugal. A Maritime Boundary treaty exists with Australia (replaced the Joint Petroleum Area)

Countering International Tax Avoidance and Evasion and International Cooperation (refer Note 11)

RESPONSIVE TAX ADMINISTRATION

Important findings from Deloitte's 2017 Tax Complexity Survey *(refer Note 12)*	% responding tax regime has become more complicated over prior 3 years	Timor-Leste was not surveyed.
	% responding tax regime has been less consistently administered over prior 3 years	
	% responding tax compliance and reporting rules are "complicated" or "very complicated"	
	Perceived fairness in tax audits	
	Perceived confidence in appeal system	
	Taxpayer relationship with authorities	
	Perceived main priority areas for reform	

	Measure	Country Ranking				World Ave.	Asia and Pacific Ave.
		2017	2018	2019	2020		
Compliance/ Regulatory Burden Indicators *(as reported in the Doing Business Series) (refer Note 13)*	Ease of Doing Business Indicator Ranking (Ranking out of 190 countries)	175	178	178	181	-	-
	Paying Taxes Indicator (Ranking out of 190 countries)	130	139	140	136	-	-
	Paying Taxes – time to comply (Hours/yr.): (all)	156	156	156	234	234	192
	Paying Taxes – time to comply (Hours/yr.): (CIT)	132	132	132	132	59	59
	Paying Taxes – time to comply (Hours/yr.): (VAT)	n.a.	n.a.	n.a.	n.a.	90	73
	Paying Taxes – time to comply (Hours/yr.): Labor taxes	24	24	24	102	85	60
	Post-Filing Index (VAT and CIT corrections)	1.4	1.4	1.4	1.4	61	57
	Time to comply with VAT refund (hours)	n.a.	n.a.	n.a.	n.a.	14.9	19.6
	Time to obtain VAT refund (weeks)	n.a.	n.a.	n.a.	n.a.	41.5	28.2
	Number of payment per year	18	18	18	18	23	21
	Trading Across Borders Rank	94	98	104	107	-	-
Observations	Timor-Leste made paying taxes costlier by introducing a social security contribution scheme paid by the employer.						

	Observations
Taxpayer rights and obligations *(refer Note 14)*	Taxpayers have the right to dispute assessments. The Appeals division provides an independent internal review. An administrative tribunal is also available followed by judicial review. A binding tax ruling regime is available.

	Observations
Corruption Perception Index Trends *(refer Note 15)*	Timor-Leste is ranked 93rd out of 180 with a score of 38/100 in 2019.

VIET NAM

AT A GLANCE

Measure	2014	2015	2016	2017	2018	2019
Total Population (million)	91.714	92.677	93.638	94.596	95.540	96.462
Age profile						
0–14	23.02	23.03	23.04	23.10	23.17	23.21
15–64	70.43	70.31	70.14	69.87	69.55	69.23
65+	6.55	6.66	6.82	7.03	7.27	7.55
Literacy level (% of population)					95	
Urbanization (%)						
Urban Population	66.89	66.19	65.49	64.79	64.08	63.40
Rural Population	76.94	76.51	76.07	76.16	76.00	75.89
Employment to Population	46.34	44.02	41.87	40.15	38.60	37.36
Agriculture	21.45	22.74	24.76	25.78	26.82	27.64
Industry	32.22	33.24	33.37	34.07	34.58	35.00
Services	33.12	33.81	34.51	35.21	35.92	36.60

Demographic Overview *(refer Note 1)*

Industrialization Indices	2012	2013	2014	ASEAN Ave.	World Ave.	
Industrialization Intensity Index	0.43	0.48	0.49	0.54	0.65	
Share of Medium & High Tech	0.3	0.38	0.38	0.44		

Main Economic Sectors: Large state-owned industries dominate in textiles, food, furniture, plastics, and paper, as well as tourism and telecommunications. Agriculture makes up 14.7% of GDP and employs 39.4% of the workforce. Economic growth is driven by labor shifting from agriculture to manufacturing and services, private investment, a strong tourist sector, and accelerating urbanization.

Trends in Income and Inequality *(refer Note 1)*

Measure	2014	2015	2016	2017	2018	2019	ASEAN Ave.
Income Index	0.593	0.6	0.609	0.616	0.624	...	0.734
Inequality in Income (%)	22	21.4	21.4	21.4	18.1	...	20.35
GNI per Capita	5,052	5,314	5,638	5,916	6,220	...	23,069
Human Development Rank				118/189			

Take-up of Technology *(refer Note 2)*

Measure	Description
E-commerce trends	87% visited an online store and 77% made an online purchase.
Internet coverage and availability	66% use the internet and 62% use social media. Internet usage remained stable in 2019. Mobile Connectivity Index = 65.0 (5th in the region)
Take-up of internet and mobile banking	50% use mobile baking and 39% make mobile payments.
Take-up of e-filing	Only certain business entities are eligible to e-file, and moves are currently underway to make e-filing compulsory for these taxpayers. No data were provided on e-filing rates.

VIET NAM: EMPLOYMENT BY SECTOR

- Employment to population ratio, 15+, total (%)
- Employment in agriculture (% of total employment)
- Employment in industry (% of total employment)
- Employment in services (% of total employment)

VIET NAM: TAKE-UP OF TECHNOLOGY

- Individuals using the internet (% of population)
- Fixed broadband subscriptions (in millions)
- Fixed broadband subscriptions (per 100 people)

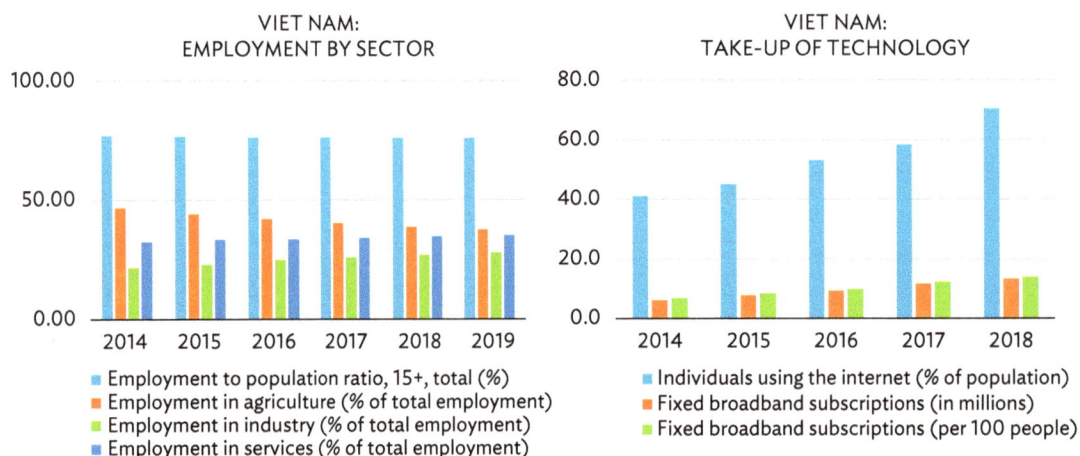

PRODUCTION STRUCTURE

	Region	Exports ($ million)				
		2014	2015	2016	2017	2018
Exports - Overall (refer Note 3)	Viet Nam	143,186	160,890	173,490	192,188	227,346
	SEA	1,606,681	1,630,770	1,508,470	1,498,265	1,676,341
	US	2,273,428	2,371,704	2,266,800	2,220,609	2,356,726
Main sector 1 Machinery and Transport Equipment	Viet Nam	43,030	48,624	60,570	70,037	90,031
	SEA	470,011	483,417	476,133	478,746	538,499
	US	639,053	665,625	647,286	627,333	645,863
Main sector 2 Office and Telecom Equipment	Viet Nam	32,305	35,843	47,329	54,950	71,680
	SEA	284,959	293,811	291,494	289,701	325,385
	US	140,971	145,946	142,274	140,473	145,475
	Region	Imports ($ million)				
		2014	2015	2016	2017	2018
Imports - Overall (refer Note 3)	Viet Nam	154,791	171,962	186,929	221,075	251,282
	SEA	1,506,926	1,372,220	1,354,024	1,525,565	1,701,449
	US	2,879,362	2,786,645	2,739,415	2,932,062	3,148,464
Main sector 1 Machinery and Transport Equipment	Viet Nam	55,014	70,323	74,516	91,803	98,264
	SEA	462,822	456,028	462,749	520,106	576,718
	US	956,716	989,206	969,943	1,040,707	1,103,063
Main sector 2 Office and Telecom Equipment	Viet Nam	27,331	33,556	37,649	50,507	57,281
	SEA	220,691	218,183	220,271	257,966	287,275
	US	314,209	321,039	316,947	350,850	362,342
Observations	Exports grew by 15.5% in 2018, compared with a regional average growth of 10.1%. Imports grew by 12.0% in 2018, compared with a regional average growth of 10.3%. The top exports are broadcasting equipment and accessories, telephones, integrated circuits, and footwear. The top imports are integrated circuits, telephones, and refined petroleum.					

	Sector	2014	2015	2016	2017	2018
Flows of Inward Foreign Direct Investment (FDI) to ASEAN Sourced from Viet Nam, by Economic Sectors ($ million) (refer Note 4)	Agriculture, forestry, and fishing	162.26	163.53	125.54	117.16	111.10
	Mining and quarrying	67.00	17.47	29.45	24.46	55.57
	Manufacturing	(15.34)	1.58	42.87	19.48	(10.18)
	Electricity, gas, steam, and air conditioning supply	0.55		0.00		4.20
	Water supply; sewerage, waste management and remediation activities			0.00		
	Construction	3.88	2.49	1.18	(0.96)	2.87
	Wholesale and retail trade; repair of motor vehicles and motorcycles	4.62	18.59	(68.28)	(26.84)	27.43
	Transportation and storage	0.04	(1.47)	(0.13)	2.47	1.41
	Accommodation and food service activities	5.39	2.35	0.11	0.00	0.10
	Information and communication	0.41	43.85	(44.49)	106.80	87.22
	Financial and insurance activities	(0.31)	(49.36)	(33.85)	76.74	157.79
	Real estate activities	41.17	1.38	0.56	64.23	96.65
	Professional, scientific, and technical activities	(3.21)	0.67	(1.42)	(0.12)	(2.37)
	Administrative and support service activities	0.00	0.00	0.99	0.01	0.08
	Education	0.12	0.00			
	Human health and social work activities				(0.01)	
	Arts, entertainment, and recreation	(0.14)	0.14			
	Other services activities	10.90	12.91	48.99	11.50	9.52
	Unspecified activity	22.79	119.75	8.06		
	TOTAL activities	**304.04**	**399.29**	**164.09**	**403.30**	**515.29**
IMF Article IV	Net FDI inflows (in percent of GDP)	4.9	6.1	6.1	6.3	6.3
	Net Direct Investment (FDI) – in $ billion	8.1	10.7	11.6	13.6	15
Observations	Viet Nam's FDI inflows in 2019 increased slightly. In recent years, FDI inflows have trended away from light industry and toward heavy industry, real estate, and tourism. The main investors are the Republic of Korea and Singapore, with the manufacturing and processing sectors attracting the most FDI followed by real estate and professional activities/science/technology. According to preliminary data from the Viet Nam government, pledged FDI reached a 10-year high of $38 billion in 2019. Viet Nam expects disbursed FDI to continue to rise as the government steps up efforts to attract factories into the country. The Ministry of Planning and Investment aims to draw more FDI into areas including export-oriented, energy, and high-technology by building a more business-friendly environment.					

Component Sector	2014	2015	2016	2017	2018	ASEAN Ave.	US 2018
Gross domestic product (GDP)	100.0	100.0	100.0	100.0	100.0	100	100
Final consumption expenditure	72.1	74.3	75.1	74.5	74.1	68.04	87
Household consumption expenditure (including NPISH)	65.8	68.0	68.5	68.0	67.7	54	70
General government final consumption expenditure	6.3	6.3	6.5	6.5	6.5	14.51	17
Gross capital formation	26.8	27.7	26.6	26.6	26.6	28.58	18
Gross fixed capital formation	23.8	24.7	23.7	23.8	26.6	27.74	17
Changes in inventories	3.0	3.0	2.9	2.8	..	1.04	1
Exports of goods and services	86.4	89.8	93.6	101.6	106.0	63.65	13
Imports of goods and services	(83.1)	(89.0)	(91.1)	(98.8)	(102.6)	(61.12)	18
Total value added	100.0	100.0	100.0	100.0	100.0	100	100

Industry Structure: GDP by type of expenditure (refer Note 5)

Observations: Capital formation is a lead indicator of economic performance and is below regional averages. Tax outcomes flowing from investment may be significantly impacted by tax incentives.

NPISH = nonprofit institutions serving households.

Component Sector	2014	2015	2016	2017	2018	ASEAN Ave.	US 2018
Agriculture, hunting, forestry, and fishing	19.7	18.9	18.1	17.0	16.2	12.11	167
Industry	36.9	37.0	36.4	37.1	38.1	38.84	1,512
Mining, manufacturing, and utilities	31.2	30.9	30.1	30.7	31.6	32	673
Manufacturing	14.7	15.2	15.9	17.0	17.8	17.29	2,321
Construction	5.7	6.0	6.2	6.4	6.5	6.99	839
Services	43.4	44.2	45.5	45.8	45.7	49.05	2,579
Wholesale, retail trade, restaurants, and hotels	15.1	15.4	15.9	16.2	16.3	16.75	2,338
Transport, storage, and communications	3.9	3.8	3.8	3.7	3.8	7.02	658
Other activities	24.3	24.9	25.8	26.0	25.7	25.28	437

Industry Structure: Value Add by kind of economic activity ($ million) (refer Note 5)

Observations: The contribution of agriculture is slightly above the regional average, but has been consistently declining, with shifts into manufacturing, mainly construction.

TAX SYSTEM AND TAX ADMINISTRATION DESIGN FEATURES

Tax Rates, Thresholds, and Overall Revenue Contribution (see Note 6)

| Taxes | Rates of Tax (%) /1 | | Thresholds | | Share (%) of Total Taxes (latest year)/9 |
	Basic/ Standard	Other	Local Currency	$	
CIT	20%	20% Branch Tax 32%–50% - Oil and gas sector /2.	No Threshold		
PIT	5%–35%	20% - nonresident	D5 million	$215.00	
PIT	0.1%–20%	Private business income	D100 million	$4,300.00	
Inheritance	10%	Also applies to gifts	> D10 million	$430.00	
VAT/ GST /3	10%	0%, 5% reduced rates	No threshold		
WHT /4	5%/20%	Resident individual/company	No threshold		
WHT /5	5%	Nonresidents	No threshold		
Excise /6	5%–150%		No threshold		
SSC /7	21.05% - employers; 10.5% - employees		No threshold		
CGT	20% (taxed as ordinary income)				
*Subnational taxes/8	0.5%–15% Rates vary	Stamp Duty Property			45.8% of general government revenue and 11.2% of GDP (2016)
Overview of Tax Incentives	Preferential tax rates of 10% for 15 years (with a possible increase to 30 years) and 17% for the next 10 years are available to taxpayers engaged in encouraged investment projects or socioeconomically disadvantaged regions. Both a tax holiday of up to 4 years and a 50% reduction for up to 9 years are available from the first profit-making year or the fourth revenue-generating year, whichever comes first. Current taxpayers with new projects may also be entitled to the incentives.				

* Viet Nam has almost 12,000 government bodies across three levels of subnational government.

/1. For FY 2020, unless otherwise indicated. /2. Rate depends upon the project. /3. Viet Nam has a WHT system for foreign entities or individuals involved in business-to-business or B2B transactions. New arrangements will extend this to those performing e-commerce activities or doing business via digital platforms in the business-to-consumer or B2C market. Businesses must directly register to file tax in Viet Nam or authorize other parties to do so on their behalf. Those already included in the existing WHT arrangements may continue or migrate to the new system. If the supplier does not comply with the requirements, the GDT has the right to enforce tax collection via commercial banks. The new requirements were introduced because the current WHT does not capture cross-border B2C transactions. /4. Dividends, interest, royalties, and fees for technical services. /5. Dividends, interest, and fees for technical services (also subject to 5% VAT). Royalties taxed at 10%. /6. Excise taxes are referred to as Special Sales Taxes. /7. Social insurance (17%), health insurance (3%), unemployment insurance (1%), and labor accident and disease insurance (0.5%) (deductible to employers). Employees must also contribute. /8. Subnational taxes include land rental taxes and land use fees and are determined and levied by municipal authorities. /9. National taxes are shown as a percentage of national tax revenue. Note that the DGT does not administer excise taxes.

Sources: IMF Art. IV reports; Deloitte Country Tax Profiles; OECD Statistics.

Tax Administration Setup and Performance

Subject Area	Aspect	Features and Performance	Overall Rating
Responsibilities of tax body	Main taxes collected	PIT, CIT, VAT, Excise (SST)	High – collect around 78% of all government revenue
	Other major roles	The GDT is a single directorate within the ministry. GDT provides policy advice and recommendations on drafting legislation and regulations.	
Tax body Autonomy	Budget flexibility, organization design	National budget management is limited as municipal offices collect most national taxes (under broad national guidance) and they are relatively autonomous.	Low
	Human resource management	Human resource management decisions are largely made at municipal office level.	
Digital services in tax administration	E-filing	**Rate (2017)** / **Comments**	Medium
	– CIT	...	Only certain business entities are eligible to e-file, and moves are currently underway to make e-filing compulsory for these taxpayers. No data were provided on e-filing rates.
	– PIT	...	
	– VAT/GST	...	
	E-payment		
	E-services (including mobile applications)	A full range of e-services are offered including tools and calculators, access to an integrated account, and a digital mailbox.	

	Measure	2014	2015	2016	2017	2018	2019	ASEAN Ave.	OECD Ave. 2018
Tax system design (refer Note 7)	Tax reliance ratio	82.9	76.8	76.2	79.9	77.9	77.9	66.9	63.8
	Tax mix	25.5	27.4	28.1	29.1	26.8	31.5	39.92	33.7
	Tax ratio	18.21	18.03	17.94	18.74	18.54	18.20	14	34.3
	CIT productivity	0.171	0.179	0.180	0.191	0.219	0.200	0.26	
	VAT productivity	0.612	0.601	0.600	0.631	0.641	0.620	0.43	
	Consolidation of tax collection and administration	The GDT provides national guidance on the application of national regulations and guidelines and on priorities and approaches. The municipal offices are largely responsible for national and local tax administration and have a degree of autonomy in determining priorities.							
Observations	The tax reliance ratio is somewhat higher than the regional average and VAT productivity is also slightly higher, all other measures are on par with regional averages.								

	Measure	Country Performance
Tax administration processes (refer Note 8)	Tax administration efficiency and effectiveness (operating expenditure as a proportion of net revenue collected)	Data not available.
	No. of labor force members/tax body FTE	Over 1,300 workers per tax officer.
	No. of citizens/tax body FTE	Over 2,300 citizens per tax officer.
	Proportion of staff assigned to support functions	26% of staff are assigned to support functions. Regional average is 29%.

REVENUE

	Measure	Country Performance						ASEAN Ave.	Asia and Pacific Ave.	OECD Ave. 2018
		2014	2015	2016	2017	2018	2019*			
Tax revenue collection performance *(all levels of government) (refer Note 9)*	Tax/GDP (%) - all	18.21	18.03	17.94	18.74	18.54	18.20	14.03	20.0	34.3
	Taxes on income & profits/GDP (%)	4.65	4.94	5.04	5.45	4.94	5.71	5.35	8.1	11.6
	Taxes on goods & services/GDP (%)	6.12	6.01	6.00	6.31	8.26	6.16	6	10.1	10.9
	Overall tax revenue trend									

(*) projected/provisional collections.

BROADENING THE TAX BASE

	Measure	Country Performance
Countering Tax Avoidance and Evasion *(refer Note 10)*	Effective anti-avoidance rules	Viet Nam has a general anti-avoidance rule and transfer pricing rules that are consistent with the OECD model. Transfer pricing reporting follows the BEPS Action 13 recommendations.
	Thin capitalization and controlled foreign corporation rules	Thin capitalization rules exist but there are no CFC, anti-hybrid rules, or economic substance rules (but there is a GAAR). Disclosure of related party transactions are required.
	Findings from OECD Forum on Harmful Tax Practices (FHTP)	Economic zones, disadvantaged areas, and IP benefits (transfer of technology) were reviewed and found to be out of scope, with no benefits for income from geographically mobile activities. Software production regime was reviewed and found to be potentially harmful but not actually harmful. Lack of substantial activities requirements, but no harmful economic effects in practice. Regime is subject to annual monitoring.
	A focus on HNWI and professions	No focus on high net worth individuals was reported.
	Dealing with the shadow economy	The shadow economy is estimated to be 14.78% of GDP (8th in the region), but this measure does not include subnational taxes, which are extensive in Viet Nam.

Measure		Country Status
Member of Global Forum on Transparency & Exchange of Information		Yes
Exchange of Information on Request Ratings	Round 1	Not reviewed
	Round 2	Scheduled 2023
Signatory to the Multilateral Convention on Mutual Assistance in Tax Matters		No
Commitment to Automatic Exchange of Information		Not committed to a specific date
Implementation of Common Reporting Standard (CRS) and Multilateral Competent Authority Agreement		No
Convention on Mutual Administrative Assistance in tax matters		No
Member of Base Erosion and Profit Shifting Inclusive Framework		Yes
Existence of harmful tax regimes (Action 5)		Not harmful (no harmful regime exists)
Exchange of information on tax rulings (Action 5)		Reviewed/recommendations made
CbC – Domestic law (Action 13)		Legal framework in place
CbC – Information exchange network (Action 13)		CbC MCAA not signed
Effective dispute resolution (Action 14)		Review scheduled
Signatory to the Multilateral Convention to Implement Treaty Related Measures to Prevent BEPS (Action 6)		Reviewed in 2018 and 2019, no recommendation. 2020 review ongoing.
Network of income tax treaties for avoidance of double taxation		81

The left sidebar label for the above table reads: **Countering International Tax Avoidance and Evasion and International Cooperation** *(refer Note 11)*

RESPONSIVE TAX ADMINISTRATION

Measure	Country Status
% responding tax regime has become more complicated over prior 3 years	72%
% responding tax regime has been less consistently administered over prior 3 years	33.9%
% responding tax compliance and reporting rules are "complicated" or "very complicated"	18%
Perceived fairness in tax audits	Low
Perceived confidence in appeal system	Low
Taxpayer relationship with authorities	neutral
Perceived main priority areas for reform	Tax officer training and timeliness and quality of audits.

The left sidebar label for the above table reads: **Important findings from Deloitte's 2017 Tax Complexity Survey** *(refer Note 12)*

	Measure	Country Ranking				Asia and Pacific Ave.	World Ave.
		2017	2018	2019	2020		
Compliance/ Regulatory Burden Indicators *(as reported in the Doing Business Series)* *(refer Note 13)*	Ease of Doing Business Indicator Ranking (Ranking out of 190 countries)	68	68	69	70	–	–
	Paying Taxes Indicator (Ranking out of 190 countries)	167	86	131	109	–	–
	Paying Taxes- time to comply (Hours/yr.): (all)	540	498	498	384	234	192
	Paying Taxes- time to comply (Hours/yr.): (CIT)	132	132	132	112	59	59
	Paying Taxes- time to comply (Hours/yr.): (VAT)	219	219	219	125	90	73
	Paying Taxes- time to comply (Hours/yr.): Labor taxes	189	147	147	147	85	60
	Post-Filing Index (VAT and CIT corrections)	73.3	49.1	49.1	49.1	61	57
	Time to comply with VAT refund (hours)	2	n.a.	n.a.	n.a.	14.9	19.6
	Time to obtain VAT refund (weeks)	61	n.a.	n.a.	n.a.	41.5	28.2
	Number of payments per year	31	14	10	6	23	21
	Trading Across Borders Rank	93	94	100	104	–	–

Observations	Viet Nam made starting a business easier by publishing the notice of incorporation online and by reducing the cost of business registration. Viet Nam made paying taxes easier by no longer requiring hard copy submission of the value added tax return and allowing joint payment of the business license tax and VAT. Viet Nam also made paying taxes less costly by reducing the employer's contribution to the labor fund. Despite this progress, the ease of doing business rank has declined by one point. No case study was conducted on VAT refunds.

Taxpayer rights and obligations *(refer Note 14)*	**Observations**
	Viet Nam reports having a formally defined set of taxpayer rights, which are set out in law. Details of complaint-handling bodies or levels of complaints were not provided. Taxpayers have a right to dispute assessments and disputes are considered in the first instance by the revenue body and may also be referred to an appellate court.

Corruption Perception Index Trends *(refer Note 15)*	**Observations**
	In 2014, Viet Nam's CPI score was 31 out of 100 and has steadily improved to 37 in 2019. This places Viet Nam at a ranking of 96th out of 180 countries. The government began tackling grand corruption in 2016 and significant sentences have been handed down in several high-level cases. The revamped 2018 anti-corruption law clarifies and enhances the legislative framework for combating corruption by strengthening the declaration of income and wealth in government and state-owned enterprises, including public access to declarations. The linking (by the end of 2019) of databases on taxation, anti-money laundering, customs, and land transactions should facilitate asset verification.

APPENDIX NOTES AND REFERENCES

General

$ = Throughout this report where dollar amounts are cited, they are shown in US dollars unless otherwise stated.

... = Data are not available for this indicator.

n.a. = Not applicable.

Note 1: Demographic overview and trends in income and inequality

Data on country demographics are sourced largely from the World Bank's Data Catalogue and ADB's Key Indicators for Asia and the Pacific. Measures used include: Gross National Income (GNI) per capita; World Bank Inequality in Income Indexes; Human Development Index Rank (which is made up of life expectancy at birth; expected years of schooling; mean years of schooling; gross national income (GNI) per capita; and GNI per capita rank minus HDI rank).

ADB. 2019. Key Indicators for Asia and the Pacific: https://www.adb.org/sites/default/files/publication/521981/ki2019.pdf

United Nations Development Program, Human Development Reports including HDIR: http://hdr.undp.org/en/content/2019-human-development-index-ranking.

World Bank Industrialization Indices:

https://tcdata360.worldbank.org/indicators/mva.ind.int?country=BRA&indicator=3793&viz=line_chart&years=1990,2014#related-link.

Note 2: Technology

Data on technology availability and usage are sourced from World Bank's World Development Indicators and Global Financial Inclusion databases, surveys conducted by HootSuite, and Mobile Connectivity analysis developed by GSMA:

https://www.wdi.worldbank.org.

https://www.juancmejia.com/wp-content/uploads/2019/03/Digital-2019-WeAreSocial-y-HootSuite.pdf.

http://www.mobileconnectivityindex.com/#year=2018&globalRankings=overall&globalRankingsYear=2018.

Note 3: Imports and Exports

Data on imports and exports are sourced from the World Trade Organization - WTO International Trade by Commodity and Commercial Services 2018.

This may also include the volume and trend of Intraregional Merchandise Exports and Imports in Asia and the Pacific. See Figures 2-4-2, 2-4-3 and Tables 2-4-13, 2-4-14 of ADB key indicator.

https://www.adb.org/sites/default/files/publication/521981/ki2019.pdf.

Data are also sourced from the Observatory of Economic Complexity:

https://oec.world/en/resources/about.

Note 4: Foreign Direct Investment

Data on FDI inflows are sourced from IMF Article IV reports and from the ASEAN FDI Data Base:

https://data.aseanstats.org/fdi-by-sources-and-sectors.

Data are also sourced from the United Nations Conference on Trade and Development's World Investment Report 2020:

https://unctad.org/en/Pages/Publications/WorldInvestmentReports.aspx.

Note 5: Industry Structure

Data on Industry Structure are sourced from the ASEAN Stats data portal:

https://data.aseanstats.org/.

TAX SYSTEM AND TAX ADMINISTRATION DESIGN FEATURES

Note 6: Overview of Taxes

Data included in this section are sourced from ADB internal sources and from various published reports such as the Deloitte and PWC country tax profiles. The report titled: The Localization of the Global Agendas: How Local Action is Transforming Territories and Communities. Asia Pacific Region Report (The GOLD Report V) was used for information on subnational governments, and is published at:

https://www.gold.uclg.org/sites/default/files/ENG-ASPAC%20REGION%E2%80%94web-final.pdf.

Note 7: Tax System Design

Data for calculation of these measures are sourced from IMF article IV reports, ADB internal data, and from the ADB comparative series on tax administration.

AREA	MEASURE	EXPLANATION
Tax reliance ratio	Tax revenue as a share of total government revenue	Reflects a country's degree of reliance on taxes as a source of government revenue
Tax mix	Direct taxes versus indirect taxes (% of total)	Indicates the relative degree of reliance on direct and indirect taxes: the tax mix.
Tax ratio	Tax collected (all levels of government) as a share of national GDP (%)	The standard international measure for comparing tax collection performance across economies.
CIT productivity	CIT revenue as a share of GDP divided by CIT standard rate	Measures the relative productivity/ efficiency of the tax, taking account of policy design choices and administrative compliance.
VAT productivity	VAT revenue as a share of GDP divided by VAT standard rate	
Consolidation of tax collection and administration	Tax revenue collected by main tax body as a share of total net tax collections (all levels of government)	Reflects the degree of reliance on the national tax body for the collection of an economy's taxes (and impacted by political factors, e.g., fiscal federalism considerations) and institutional design choices.

Note 8: Tax Administration

Data for calculation of these measures are sources from IMF article IV reports, ADB internal data, and from the ADB Comparative Series on Tax Administration. Other sources include:

WB database: https://data.worldbank.org/indicator/GC.DOD.TOTL.GD.ZS.

OECD Revenue Statistics: https://www.oecd.org/tax/tax-policy/revenue-statistics-highlights-brochure.pdf

and OECD. 2019. Revenue Statistics in Asian and Pacific Economies, OECD Library 2019.

AREA	MEASURE	EXPLANATION
Tax administration efficiency and effectiveness	Administrative expenditure of the national tax body as a proportion of total net tax collected	Reflects the relative amount expended to collect taxes for a fiscal year. Viewed over time, the measure may reflect changes in efficiency and effectiveness; the measure needs to be used carefully in international comparisons given the potential for it to be impacted by extraneous factors.
Tax administration staff resourcing comparability	No. of labor force members/ tax body FTE	Broad measures that reflect the extent of resources allocated by government for national tax administration purposes.
	No. of citizens/ tax body FTE	

REVENUE

Note 9: Tax Revenue Collection Performance (all levels of government)

Data on tax revenue collections and on revenue mobilization have been obtained largely from IMF Article IV reports published in 2017, 2018, and 2019. The OECD's publication Revenue Statistics in Asian and Pacific Countries has also been used as a reference.

BROADENING THE TAX BASE

Note 10: Countering Tax Avoidance and Evasion

This item is based on a range of factors, including the legal framework and the revenue body's administrative arrangements. Most data are sourced from the OECD. Shadow economy data are sourced from:

https://www.theglobaleconomy.com/rankings/shadow_economy/.

Harmful tax practices data are sourced from the OECD's 2019 review:

https://www.oecd.org/tax/beps/harmful-tax-practices-peer-review-results-on-preferential-regimes.pdf.

Note 11: Countering International Tax Avoidance and Evasion

This item is based on a range of factors, including membership of the specified body committed to collaboration in tax reform, a signatory to the named convention, and the scale of the treaty network.

RESPONSIVE TAX ADMINISTRATION

Note 12: Important findings from Deloitte's 2017 Tax Complexity Survey

The referenced findings are from the third edition of Deloitte's publication published in early 2017. Previous editions were published in 2011 and 2014. Deloitte notes that its latest survey covered the views and perceptions of 331 business executives across the region, from 20 jurisdictions. To be updated if a new survey is released or if additional sources are identified.

Note 13: Compliance/ Regulatory Burden Indicators

The Doing Business Series presents quantitative indicators on business regulations and the protection of property rights that can be compared across 190 economies and over time. This includes the area of taxation for which a *Paying Taxes* indicator has been designed. The *Paying Taxes* indicator takes account of the number of payments, the estimated time to comply for a defined range of taxes, and the total tax and contribution rate for a **standardized case study company** to comply with all tax regulations as well as post-filing processes. The Doing Business Series is prepared and published annually, with its most recent (17th edition) published in late 2019. In the absence of any other comparable set of measures, the Doing Business series has become the *de facto* standard for measure compliance/regulatory burden.

Time to Comply: The time it takes to prepare, file, and pay (or withhold) the corporate income tax, value-added or sales tax, and labor taxes, including payroll taxes and social contributions (in hours per year).

Customs: The World Bank's Doing Business Series includes an indicator '*Trading Across Borders*' to gauge the burden imposed on businesses by regulations governing cross-border trading. The indicator is derived from eight sub-indicators that reflect the time and costs of exports and imports, and aspects of border compliance.

Note 14: Taxpayer rights and obligations

Data for this item are based on ADB's comparative series, published taxpayer surveys, and on Asia Oceania Tax Consultants' Association (AOTCA), Confédération Fiscale Européenne (CFE), and Society of Trust and Estate Practitioners (STEP). 2015. Taxpayer Charter Survey. www.taxpayercharter.com.

Note 15: Corruption Index Trend

Data for this item are based on the World Bank's CPIA transparency, accountability, and corruption in the public sector rating, and Transparency International's Corruption Perception Index, which can be accessed at: https://www.transparency.org/en/cpi.

REVENUE BODIES

Brunei Darussalam
Revenue Division of the Ministry of Finance and Economy: https://www.mofe.gov.bn/SitePages/Home.aspx

Cambodia
The General Department of Taxation (GDT): https://www.tax.gov.kh/en/index.php

Indonesia
Directorate General of Taxation (DGT): www.pajak.go.id

Lao People's Democratic Republic
Ministry of Finance – Tax Department, Tax Division of Vientiane Capital and Tax District: https://www.mof.gov.la/index.php/en/home/

Malaysia
Inland Revenue Board of Malaysia (IRBM): http://www.hasil.gov.my/index1.php?bt_lgv=2

Philippines
Bureau of Internal Revenue (BIR) Philippines: https://www.bir.gov.ph/

Singapore
Inland Revenue Authority of Singapore (IRAS): https://www.iras.gov.sg

Thailand
Thai Revenue Department (TRD): http://www.rd.go.th/publish/index_eng.html

Timor-Leste
The Ministry of Finance, Directorate-General for Revenues: https://www.mof.gov.tl/about-the-ministry/organisation-structure-roles-and-people/generals-directorate/general-diretore-of-revenue/?lang=en

Viet Nam
The General Department of Taxation (GDT): http://www.gdt.gov.vn/wps/portal/english

References

Asian Development Bank (ADB). 2020. *A Comparative Analysis of Tax Administration in Asia and Pacific: 2020 Edition*. Manila. https://www.adb.org/publications/comparative-analysis-tax-administration-asia-pacific-2020.

———. 2019. *Key Indicators for Asia and the Pacific*. Manila. https://www.adb.org/sites/default/files/publication/521981/ki2019.pdf.

———. 2019. *Intraregional Merchandise Exports and Imports in Asia and the Pacific*. Manila. https://www.adb.org/sites/default/files/publication/521981/ki2019.pdf.

Asia Oceania Tax Consultants' Association, Confédération Fiscale Européenne, and Society of Trust and Estate Practitioners. 2015. Taxpayer Charter Survey. www.taxpayercharter.com.

Association of Southeast Asian Nations. 2020. Online ASEAN FDI Data Base Tool. https://data.aseanstats.org/.

Crivelli, Ernesto, Ruud A. de Mooij, and Michael Keen. 2015. Base Erosion, Profit Shifting and Developing Countries. *IMF Working Paper 15/118*. Washington, DC: International Monetary Fund.

Deloitte. 2020. Country Tax Profiles.

———. 2019. *International Tax Highlights*. Deloitte.

———. 2017. *Asia Pacific Tax Complexity Survey*. Deloitte.

Ernst and Young. 2020. Country Tax Profiles.

International Monetary Fund (IMF), Finance and Development. 2019. *The True Cost of Tax Havens*. Washington, DC.

IMF. 2018 and 2019. IMF Article IV Reports for relevant countries. Washington, DC.

Klynveld, Peat, Marwick, Goerdeler (KPMG). 2017. *Asia Pacific Indirect Tax Guide*. KPMG.

KPMG. 2020. Country Tax Profiles.

The Observatory of Economic Complexity. https://oec.world/en/resources/about.

Organisation for Economic Co-operation and Development (OECD). 2018 and 2019. *Revenue Statistics*. Paris: OECD Publishing. https://www.oecd.org/tax/tax-policy/revenue-statistics-highlights-brochure.pdf.

OECD. 2019. *Review of Harmful Tax Practices*. Paris: OECD Publishing. https://www.oecd.org/tax/beps/harmful-tax-practices-peer-review-results-on-preferential-regimes.pdf.

Transparency International. 2019. Corruption Perception Index. https://www.transparency.org/en/cpi.

United Cities and Local Government (UCLG). 2020. *The Localization of the Global Agenda, Asia Pacific Region Report (The GOLD Report V)*. Barcelona: UCLG. https://www.gold.uclg.org/sites/default/files/ENG-ASPAC%20 REGION%E2%80%94web-final.pdf.

United Nations. 2020. *Conference on Trade and Development World Investment Report 2020*. https://unctad.org/en/ Pages/Publications/WorldInvestmentReports.aspx.

United Nations. 2019. *Development Program: Human Development Reports*. http://hdr.undp.org/en/content/2019-human-development-index-ranking.

World Bank. 2020. *CPIA Transparency, Accountability, and Corruption in the Public Sector Rating*. Washington, DC: WB Publishing.

———. 2020. Online Data Catalogue, World Development Indicators, and Global Financial Inclusion Data. Washington, DC: WB Publishing. https://data.worldbank.org/indicator/GC.DOD.TOTL.GD.ZS.

———. 2019. *WB Doing Business Series, 2020*. Washington, DC: WB Publishing.

———. 2014. *Industrialization Indices*. Washington, DC: WB Publishing. https://tcdata360.worldbank.org/indicators/ mva.ind.int?country=BRA&indicator=3793&viz=line_chart&years=1990,2014#related-link.

World Trade Organization. 2018. *International Trade by Commodity and Commercial Services 2018*.